"What a tour de force! *In Business Strategy Formulation* Bassil Yaghi masterfully presents a fantastic range of strategy tools. Thoroughly recommended to all those interested in developing and deploying winning strategies".

Andy Neely, *University of Cambridge and Chair of Innovate Cambridge*

"The field of strategy is rich and complex. And new ideas come along all the time. This book does a terrific job of making sense of this complexity through the 7C Strategy Wheel. It's an important reference for anyone who has responsibility for developing strategy in their company, or as an advisor to others".

Julian Birkinshaw, *Dean, Ivey Business School, Canada*

"There are many books on business strategy, but few that are so clear, well-written and grounded in research and evidence. This is an invaluable guide for senior managers and practitioners in both the public and private sector".

Jonathan Portes, *Professor of Economics and Public Policy and Senior Fellow, UK in a Changing Europe, King's College London*

"*Business Strategy Formulation: The 7C Strategy Wheel* offers a great overview of strategy approaches, frameworks, and tools developed over the past seven decades. It's a well-structured synthesis grounded in very extensive research that not only categorizes these concepts clearly but also explains how they interrelate. A must-read for anyone who wants to stand on the shoulders of strategy's intellectual giants and apply their insights with confidence".

Marc Baaij, *Associate Professor of Strategic Management, Rotterdam School of Management, Erasmus University*

"Bassil Yaghi has accomplished what no strategic management researcher has before: organize decades of fragmented strategy making tools and methods into a single, comprehensive, easy to understand typology. His 7C Strategy Wheel enables practitioners to not only pick the right tool for the job but also consider what the job of their strategy is to begin with. Leaders who want to increase their odds of strategy success should consult the meticulously researched *Business Strategy Formulation: The 7C Strategy Wheel* before they do anything else".

Edward Barrows, *DBA, Professor of the Practice of Leadership and Academic Director, Master of Science in Organizational Leadership, Brown University*

"A highly impressive and timely contribution to the strategy field. *Business Strategy Formulation* offers leaders a robust, context-sensitive framework grounded in scholarly rigor and practical relevance. An essential guide for navigating complexity and shaping strategic futures".

Luís Serra Coelho, *Dean of the School of Economics, University of Algarve*

"At last! A comprehensive review of the myriad of strategy tools and approaches – and, as importantly, a practical guide to the question of when to use them. A must read for any strategy practitioner. A book that is as impressive in scope, as it is in practical value. If you're looking to make sense of strategy, and don't know what you don't know, this book should be your starting point. Essential reading. A truly impressive undertaking and an invaluable contribution for anyone looking to deliver superior strategy formulation results. In presenting *Business Strategy Formulation*, Yaghi has crystalised a field of considerable complexity, to something that can be immediately and practically applied by all".

Ian Richardson, *Director of Executive Education, Stockholm Business School, Stockholm University*

"One size does not fit all when it comes to developing a strategy. In his thoroughly researched work, Bassil Yaghi makes sense of the bewildering plethora of strategic frameworks, approaches, and methods developed over the last 60 years. In dynamic, fast-changing markets, companies adopt – either by design or neglect – differing strategic postures, Yaghi's '7 Cs'. This book recognises the complexity and diversity of strategy development in today's world and provides a practical guide to the most relevant strategic approaches and methods for each strategic posture".

Rolf Meakin, *Former PwC Strategy& Partner and Global Telecoms Advisory Leader*

Business Strategy Formulation

This book introduces the innovative 7C Strategy Wheel framework, an extensive toolkit designed to transform how businesses select appropriate strategy approaches.

In today's rapidly evolving business environment characterized by volatility, uncertainty, complexity, and ambiguity, businesses face mounting pressures that demand more robust, agile, innovative, and adaptable strategic approaches. Despite acknowledging the importance of aligning strategy with specific strategic contexts, many continue to rely on a limited set of traditional tools that are better suited for stable environments. *Business Strategy Formulation* addresses key challenges in strategy selection by providing a comprehensive framework comprising seven strategic postures, 28 approaches, and 59 methods. Built on a thorough integrative review of theoretical, empirical, and practitioner knowledge bases, it synthesizes insights from disciplines such as strategic management, economics, sociology, and public policy. This interdisciplinary approach creates a common strategic language, reduces ambiguities, and fosters better understanding and alignment between boards, executives, and managers.

This framework serves as a powerful guide for strategic leaders, strategists, planners, and practitioners, enabling them to navigate the complex competitive strategy landscape with confidence.

Bassil A. Yaghi, CEO of StrategistMind, is a strategy educator, advisor, and author with over 25 years of experience bridging theory and practice to help organizations master strategy formulation and approach selection.

Business Strategy Formulation

The 7C Strategy Wheel

Bassil A. Yaghi

Routledge
Taylor & Francis Group
LONDON AND NEW YORK

Designed cover image: Background image Getty Images – enjoynz
Foreground image Bassil A. Yaghi

First published 2026
by Routledge
4 Park Square, Milton Park, Abingdon, Oxon OX14 4RN

and by Routledge
605 Third Avenue, New York, NY 10158

Routledge is an imprint of the Taylor & Francis Group, an informa business

British Library Cataloguing-in-Publication Data
A catalogue record for this book is available from the British Library

ISBN: 978-1-041-16344-2 (hbk)
ISBN: 978-1-041-16342-8 (pbk)
ISBN: 978-1-003-68406-0 (ebk)

DOI: 10.4324/9781003684060

Typeset in Goudy
by Newgen Publishing UK

Contents

Preface

This book was born during an extraordinary period of global disruption. In April 2020, as the world came to a standstill during the COVID-19 lockdowns, I found myself in London, grounded, immobile, and distanced from the usual rhythm of travel, meetings, and client engagements. But amidst that stillness emerged a rare opportunity: the time and space to reflect deeply on a strategy paradox that had long puzzled me.

I had encountered this paradox repeatedly in executive education programs I taught, in strategy workshops I facilitated, and in high-stakes strategy advisory engagements with intelligent, capable leaders. It was this: while the majority of senior executives (over 75 percent, according to research) understand that different strategic situations demand different strategy approaches, only a quarter of them actually adapt how they formulate strategy to match the nature of the challenge they face.

This disconnect is not due to ignorance, incompetence, or lack of effort. These are smart people working with serious intent. Rather, it reflects something more structural and pervasive, what I call The Strategy Gap. It is the systematic failure to align strategy formulation approaches with the complexity, uncertainty, and context-specific challenges organizations confront.

This book, *Business Strategy Formulation: The 7C Strategy Wheel*, is the first in a series of publications dedicated to understanding and closing that gap. It presents the results of an ambitious research program that began in those early months of the pandemic and has since evolved into a multiyear effort to rethink how strategy is selected, designed, and practiced.

Drawing on over 300 strategy tools, more than 25 theoretical perspectives, and over 2,000 literature pieces, the 7C Strategy Wheel offers a practical and comprehensive framework to help leaders, strategists, and consultants tailor their strategy formulation process to the demands of their context. It is a book for those who refuse to settle for one-size fits-all solutions and who are committed to navigating strategy with rigor, nuance, and adaptability.

My hope is that this book challenges prevailing assumptions, provokes critical reflection, and above all, equips you to close the strategy gap in your organization and in your practice.

Bassil A. Yaghi, PhD
July 2025

Acknowledgments

The journey of writing *Business Strategy Formulation: The 7C Strategy Wheel* has been profoundly enriching, made possible by the invaluable support and encouragement of many individuals and institutions to whom I owe my deepest gratitude.

First and foremost, I extend my sincere appreciation to the acquisition team and the editorial board at Routledge for their belief in this project and their professional guidance throughout the publishing process. I would also like to thank the reviewers whose constructive feedback helped refine the manuscript and sharpen its arguments.

Special thanks are due to Basma Yaghi, whose persistent efforts and thoughtful insights helped shape this book from the earliest drafts to the final version. Her meaningful contributions and careful reading of the manuscript added notable value to the work.

I also wish to thank the many MSc, MBA, and Executive MBA students I have had the privilege of teaching. Their probing questions and real-world reflections continually pushed me to refine my thinking on strategy. Equally, I am indebted to the participants of my executive education courses and corporate programs, whose engagement and feedback offered vital practical grounding for the ideas presented in this book.

My consulting clients across both the private and public sectors deserve distinct appreciation for entrusting me with their strategic challenges. Their organizations provided rich learning environments that inspired many of the concepts and frameworks developed in this book.

As this work is built upon decades of research, I am immensely grateful to the hundreds of scholars and practitioners whose insights I have drawn upon and integrated into the 7C Strategy Wheel. Their collective wisdom and diverse perspectives form the intellectual backbone of this book.

Finally, I am wholeheartedly thankful to my wife and children, whose unwavering support, patience, and encouragement sustained me throughout the writing of this book. Their presence made all the difference.

1
Introduction

1.1 Background and Aims

In today's rapidly evolving and increasingly complex business environment, characterized by volatility, uncertainty, complexity, and ambiguity (VUCA), the role of effective strategy has become more critical than ever. Businesses across the globe, regardless of their size, sector, or industry, are facing a multitude of unprecedented challenges and opportunities that demand a strategic approach to navigate successfully.

The sources of these challenges are diverse and far-reaching, encompassing a wide range of factors that shape the current business landscape. Economic shifts, such as the increasing interconnectedness of global markets, global value chains, the rise of emerging economies, and the impact of financial crises, have created a more dynamic and unpredictable business environment. Moreover, the rapid pace of technological change has emerged as a key driver of disruption and transformation across industries. The proliferation of digital technologies, such as digital platforms, artificial intelligence, the Internet of Things, and blockchain, has fundamentally altered the way businesses operate, compete, and create value.

Geopolitical tensions and trade conflicts have further intensified the complexity of the strategic landscape. The resurgence of protectionist policies, escalating tariff wars between major economies, and the weaponization of trade relationships have disrupted established supply chains and forced organizations to reconsider their global strategies. These developments have created new uncertainties around market access, regulatory compliance, and operational continuity, compelling businesses to develop more resilient and adaptable strategies that can navigate an increasingly fragmented and politically volatile international environment.

DOI: 10.4324/9781003684060-1

Alongside this, ecological concerns, particularly those related to climate change and sustainability, as well as societal transformations such as changing demographics, have created new expectations and demands for organizations and challenged them to rethink their strategic priorities. Environmental pressures now encompass not only regulatory compliance with carbon emissions targets and waste reduction mandates, but also stakeholder demands for transparent environmental, social, and governance reporting and genuine commitment to circular economy principles. Simultaneously, demographic shifts, including aging populations in developed markets, urbanization trends, evolving workforce expectations around purpose-driven employment, and the rise of socially conscious consumers, have fundamentally altered market dynamics and talent acquisition strategies.

Neither the public nor the private sectors are exempt from these rising pressures. Public sector organizations grapple with the dual challenges of delivering more with less. The greater demand for public services rooted in citizen-centric delivery, coupled with the need to tackle "wicked problems" such as income inequality and public health crises in the backdrop of highly polarized societies and tighter budgets, places significant pressure on government organizations. Private sector firms encounter their own challenges. They contend with increasingly evolving consumer preferences and the compulsion to continuously innovate and swiftly respond to emerging technologies amidst shorter product life cycles and fiercer market competition.

These mounting challenges on the macro level, as well as the meso level, across sectors drive an unprecedented need for organizations to develop robust strategies and update them more frequently than ever before.

To navigate this complex and ever-changing landscape, strategy scholars, consultants, and practitioners have been actively developing and refining a wide array of strategy tools and frameworks since the 1960s. These tools are designed to help organizations make sense of their environment, identify opportunities and threats, and formulate effective strategies to achieve their objectives. They cover a broad spectrum of strategic considerations, from analyzing industry dynamics and competitive forces to assessing internal capabilities and resources, and from scenario planning and foresight to innovation and business model design. The sheer diversity and richness of this toolkit reflect the multifaceted nature of the strategic challenges organizations face and the need for a range of approaches to address them effectively.

However, despite the recognized importance of aligning strategy approaches with specific organizational contexts and challenges, many companies, government organizations, leaders, strategists, and strategy practitioners continue to rely on a limited set of strategy approaches better suited for stable environments. This misalignment can be attributed to several barriers that hinder the selection of appropriate strategy approaches.

First, many strategy practitioners and executives are only exposed to a limited set of strategy tools, primarily through business school curricula, which tend to focus on foundational tools geared toward stable environments and noncomplex problems. This narrow exposure, combined with the tendency for strategic management tools to adopt a one-size-fits-all approach, leads to a lack of awareness of the diverse range of strategy tools available.

Second, the absence of a comprehensive and continuously updated inventory of strategy tools magnifies the problem, making it challenging for leaders and strategists to access and leverage lesser known but potentially valuable tools.

Third, cognitive and psychological factors also play a significant role in the selection of strategy approaches. Familiarity with specific tools often drives their use, as managers gravitate toward methods they are accustomed to and have successfully applied in the past. This familiarity bias is reinforced by the legitimacy certain tools gain through their widespread adoption and endorsement by prestigious institutions, leading to a self-perpetuating cycle of reliance on a limited set of approaches.

Furthermore, the lack of key competencies among managers, such as strategic thinking, paradoxical thinking, and the ability to embrace complexity, hinders the effective selection and application of diverse strategy tools. The prevalence of traditional, linear thinking and the tendency to avoid uncertainty due to cognitive biases like overconfidence and confirmation bias also contribute to the resistance to adopt new approaches.

Lastly, the use of template-based strategies, often mandated by government agencies or corporate centers, encourages a standardized, "fill-in-the-blank" approach to strategy formulation. This practice often results in a lack of critical thinking and a failure to adapt strategies to the unique challenges and opportunities faced by organizations.

These multifaceted challenges create significant barriers to selecting and implementing the most appropriate strategy approaches, leading organizations to rely on a narrow set of tools that may not be well-suited to their specific contexts and hindering their ability to effectively navigate an increasingly complex and uncertain business landscape.

With the aim of transforming how organizations select appropriate strategy approaches, this book unveils the 7C Strategy Wheel. This comprehensive framework serves as a powerful strategy guide for strategic leaders, strategists, strategic planners, policy analysts, and strategy practitioners, empowering them to navigate the complex strategy landscape effectively with a level of precision and confidence previously unattainable.

The 7C Strategy Wheel is specifically designed to tackle the key challenges to choosing the right strategy approaches. It consists of 7 strategic postures, 28 approaches, and 59 methods, providing a nuanced and comprehensive guide for organizations. The inclusion of 28 distinct strategy approaches makes it one of the most extensive strategy toolkits available. This broad coverage addresses the issue of limited exposure to strategy tools and helps leaders and strategy practitioners expand their repertoire. By showcasing a diverse range of strategies spanning various disciplines and sectors, the framework encourages a more adaptable and context-specific approach to strategy formulation.

Moreover, the 7C Strategy Wheel is grounded in a thorough integrative review of theoretical, empirical, and practitioner knowledge bases, ensuring its relevance and applicability to real-world challenges.

Finally, the 7C Strategy Wheel challenges the use of template-based strategies by providing a flexible and adaptable approach to strategy formulation. By highlighting the importance of aligning strategy approaches with specific strategic postures, the framework promotes critical thinking and encourages organizations to develop strategies tailored to their unique contexts.

1.2 Audience

The primary intended audience for this book is the leaders, practitioners, and consultants who are involved directly with setting the strategic direction, formulating strategies, making strategic decisions, or solving strategic problems. They include:

- Business executives, strategic planners, and managers responsible for steering their organizations through the challenges and opportunities of the 21st century.
- Policymakers and public sector leaders tasked with effective policy-making and public sector leadership in an era of political, economic, technological, and societal upheavals.
- Strategy practitioners and consultants who guide organizations through the intricate process of strategy formulation and execution.

The secondary intended audience for this book comprises:

- Students and educators of business strategy, business management, public administration, and public policy seeking to bridge the gap between theory and practice in strategic management.
- Researchers and academics in the fields of strategic management, organizational studies, and policy sciences seeking a fresh perspective on strategy formulation grounded in rigorous integrative research.

1.3 The Evidence Supporting This Book

The 7C Strategy Wheel is built on a thorough integrative evaluation of the theoretical, empirical, and practitioner knowledge bases. According to Torraco (2005), an integrative review is "a form of research that reviews, critiques, and synthesises representative literature on a topic in an integrated way such that new frameworks and perspectives on the topic are generated" (p. 356). Elsbach and van Knippenberg (2020) emphasize that "these reviews move beyond a description of the field and yield value-added insights through integration and critical assessment of the extant knowledge base" (p. 1).

The work developed in this book is based on a synthesis of the following:

- Catalog of over 300+ strategy tools over the past 100 years. Strategy tools are broadly defined here "to encompass the full range of concepts, ideas, techniques and approaches that structure or influence this activity" (Knott, 2006, p. 1090).
- Review of 25+ theoretical perspectives. In recognition of the interdisciplinary nature of the strategy field, we reviewed not only strategic management theories but also theories from other fields that have strategic implications. These include organization theories, economic theories, sociological theories, public policy theories, future studies, sustainability, and critical management studies.
- Evaluation of 20+ strategy selection frameworks. This review involved a comprehensive assessment of frameworks designed to guide organizations in choosing appropriate strategy approaches. These frameworks span both academic contributions from leading business schools and strategy scholars, and proprietary methodologies developed by major consulting firms like McKinsey, BCG, Kearney, and others.
- Evaluation of 15+ strategic contextual variables that impact strategy formulation. This comprehensive analysis examined the critical environmental

and organizational factors that fundamentally shape how strategies are formulated. These contextual variables included uncertainty, complexity, ambiguity, resources, agency, power, knowledge, organization DNA, and predictability.

- Review of 2,000+ literature pieces on strategic management. This extensive literature review encompassed both peer-reviewed academic research and practitioner-oriented publications spanning decades of strategic management thinking. The review covered seminal works from strategy pioneers like Porter, Mintzberg, and Barney, contemporary research on dynamic capabilities, platform strategies, and digital transformation, as well as industry reports, case studies, and white papers from consulting firms and business publications.
- Review of 200+ business and public strategies. This involved analyzing actual strategic documents, plans, and implementations from both private sector organizations and public sector entities. The review examined strategies across different industries, organizational sizes, and geographic regions, including corporate strategies, business unit strategies, functional strategies, and public policy strategies.

The integrative review and interdisciplinary approach of the 7C Strategy Wheel significantly enrich the strategic management discourse by offering a unique amalgamation of theory, empirical evidence, and practical insights. This synthesis not only closes the gap between academic research, commercial practice, and strategy but also promotes a more sophisticated understanding of strategy formulation processes.

1.4 Strategy Tools – Overview

1.4.1 Definition

Strategy tools are an integral part of strategic management, widely used by practitioners, consultants, and taught in business, public policy, and public management programs (Jarzabkowski et al., 2013). In essence, strategy tools as used in the academic literature encompass concepts, frameworks, approaches, methodologies, methods, models, and techniques that assist and guide strategy practitioners in formulating and executing strategies (Clark, 1997; Knott, 2006). They encapsulate management concepts and techniques, providing frameworks and processes to structure strategic thinking and strategy work (Wright et al., 2013). Within this book, strategy tools help us understand the available strategic postures, approaches, and methods, with the 7C Strategy Wheel having emerged as a distillation of over 300 such tools.

1.4.2 Conceptualizations

Strategy tools have been conceptualized in various ways in the literature. One prominent view is of strategy tools as "technologies of rationality" (March, 2006, p. 201). This perspective suggests that tools embody rational, analytical approaches to strategy, helping managers to collect and process information systematically to make optimal choices. However, the assumption of rationality has been questioned, with scholars pointing out that tool use is often driven by social and political factors rather than pure rational analysis (Jarzabkowski & Kaplan, 2015).

Another conceptualization is of strategy tools as sensemaking devices, helping managers and organizations make sense of complex and ambiguous situations. These tools facilitate the interpretation and understanding of strategic issues (Dameron et al., 2015). Strategy tools can form "the basis of discursive, narrative, or rhetorical structures, thus complementing the language-based view in strategy process and practice research" (Jalonen et al., 2018, p. 2795).

Strategy tools are also conceptualized as boundary objects (Spee & Jarzabkowski, 2009). This view highlights the role of tools in enabling communication and coordination across different organizational groups and levels involved in strategy work. By providing a shared language and framework for discussing strategic issues, they help align understanding, surface assumptions, foster collaboration, generate insights, enable constructive debate among stakeholders, and build consensus around strategic choices (Spee & Jarzabkowski, 2009).

A further conceptualization of strategy tools is as cognitive frames. They influence how strategists perceive and interpret strategic issues and shape the mental models, assumptions, and biases that underlie strategic thinking. By providing specific lenses through which to view strategic problems, tools can guide attention, filter information, and shape the formulation of strategic options (Gavetti & Rivkin, 2005). This means that strategy tools are "knowledge artifacts" that impose "cognitive dimensions" on their users, with our deeper understanding of them allowing for better use and design (Wright et al., 2013, p. 115).

Additionally, strategy tools are conceptualized as routines when they are deeply embedded in the day-to-day activities of strategists. They are not merely theoretical constructs but are actively used and adapted in the practice of strategy.

Managers rely on these tools to gather and analyze data, generate strategic options, and make decisions. The routinization of tool usage helps institutionalize strategic thinking and ensures consistency in strategic processes (Jarzabkowski & Kaplan, 2015).

Strategy tools can also be used as instruments of power and politics within organizations. They can be employed to legitimize certain viewpoints, decisions, and actions while marginalizing others. Managers may selectively use tools to advance their agendas, influence decision-making, and shape organizational narratives (Jarzabkowski & Kaplan, 2015). The choice and application of tools can reflect and reinforce existing power dynamics (Vuorinen et al., 2018).

There has been growing interest in the materiality of strategy tools (Dameron et al., 2015). This perspective draws attention to the physical features and properties of tools, such as the visual format, information categories, and procedural steps. It suggests that these material aspects are not neutral but actively shape cognition and action in strategy work.

1.4.3 Limitations

Despite their potential benefits, as evident in their different conceptualizations, strategy tools also have several disadvantages that can limit their effectiveness or even lead to negative outcomes. One major disadvantage is the risk of oversimplification. Many strategy tools, such as SWOT analysis or the BCG Matrix, provide simplified representations of complex strategic realities (Wright et al., 2013). While this simplification can make issues more manageable, it can also lead to the omission of important nuances and contingencies. Managers may adopt a reductionist approach of relying too heavily on the outputs of tools without considering the limitations of their underlying assumptions and frameworks (Jarzabkowski & Kaplan, 2015).

A related disadvantage is the potential for misuse or overuse of strategy tools. When tools are applied mechanistically or in situations for which they are ill-suited, they can lead to suboptimal or even disastrous decisions (Vuorinen et al., 2018). For example, the use of financial forecasting models based on historical data may be inappropriate in highly uncertain or disrupted environments, leading to flawed projections and strategies (Wright et al., 2013). Similarly, the overuse of certain popular tools like Porter's Five Forces can lead to generic, "cookie-cutter" strategies that fail to account for an organization's unique circumstances (Jarzabkowski et al., 2013).

Another disadvantage of strategy tools is their potential to constrain creative thinking and innovation. By providing predetermined frameworks and categories, tools can channel strategic thinking along narrow, well-worn paths (Wright et al., 2013). Managers may become overly focused on the dimensions and variables highlighted by a particular tool, overlooking other potentially relevant factors or novel solutions. This can lead to a form of tool myopia where strategic options are constrained by the scope of the tools being used (Jarzabkowski & Kaplan, 2015).

Strategy tools can also have political and symbolic drawbacks. The selection and use of particular tools can serve as a means of legitimizing certain perspectives or agendas while marginalizing others (Jarzabkowski & Kaplan, 2015). For instance, a manager may use a financial analysis tool to justify a preferred course of action, even if the tool's outputs are based on questionable assumptions. The use of strategy tools can also become a symbolic ritual, performed to signal rationality and competence to stakeholders while seeking legitimacy, rather than to genuinely inform strategic decisions (Jarzabkowski et al., 2013).

Furthermore, an overemphasis on strategy tools can lead to a false sense of certainty and control. Many tools, particularly those based on quantitative analysis, can create an illusion of precision and predictability in an inherently uncertain and changeable strategic environment (Vuorinen et al., 2018). This can lead managers to underestimate risks, overlook weak signals, and fail to adapt to changing circumstances. An overreliance on tools can also result in neglecting intangible factors such as organizational culture, employee morale, and stakeholder perceptions, which are critical to strategic success but difficult to capture in formal frameworks (Wright et al., 2013).

Lastly, the use of strategy tools can be time and resource intensive. Learning to use tools effectively requires training and practice, and applying them to specific strategic issues often involves extensive data gathering and analysis (Jarzabkowski & Kaplan, 2015). In fast-moving environments, the time required to conduct formal strategic analysis using tools may be a luxury that organizations cannot afford. This is intensified when considering that the costs of purchasing, implementing, and maintaining some tools, particularly those based on specialized software or databases, can be substantial (Vuorinen et al., 2018).

1.5 Strategy Tools – State of the Field

1.5.1 Taking Inventory

The landscape of strategy tools has evolved significantly over the past 80 years, resulting in a rich and diverse array of frameworks, methodologies, and concepts.

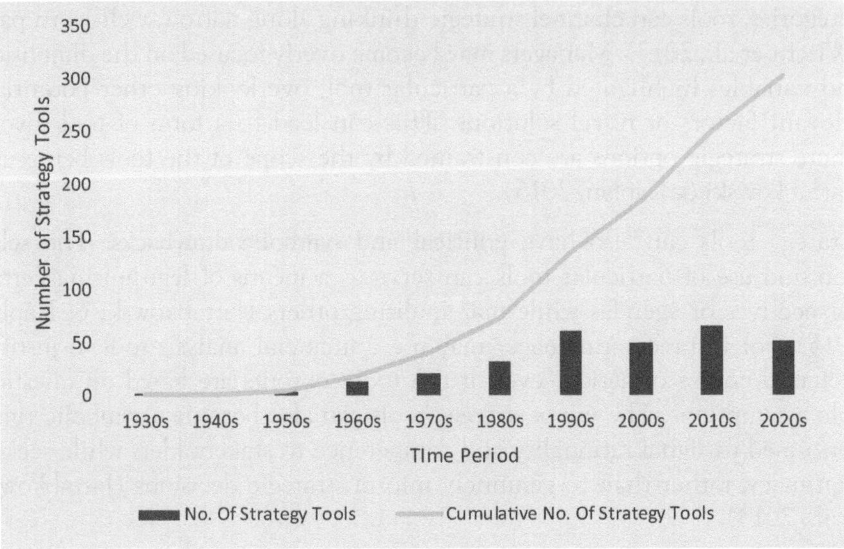

Figure 1.1 Evolution of Strategy Tools.

The following observations provide insights into the current state of the field, reflecting the development and complexity of strategy tools available today.

Enormous number of strategy tools: As shown in Figure 1.1 that plots the number of strategy tools over the periods spanning 80 years, there has been a great increase in the number of tools available. This proliferation showcases a dynamic and evolving field, continually adapting to new challenges and environments. The increase in the number of tools reflects the ongoing innovation in strategic thinking, indicating how the strategic management discipline has expanded to incorporate new ideas and refine existing ones. This growth also highlights the importance of being well-versed in various tools to select the most appropriate ones for specific strategic challenges.

Diversity of perspectives: The concepts, frameworks, approaches, methodologies, methods, models, and techniques originate from various schools of thought, such as the industrial organization (IO) perspective, the Resource-Based View (RBV), and Dynamic Capabilities. This diversity highlights the multifaceted nature of strategic management and the different lenses through which strategies can be formulated and analyzed.

Internal and external focus: Various tools, such as the value chain and the value, rarity, imitability, and organization (VRIO) framework, emphasize the internal aspects of the firm, while others, such as the Five Forces and PESTEL, focus on the external environment. This underscores the need for firms to consider both internal capabilities and external factors when crafting strategies.

Prescriptive and descriptive approaches: The tools include both prescriptive tools that offer guidelines for strategy formulation (e.g., the BCG Matrix and the GE-McKinsey Matrix) and descriptive frameworks that help explain and analyze strategic phenomena (e.g., the Upper Echelons Theory and the Stakeholder Theory).

Static and dynamic perspectives: Some tools, like the Industry Life Cycle and the Product Life Cycle, emphasize the dynamic nature of the business environment, while others, such as the Value Chain and the McKinsey 7S Framework, provide a more static view of the firm and its strategies.

Increasing complexity: As the tools progress chronologically, they tend to become more complex and nuanced, reflecting the growing intricacy of the business landscape. For example, earlier tools such as the Experience Curve and the BCG Matrix are relatively simple compared to more recent ones such as the Ecosystem Strategy and the Business Model Canvas.

Adapting to new realities: The emergence of new tools and frameworks over time mirrors the changing business environment. For instance, the growing importance of technology and innovation is reflected in the appearance of concepts including Disruptive Innovation, the Gartner Hype Cycle, and Digital Transformation in the recent years.

Interconnectedness: Despite the diversity of the tools and frameworks, many of them are interconnected and build upon each other. For example, the RBV and the Dynamic Capabilities Framework are closely related, while the Industry Life Cycle and the Product Life Cycle share similar underlying principles.

These themes highlight the richness and diversity of the strategy tools landscape and draw attention to the importance of understanding their evolution and interconnectedness for effective strategic management.

1.5.2 History of Strategy and Strategy Tools

Strategy tools or "knowledge artifacts" represent the concrete application of underlying strategic theories or theoretical frameworks that facilitate the translation of theoretical insights into everyday strategizing practices (Jarzabkowski & Wilson, 2006, p. 348). These "tools of rationality" serve as the practical

Table 1.1 History of Strategy

Period	Key Developments	Key Strategy Tools	Key Contributors
Origins of Strategy			
~500 BCE	Statecraft; strategic maneuvering; Strategic intelligence; strategic deception	The five fundamental factors (strategy analysis); The concept of Shi (strategic advantage)	Sun Tzu
1532	Realpolitik; Pragmatism	Political analysis; Stakeholder analysis	Niccolò Machiavelli
1832	Holistic approach to strategy	Friction; Uncertainty; Center of gravity; Means-End	Carl von Clausewitz
Foundations of Strategy			
Late 19th C. and Early 20th C.	Theory of scientific management	Time and Motion Studies; Standardization	Frederick Taylor
	14 Principles of Management	Planning, Organizing, Staffing, Directing, Coordinating, Reporting, and Budgeting (POSDCORB) model	Henri Fayol
1930s	Foundation for transaction cost economics (TCE)	Transaction costs; Property rights; Firm boundary and structure	Ronald H. Coase
	Gause's Principle of Competitive Exclusion	Competitive exclusion principle; Niche differentiation	Georgy F. Gause
	The theory of economic development	Creative destruction; Innovation; Entrepreneurship; Economic change	Joseph Schumpeter
	Foundational work in organization theory and management theory	Theory of cooperation and organization; Organizational purpose; Formal organization; Strategic factors	Chester I. Barnard

Table 1.1 (Continued)

Period	Key Developments	Key Strategy Tools	Key Contributors
1940s	Theory of Games and Economic Behavior (Foundation for game theory)	Mathematical Modeling of Strategic Interaction; Expected utility theory; Zero-sum games	John von Neumann and Oskar Morgenstern,
1950s	Systems theory	General Systems Theory	Ludwig von Bertalanffy
	Industrial organization (IO) economics	Structure-conduct-performance; Barrier to entry	Joe S. Bain
	Foundation for Resource-Based View (RBV)	Firm as a collection of productive resources; Distinctive competence	Edith Penrose; Philip Selznick
The Emergence of The Field of Strategy			
1960s	Strategic planning school	Gap analysis; Ansoff Matrix (1958)	H. Igor Ansoff
	Harvard business policy (Design school)	SWOT	Edmund P. Learned; C. Roland Christensen; Kenneth R. Andrews; William D. Guth
	BCG was established ushering the rise of the influence of strategy consulting	Experience curve; BCG Growth Matrix	Bruce Henderson
	Strategic Foresight	Scenario planning	Herman Kahn
The Proliferation of Corporate Portfolio Management			
1970s	Corporate Portfolio Management	BCG Growth-Share Matrix; Shell Directional Policy Matrix; McKinsey Nine Box Industry Matrix; ADL Portfolio Matrix	Bruce Henderson; Frederick W. Gluck

(*Continued*)

Table 1.1 (Continued)

Period	Key Developments	Key Strategy Tools	Key Contributors
	Real Options Theory	Real Options Valuation Models	Stewart C. Myers
	Logical incrementalism	The 5 Stages of Logical incrementalism	James Brian Quinn
	Agency Theory	Agency Costs; Incentive Structures; Moral Hazard; Adverse Selection	Michael C. Jensen & William H. Meckling
	Resource Dependency	The framework of social control; Assessment of External Demands	Jeffrey Pfeffer; Gerald R. Salancik
Influence of IO economics on strategic management and the rise of competitive strategy and competitive advantage			
1980s	Market-Based View (MBV)	Five Forces Model; Generic Competitive Strategies; Value chain analysis; Competitive Advantage	Michael Porter; Chamberlain, 1932; Bain, 1959; Caves and Porter, 1977, 1978; Porter, 1979; Gilbert, 1989)
	Evolutionary economics	Organizational Routines; Path Dependence	Richard R. Nelson; Sidney G. Winter
	TCE	Comparative institutional analysis; Transaction cost analysis; Governance structures	Oliver E. Williamson
Shift toward internal resources and capabilities with the rise of the RBV in strategic management theory.			
1990s	RBV	VRIO Framework; Core Competence Analysis,	Birger Wernerfelt Wernerfelt; Richard P. Rumelt; Jay Barney; Cynthia A. Montgomery

Table 1.1 (Continued)

Period	Key Developments	Key Strategy Tools	Key Contributors
	Dynamic capability theory	Dynamic capability framework	David J. Teece; Gary Pisano; Amy Shuen
	Knowledge-Based View	Combinative capabilities	Bruce Kogut; Udo Zander; Robert M. Grant
	Neo Institutional Theory	Institutional analysis; Path dependence analysis	Douglass C. North
	Nonmarket Strategies	Nonmarket strategies	David P. Baron
	Coopetition	Value Net analysis; Complementors; PART	Adam M. Brandenburger; Barry J. Nalebuff
	Competitive dynamics	Framework for competitor analysis and interfirm rivalry	Ming-Jer Chen
	Disruptive innovation	The Disruptive Innovation Model; Jobs to Be Done framework	Joseph L. Bower; Clayton M. Christensen
	Value innovation	Value curve; The Three Platform	W. Chan Kim; Renée Mauborgne
	Corporate Political Strategy	Framework for Corporate Political Strategy	Amy J. Hillman; Michael A. Hitt
	Strategic Performance Management	Balanced Scorecard; Strategy Maps; Performance Prism	Andy Neely; Robert Kaplan; David Norton
	Competing for the future	Strategic Intent; Strategic Architecture; Core Competencies	C. K. Prahalad and Gary Hamel
	Complexity Perspective	Stacey's Agreement & Certainty Matrix; Strategy as Structured Chaos	Ralph D. Stacey; Peter Allen; Steve Maguire; Bill McKelvey; Shona L. Brown; Kathleen M. Eisenhardt

(*Continued*)

Table 1.1 (Continued)

Period	Key Developments	Key Strategy Tools	Key Contributors
	Strategy Under Uncertainty	Four Level Uncertainty Framework; The Strategic Postures; The Portfolio of Actions; Strategy Under Uncertainty Process	Hugh Courtney; Jane Kirkland; Patrick Viguerie
	Strategic Flexibility	An Integrative Framework; Archetypal maneuvers;	J. Stuart Evans; Henk W. Volberda; Ron Sanchez; Michael A. Hitt
Growth of MBV and RBV and the introduction of new strategy tools emphasizing innovation, agility, and design thinking in response to digital technologies and increasing complexity.			
2000s	Demand-Based View	Demand heterogeneity analysis;	Adner (2002); Adner and Zemsky (2006)
	Blue Ocean Strategy	Value Innovation; Strategy Canvas; Four Actions Framework; Six Paths Framework; Buyer Utility Map; Three Tiers of Noncustomers; Pioneer-Migrator-Settler Map	W. Chan Kim; Renée Mauborgne
	Open innovation		Henry W. Chesbrough
	Business model innovation	Business Model Canvas; Value Proposition Canvas; The Business Model Innovation Process; Dual Business Model	Alexander Osterwalder; Yves Pigneur; Mark Johnson; Clayton Christensen; Raphael Amit; Christoph Zott; Constantinos Markides

Table 1.1 (Continued)

Period	Key Developments	Key Strategy Tools	Key Contributors
	The economic theory of platforms	Pricing Strategies for Multisided Platforms; Two-sided Markets	Jean-Charles Rochet; Jean Tirole; Annabelle Gawer; Michael A. Cusumano; Andrei Hagiu
	Organizational Ambidexterity	Structural Ambidexterity; Contextual Ambidexterity	Julian Birkinshaw; Cristina Gibson; Charles O'Reilly; Michael Tushman
Continued emphasis on adaptability and strategic innovation; tools for fostering continuous learning and scenario planning gained prominence.			
2010s	Strategic Agility	Strategic Agility Framework; The Agility Factor; Agility Assessment Framework; Disruptive Inflection Points	Yves Doz; Mikko Kosonen; Donald Sull; Rita G. McGrath; Thomas D. Williams; Christopher G. Worley; Edward E. Lawler, III
	Lean Startup	The Build-Measure-Learn feedback loop; Minimal Viable Product (MVP); Customer Development methodology; Lean Canvas; Customer Factory Framework;	Eric Ries; Steve Blank; Ash Maurya
	Ecosystems Strategy	Theory of Ecosystems; Ecosystem Development Framework	Michael G. Jacobides; Carmelo Cennamo; Annabelle Gawer;

(*Continued*)

Table 1.1 (Continued)

Period	Key Developments	Key Strategy Tools	Key Contributors
	Platforms Strategy	Platforms Strategy	
	Open Strategy		Richard Whittington; David Seidl; Georg von Krogh
Focus on digital transformation and sustainability; strategy tools incorporate digital analytics, big data, and AI; increased emphasis on resilience and adaptability due to the COVID-19 pandemic.			
2020s	Artificial Intelligence (AI)	AI Strategy Framework; AI Governance Framework	Thomas H. Davenport; Nitin Mittal Marco Iansiti; Karim R. Lakhani; Georg von Krogh; Ajay Agrawal; Avi Goldfarb
	Strategic Resilience		Julia Hillmann;

embodiments of abstract theories, translating complex ideas into actionable guidelines for practitioners (March, 2006, p. 203). For these strategy tools to be truly effective and useful in real-world applications, the underlying theories must possess pragmatic validity (Worren et al., 2002). Pragmatic validity ensures that the theories are not only theoretically sound but also practically applicable, providing real utility to those implementing them in dynamic and complex environments.

Given the critical role that strategic theories and theoretical frameworks play in gaining a deeper understanding of strategy tools, it is essential to conduct a review of the theories that inform their selection. Such a review provides deeper insights into the evolution of strategic thought and the practical instruments that emerge from these theoretical foundations. By understanding the historical development and practical implications of these theories and tools, we can develop better strategy selection frameworks. This thorough understanding enables the continuous refinement of the strategy selection frameworks, ensuring they remain relevant and effective in guiding strategic decision-making in an ever-evolving landscape.

Our historical account of strategy tools development is based on the database of strategy tools we built and the historical account of strategy evolution presented in the strategic management literature (Aurik et al., 2014; Freedman, 2013, 2017, 2018; Ghemawat, 2002, 2016; Gluck et al., 1980; Henderson, 1989; Kiechel, 2010; Mahoney & McGahan, 2007; Mintzberg et al., 1998) We also considered recent reviews of theoretical developments in strategy published in the edited book *Strategic Management: State of the Field and Its Future* (2021). Additionally, we considered other theoretical reviews such as foundations of strategy (Leiblein & Reuer, 2020), four dominant strategy theories (Makadok, 2011), corporate strategy (Feldman, 2020), and strategic organization (Mahoney & McGahan, 2007).

Given the multidisciplinary character and variety of viewpoints within the vibrant and rapidly evolving field of strategy, our historical account is necessarily limited and simplified as shown in Table 1.1. The aim is to provide a broad outline of the intellectual terrain that strategy encompasses.

1.6 Challenges to Choosing the Right Strategy Approaches

Although many companies, government organizations, and strategy practitioners acknowledge the importance of tailoring their strategy approaches to the specific problems they face and their contexts, they continue using a limited set of strategy approaches that are more suitable for stable environments. This results in a misalignment with their contexts, as evidenced by Boston Consulting Group research revealing that although 75% of executives surveyed agreed that they needed to utilize different strategic approaches in different situations, only 25% of executives were using approaches that are suitable for unpredictable environments (Reeves et al., 2012).

This discrepancy reflects a structural and pervasive phenomenon which we term the "Strategy Gap". This is the systematic failure to align strategy formulation approaches with the complexity, uncertainty, and context-specific challenges organizations confront. Its existence is, perhaps, unsurprising given that there are several barriers to choosing the right strategy approaches.

We have drawn on behavioral strategy research – which applies insights from cognitive and social psychology into strategic management to examine how cognitive biases, emotions, and social factors influence how decision-makers and strategists actually formulate strategies, rather than assuming perfectly rational choices – and more specifically, have utilized the framework developed by Powell et al. (2011). This has enabled us to categorize strategic selection barriers into three interdependent levels: Individual, Knowledge and Capability, and Institutional and Social. These levels correspond to different sources of constraint: cognitive, developmental, and institutional that inhibit the effective matching of strategy approaches to contextual demands.

1.6.1 Individual-Level Barriers

Cognitive biases and limited mental models shape how strategists perceive complexity, uncertainty, and causality.

1.6.1.1 *Familiarity*

Familiarity with a strategy tool often plays a significant role in its selection and use. Managers tend to prefer tools they are accustomed to and have previously used successfully. Familiarity breeds confidence in the tool's applicability and effectiveness, making managers more likely to employ it in their strategic processes (Clark, 1997; Frost, 2003). Several factors contribute to the familiarity of certain strategy tools. First, many strategy tools are taught extensively in business and management schools and universities, making them familiar to graduates entering the workforce. Academic curricula often include foundational tools such as SWOT, PESTLE, and Porter's Five Forces, ensuring that future managers are well-versed in their application (Wright et al., 2013).

Second, consulting firms frequently employ established strategy tools in their work with clients. The widespread use of these tools by prestigious firms lends them credibility and reinforces their familiarity among managers who engage with consultants (Jarzabkowski & Kaplan, 2015). Furthermore, some strategy tools are popularized by business and management publications who are usually affiliated with prestigious educational institutions or top strategy consulting firms (Kiechel, 2010). However, these familiar strategy tools represent only a small number of the strategy tools that are available and could enhance strategic thinking and aid in the development of effective strategies (Hakala & Vuorinen, 2020).

1.6.1.2 *The Lack of Complexity Perspective*

The traditional analytical thinking in strategy development is deeply rooted in linear and mechanistic worldviews (Newtonian-Cartesian), assuming that problems exist within closed, predictable systems (Capra, 1996). Such a mindset, which simplifies the intricate reality of these challenges into linear and compartmentalized components, favors the use of analytical strategy tools. This traditional perspective fails to account for the dynamic, interconnected nature of modern business challenges, which demand the use of different strategy tools (Wright et al., 2013).

Adopting a complexity mindset helps in tackling this challenge. However, it requires different strategy tools that help managers to think in terms of systems, interrelationships, and patterns, rather than in isolated silos. This shift not only allows for a more holistic understanding of challenges but also opens up new avenues for innovation and creative problem-solving.

1.6.1.3 *Avoiding Uncertainty*

Humans are cognitively prone to avoid uncertainty, a trait that creates systematic blind spots in strategy formulation. This uncertainty avoidance manifests through interconnected cognitive biases that make strategists underestimate, dismiss, or artificially reduce uncertainty in strategic decision-making. Three cognitive biases combine to create systematic resistance to uncertainty-appropriate strategy approaches: overconfidence bias, confirmation bias, and the ostrich effect (Meyer & Kunreuther, 2017).

Overconfidence bias leads strategists to systematically overestimate their predictive capabilities, particularly regarding market conditions and competitive responses (Moore & Healy, 2008). Senior leaders place excessive confidence in intuitive judgment or past experience, choosing strategy approaches based on gut feeling rather than evidence-based contextual diagnosis (Russo & Schoemaker, 1992). This connects to the illusion of validity, where decision-makers have excessive confidence in judgments based on limited or unreliable information (Kahneman, 2011), as well as research on managerial overconfidence demonstrating how executives' inflated self-assessments lead to sub-optimal strategic decisions (Malmendier & Tate, 2005). Ultimately, it indicates that strategic leaders often fail to recognize the conditions under which intuitive expertise is unreliable, particularly in uncertain environments where feedback is delayed or ambiguous (Kahneman & Klein, 2009).

Confirmation bias reinforces these choices by seeking information supporting chosen frameworks while dismissing contradictory evidence (Courtney, 2001). Strategic planning becomes validation of predetermined conclusions rather than genuine environmental analysis that might reveal uncertainty requiring adaptive approaches.

The ostrich effect manifests when environmental uncertainty reaches uncomfortable levels, causing leaders to intensify reliance on familiar analytical frameworks rather than embracing uncertainty-designed approaches like scenario planning or adaptive management (Meyer & Kunreuther, 2017).

This combination of human errors systematically biases strategy approach selection toward approaches that dismiss uncertainty regardless of environmental realities, preventing organizations from embracing dynamic, experimental, and emergent approaches that could provide competitive advantage in VUCA environments.

1.6.1.4 Attribution Bias

Attribution bias represents a critical individual-level cognitive barrier that systematically distorts strategy approach selection through misinterpretation of past strategic outcomes. This attribution bias manifests when strategists disproportionately credit their chosen methodologies for strategic successes while downplaying the role of environmental factors, timing, or contextual variables beyond their control in both successes and failures (Bettman & Weitz, 1983; Miller & Ross, 1975). This false attribution creates inflated confidence in particular methodologies and increases likelihood of inappropriate application in different contexts. Success bias creates "competency traps" where past success prevents adaptation to new contexts requiring different approaches (Levitt & March, 1988). This creates systematic distortion in learning from strategic experience that profoundly impacts future strategy approach selection. Attribution bias connects to outcome bias, evaluating strategy effectiveness based solely on results rather than decision-making process appropriateness (Baron & Hershey, 1988). Organizations may abandon appropriate strategy approaches due to short-term results while persisting with inappropriate analytical frameworks that coincided with favorable conditions. Breaking attribution bias requires fostering cognitive discipline and reflective practices, which might be termed "strategic humility", to critically examine the true sources of strategic outcomes. This involves structured post-mortem processes that distinguish between environmental factors and methodological effectiveness (Kahneman, 2011).

1.6.1.5 Cognitive Rigidity

Strategists often exhibit cognitive rigidity, a resistance to updating entrenched mental models shaped by past experiences, education, and cultural norms (König et al., 2013). While these models help simplify complexity, they can become misaligned with dynamic environments, narrowing perception and interpretation of strategic challenges. This rigidity can distort diagnosis, leading to premature dismissal of novel or context-based approaches and repeated reliance on outdated strategy approaches. It may be reinforced through escalation of commitment (Staw, 1981), wherein strategists persist in investing in a strategic approach they recognize as ineffective due to prior commitments, or collective groupthink dynamics (Janis, 1982), which discourage dissent and critical reassessment. Research in organizational learning linked this barrier to cognitive inertia, where frames become embedded in organizational systems, thus creating resistance to change (Kaplan & Tripsas, 2008; Tripsas & Gavetti, 2000).

1.6.2 Knowledge and Capability-Level Barriers

Gaps in exposure, access, and analytical competence inhibit effective selection and use of strategy approaches.

1.6.2.1 The Availability of Strategy Selection Tools

While there are many strategy approaches, frameworks, methods, and techniques available today (Vuorinen et al., 2018), there is limited guidance on how to choose between them to formulate strategies in the different strategic contexts organizations operate in and the strategic problems they seek to address. "The problem managers face is not a lack of appropriate tools... But the sheer variety can be overwhelming without clear guidance about when to use one tool or combination of tools over another" (Courtney et al., 2013, p. 63). This shortage of strategy selection tools to help practitioners choose the right strategy approach is often the reason why they fail to determine suitable strategy approaches (Reeves et al., 2015).

1.6.2.2 The Quality of Strategy Selection Tools

In addition to the paucity of strategy selection methods, most strategy selection tools are either outdated or lack the robustness critical to handle today's dynamic environment. This will become very clearer in our extensive review of the existing strategy selection methods in Chapter 4.

Notably, strategy tools are developed at a faster pace than the strategy selection frameworks that could provide guidance on their use. Although some of them remain useful in specific sectors and for some strategy approaches, they are becoming outdated because they do not cover many of the strategy approaches that have been created or have evolved since their creation. For example, the underlying competition logic for some of the frameworks is based on the dynamic structure, structure-conduct-performance perspective, which emphasizes industry structures and its players (Bain, 1959). This perspective is still valid for some industries, but it is less valid when analyzing new bases of competition, such as ecosystems, the rates of learning, resilience, imagination, and the dual world of the digital and physical (Kimura et al., 2021)

1.6.2.3 *Exposure to a Limited Set of Strategy Tools*

Most strategy practitioners and executives are exposed to a limited set of strategy approaches, and these strategy tools tend to be geared toward stable environments and noncomplex problems (Frost, 2003). There are several reasons for this. First, most strategy courses offered by business and management schools teach a limited set of strategy tools. They often include foundational tools such as SWOT, PESTLE, and Porter's Five Forces, ensuring that future managers are well-versed in their application (Wright et al., 2013). Most of these tools emphasize the use of structured analytical strategy approaches suitable for predictable environments (Jarzabkowski et al., 2013).

Second, due to disciplinary and sectoral silos, many strategy approaches remain unknown outside the domains where they are practiced. Tools developed by sustainability practitioners and academics, such as transition approaches to managing complex environmental and socioeconomic challenges, serve as an example of this, with limited visibility outside of the sustainability field. Third, the repeated use of these few strategy approaches helps build competency, which could turn into "core rigidity" (Leonard-Barton, 1992) when users insist on using them in the wrong contexts. Lastly, there has been a tendency for strategic management tools to adopt a one-size-fits-all, or generic applicability regardless of culture, industry, and sector. Most developers of strategy tools are overoptimistic of the power of their tools to solve most of the strategic issues regardless of the environments they are situated in. They rarely specify the boundary conditions of their tools.

1.6.2.4 *Lack of Comprehensive Inventory of Strategy Tools*

There is a large pool of strategy tools, which remains undiscovered by practitioners because they are less disseminated through the common channels of diffusion (Sahlin-Andersson & Engwall, 2002). However, these less-known strategy tools are valuable for leaders, strategists and practitioners who want to advance their strategic thinking and build a broader strategy tool kit that allow them to develop more creative, competitive or differentiated strategies.

To increase the accessibility to a wide range of strategy tools, some authors have developed inventories of strategy tools (Hakala & Vuorinen, 2020; Pascale, 1990; Reeves et al., 2015; Rigby et al., 2023; Vuorinen et al., 2018). These efforts are helpful as a building block that can be built but as it is, they fall short for two reasons. First, they are not comprehensive in their coverage. Second, inventories should be continually updated to remain relevant.

1.6.2.5 *Competency of Managers*

The selection and effective use of strategy tools require managers to possess key competencies. One of these competencies is strategic thinking, which involves understanding systemic relationships, having clear direction, seizing emerging opportunities, considering temporal implications, and testing strategic hypotheses, thereby enabling the use of more complicated tools (Liedtka, 1998). Other competencies include paradoxical thinking, which entails recognizing and managing contradictory yet interrelated elements, facilitating the selection of more nuanced and adaptable strategy tools (Smith & Lewis, 2011).

Peripheral vision is another important competency, referring to the skill in identifying and interpreting weak signals from the periphery of the organization's environment, which can be crucial for anticipating and responding to emerging trends (Day & Schoemaker, 2006). Connected thinking is the capability to see the interconnectedness of various strategic issues and understand how changes in one area can impact others (Senge, 1990). Managers should also be encouraged to adopt multiple viewpoints to gain a more comprehensive understanding of strategic challenges (Bolman & Deal, 2017). Lastly, differentiation and integration refer to the skill of distinguishing between complex issues and integrating diverse elements into a coherent strategy (Kurtz & Snowden, 2003).

These competencies are lacking in many organizations, to develop these competencies, organizations must actively nurture them through deliberate practice, multidisciplinary teams, and fostering an environment where managers are encouraged to seek ideas from outside their immediate fields and consider historical and future contexts (Wright et al., 2013).

1.6.3 Organizational and Social Barriers

Institutional norms, social pressures, and structural routines constrain strategic choice and reinforce conformity.

1.6.3.1 Legitimacy

Legitimacy refers to the perceived validity and acceptance of a strategy tool within the organization and the broader strategic community. Institutional theory and mimetic processes play a significant role in establishing this legitimacy. According to institutional theory, organizations adopt practices and structures that are considered legitimate within their institutional environment to gain acceptance and support (DiMaggio & Powell, 1983).

Mimetic processes, where organizations imitate the successful practices of peers or industry leaders, further enhance the legitimacy of strategy tools. When a tool is widely adopted and endorsed by reputable organizations, it gains legitimacy, encouraging other organizations to follow suit to maintain or enhance their legitimacy (DiMaggio & Powell, 1983; Scott, 2014). Tools such as Porter's Five Forces and the Balanced Scorecard have achieved high legitimacy due to their widespread acceptance and robust theoretical foundations, making them popular choices among managers (Spee & Jarzabkowski, 2009). Attaining legitimacy is helped by the routinization of a select, well-known set of strategy tools (Jarzabkowski & Kaplan, 2015) and the adoption of accepted best practices even if they do not fit the fast-paced environment they operate (Snowden & Boone, 2007).

1.6.3.2 Template-Based Strategy

The template-style strategy has been mandated by many government agencies, incorporating a uniform approach to formulating strategy consisting of standardized templates to be filled in with each prescribed step (Bryson, 2018). Some corporate centers also mandate their use for their subsidiaries (Grant, 2003). One version of such templates calls for filling in the blanks with vision, mission, values, and strategies. This is problematic because such strategic planning often becomes a routine, "tick box" exercise carried out with little critical thinking concerning the realistic challenges and opportunities faced by organizations (Rumelt, 2011).

1.6.3.3 Strategic Theater

Organizations often select strategy approaches to manage external perceptions rather than address internal strategic challenges. This includes adopting strategy approaches such as balanced scorecards and strategy maps, not because they fit the context or are analytically superior, but because they signal innovation, responsiveness, or legitimacy to external stakeholders. This phenomenon reflects how organizations use signaling to communicate information about their beliefs, competencies, and intentions through specific behaviors that lend credence to underlying values (Connelly et al., 2011), even when those behaviors may not enhance actual performance. Organizations engage in ceremonial adoption of practices to gain legitimacy benefits while performing little or none of the activities typically associated with such practices.

This behavior is grounded in impression management (Goffman, 1959), signaling theory (Spence, 1973), and institutional theory, particularly the concept of ceremonial adoption to maintain legitimacy (Meyer & Rowan, 1977). Impression management, as conceptualized by Goffman, involves the deliberate control of information and behaviors in social interactions to influence how others perceive an individual or organization, much like actors performing on a stage for their audience. In the organizational context, this translates to carefully orchestrated "front stage" performances of strategic sophistication for external stakeholders, while the actual "backstage" strategic work may remain unchanged or underdeveloped.

1.6.3.4 Multi-actor Strategy Complexity

In many organizations, strategy formulation involves multiple departments, actors, and hierarchical levels, creating coordination challenges that impair the selection of appropriate strategy approaches. This multi-stakeholder environment generates conflicting interpretations, competing priorities, and political compromises that prevent clear strategic alignment. The resulting complexity contributes to organizational inertia and the adoption of least-resistance strategies that satisfy multiple constituencies rather than choosing the right strategy approach. This barrier is grounded in theories of distributed decision-making and organizational ambiguity (March & Olsen, 1976) and the political dynamics that shape strategic outcomes (Pettigrew, 1973). The coordination challenges inherent in multi-stakeholder strategic processes often overwhelm analytical considerations, leading to suboptimal strategy selection.

1.6.3.5 Temporal Misalignment

Organizations often become trapped in rigid strategic planning cycles that are dictated by budgeting processes, board review timetables, or regulatory reporting requirements rather than by the actual pace of environmental change. These institutionalized temporal structures create systematic delays, limit strategic iteration, and prevent organizations from selecting or shifting strategy approaches in response to emerging complexity or discontinuous change. This temporal rigidity forces leaders to defer strategic responses until the next formal planning cycle, even when the need for strategic response is immediate and obvious. The mismatch between organizational planning rhythms and environmental change tempo becomes particularly problematic during turbulent periods that demand fast feedback loops, real-time strategic adjustment, or mid-cycle reformulation.

This barrier is grounded in research on temporal structuring in organizations, which demonstrates how time becomes socially constructed through institutionalized routines and formal structures (Orlikowski & Yates, 2002). The strategy-as-practice (SAP) literature shows how embedded practices like annual planning sessions and quarterly reviews shape and constrain strategic behavior (Vaara & Whittington, 2012). When strategic timing is driven by calendars rather than context, organizations often fail to adopt exploratory strategies, experimentation, or adaptive learning approaches precisely when they are most needed.

1.7 How to Use This Book

This book is organized into nine chapters and is designed to be both a comprehensive guide and a practical reference. Readers can approach the book in a linear fashion, beginning with Chapter 1 and progressing through to Chapter 9, or they can navigate directly to specific chapters based on their immediate interests or strategic challenges.

To understand the foundation of this book, readers are encouraged to begin with Chapter 2, which introduces the 7C Strategy Wheel. This chapter explains the rationale behind the model, defines its seven strategic postures, and outlines how each posture connects to distinct strategy approaches. Gaining a clear understanding of this framework early on will help readers make better sense of the strategy selection process and navigate the remaining chapters with greater clarity and purpose.

Chapters 3–9 focus on one of the seven strategic postures. These chapters are self-contained and include their own references, allowing you to explore specific strategic situations without having to read the entire book. For instance, if your organization is dealing with high levels of complexity and uncertainty, you may turn directly to Chapter 5, which explores the Coping strategic posture. This chapter provides a detailed discussion of how to build resilience, robustness, and flexibility using strategy approaches such as strategic resilience, dynamic robustness, and strategic flexibility. It draws on multiple theoretical perspectives and introduces practical methods such as worst-case planning, scenario planning, and dynamic adaptive planning. Readers facing other types of strategic contexts will find equally focused guidance in the corresponding posture chapters.

The book can be used in several ways:

- As a **diagnostic tool** to help determine which strategic posture and strategy approaches best fit your organization's context.
- As a **learning resource** for educators and students exploring the diversity of strategy approaches and strategic thinking.
- As a **practical reference** for consultants and practitioners seeking applicable frameworks, theories, and tools for diverse strategic challenges.
- As a **design guide** for strategy leaders developing custom strategy processes, toolkits, and roadmaps aligned with specific organizational contexts.
- As a **strategic evaluation aid** for senior decision-makers and boards assessing the coherence, relevance, and adaptability of their current strategy formulation practices.

Whether you choose to read the book from start to finish or dive into a specific chapter, the aim is to help you make more informed strategic choices. Each chapter stands on its own, but when read together, they offer a coherent and integrated approach to strategy formulation that aligns with the complexity and diversity of real-world strategic challenges.

References

Adner, R. (2002). When are Technologies Disruptive? A Demand-based View of the Emergence of Competition. *Strategic Management Journal*, 23(8), 667–688.

Adner, R., & Zemsky, P. (2006). A demand-based perspective on sustainable competitive advantage. *Strategic Management Journal*, *27*(3), 215–239.

Aurik, J. C., Fabel, M., & Jonk, G. J. (2014). *The Future of Strategy: A Transformative Approach to Strategy for a World That Won't Stand Still*. McGraw-Hill.

Bain, J. S. (1959). *Industrial Organization*. John Wiley & Sons.

Baron, J., & Hershey, J. C. (1988). Outcome Bias in Decision Evaluation. *Journal of Personality and Social Psychology*, 54(4), 569–579.

Bettman, J. R., & Weitz, B. A. (1983). Attributions in the Board Room: Causal Reasoning in Corporate Annual Reports. *Administrative Science Quarterly*, *28*(2), 165–183.

Bolman, L. G., & Deal, T. E. (2017). *Reframing Organizations: Artistry, Choice, and Leadership* (6th ed.). Jossey-Bass.

Bryson, J. M. (2018). *Strategic Planning for Public and Nonprofit Organizations: A Guide to Strengthening and Sustaining Organizational Achievement* (5th ed.). John Wiley & Sons.

Capra, F. (1996). *The Web of Life: A New Scientific Understanding of Living Systems* (1st ed.). Anchor Books.

Caves, R.E. and Porter, M.E. (1977). From entry barriers to mobility barriers: Conjectural decisions and contrived deterrence to new competition. *The Quarterly Journal of Economics*, *91*, 241–261.

Caves, R. E., & Porter, M. E. (1978). Market structure, oligopoly, and the stability of market shares. *Journal of Industrial Economics*, *26*(4), 289–313.

Clark, D. N. (1997). Strategic Management Tool Usage: A Comparative Study. *Strategic Change*, *6*(7), 417–427.

Connelly, B. L., Certo, S. T., Ireland, R. D., & Reutzel, C. R. (2011). Signaling Theory: A Review and Assessment. *Journal of Management*, *37*(1), 39–67.

Courtney, H. (2001). *20/20 Foresight: Crafting Strategy in an Uncertain World*. Harvard Business School Press.

Courtney, H., Lovallo, D., & Clarke, C. (2013). Deciding How to Decide. *Harvard Business Review*, *91*(11), 62–70.

Dameron, S., Lê, J. K., & LeBaron, C. (2015). Materializing Strategy and Strategizing Material: Why Matter Matters. *British Journal of Management*, *26*(S1), S1–S12.

Day, G. S., & Schoemaker, P. J. H. (2006). *Peripheral Vision: Detecting the Weak Signals That Will Make or Break Your Company*. Harvard Business School Press.

DiMaggio, P. J., & Powell, W. W. (1983). The Iron Cage Revisited: Institutional Isomorphism and Collective Rationality in Organizational Fields. *American Sociological Review*, *48*(2), 147–160.

Duhaime, I. M., Hitt, M. A., & Lyles, M. A. (2021). *Strategic Management: State of the Field and Its Future*. Oxford University Press.

Elsbach, K. D., & van Knippenberg, D. (2020). Creating High-Impact Literature Reviews: An Argument for 'Integrative Reviews'. *Journal of Management Studies*, *57*(6), 1277–1289.

Feldman, E. R. (2020). Corporate Strategy: Past, Present, and Future. *Strategic Management Review*, *1*(1), 179–206.

Freedman, L. (2013). *Strategy: A History*. Oxford University Press.

Freedman, L. (2017). The Meaning of Strategy: Part I: The Origin Story. *Texas National Security Review*, *1*(1), 90–105.

Freedman, L. (2018). The Meaning of Strategy: Part II: The Objectives. *Texas National Security Review*, *1*(2), 34–56.

Frost, F. A. (2003). The Use of Strategic Tools by Small and Medium-Sized Enterprises: An Australasian Study. *Strategic Change*, *12*(1), 49–62.

Gavetti, G., & Rivkin, J. W. (2005). How Strategists Really Think. *Harvard Business Review*, *83*(4), 54–63.

Ghemawat, P. (2002). Competition and Business Strategy in Historical Perspective. *The Business History Review*, *76*(1), 37–74.

Ghemawat, P. (2016). Evolving Ideas about Business Strategy. *Business History Review*, *90*(4), 727–749.

Gilbert, R. J. (1989). The role of potential competition in industrial organization. *Journal of Economic Perspectives*, *3*(3), 107–127.

Gluck, F. W., Kaufman, S. P., & Walleck, A. S. (1980). Strategic Management for Competitive Advantage. *Harvard Business Review*, *58*(4), 154–161.

Goffman, E. (1959). *The Presentation of Self in Everyday Life*. Anchor Books.

Grant, R. M. (2003). Strategic Planning in a Turbulent Environment: Evidence from the Oil Majors. *Strategic Management Journal*, *24*(6), 491–517.

Hakala, H., & Vuorinen, T. (2020). *Tools for Strategy: A Starter Kit for Academics and Practitioners*. Cambridge University Press.

Henderson, B. D. (1989). The Origin of Strategy. *Harvard Business Review*, *67*(6), 139–143.

Jalonen, K., Schildt, H., & Vaara, E. (2018). Strategic Concepts as Micro-Level Tools in Strategic Sensemaking. *Strategic Management Journal*, *39*(10), 2794–2826.

Janis, I. L. (1982). *Groupthink: Psychological Studies of Policy Decisions and Fiascoes*. Houghton Mifflin.

Jarzabkowski, P., Giulietti, M., Oliveira, B., & Amoo, N. (2013). "We Don't Need No Education"—Or Do We? Management Education and Alumni Adoption of Strategy Tools. *Journal of Management Inquiry*, *22*(1), 4–24.

Jarzabkowski, P., & Kaplan, S. (2015). Strategy Tools-in-Use: A Framework for Understanding "Technologies of Rationality" in Practice. *Strategic Management Journal*, *36*(4), 537–558.

Jarzabkowski, P., & Wilson, D. C. (2006). Actionable Strategy Knowledge: A Practice Perspective. *European Management Journal*, *24*(5), 348–367.

Kahneman, D. (2011). *Thinking, Fast and Slow* (1st ed.). Farrar, Straus and Giroux.

Kahneman, D., & Klein, G. (2009). Conditions for Intuitive Expertise: A Failure to Disagree. *American Psychologist*, *64*(6), 515–526.

Kaplan, S., & Tripsas, M. (2008). Thinking About Technology: Applying a Cognitive Lens to Technical Change. *Research Policy*, *37*(5), 790–805.

Kiechel, W. I. (2010). *Lords of Strategy: The Secret Intellectual History of the New Corporate World*. Harvard Business School Press.

Kimura, R., Reeves, M., & Whitaker, K. (2021). The New Logic of Competition. In M. Reeves & F. Candelon (Eds.), *Dynamic Business Strategy: Competing in a Fast-changing, Uncertain Context* (pp. 71–80). De Gruyte.

Knott, P. (2006). A Typology of Strategy Tool Applications. *Management Decision*, *44*(8), 1090–1105.

König, A., Kammerlander, N., & Enders, A. (2013). The Family Innovator's Dilemma: How Family Influence Affects the Adoption of Discontinuous Technologies by Incumbent Firms. *Academy of Management Review*, *38*(3), 418–441.

Kurtz, C. F., & Snowden, D. J. (2003). The New Dynamics of Strategy: Sense-Making in a Complex and Complicated World. *IBM Systems Journal*, *42*(3), 462–483.

Leiblein, M. J., & Reuer, J. J. (2020). Foundations and Futures of Strategic Management. *Strategic Management Review*, *1*(1), 1–33.

Leonard-Barton, D. (1992). Core Capabilities and Core Rigidities: A Paradox in Managing New Product Development. *Strategic Management Journal*, *13*(S1), 111–125.

Levitt, B., & March, J. G. (1988). Organizational Learning. *Annual Review of Sociology*, *14*(1), 319–338.

Liedtka, J. M. (1998). Strategic Thinking: Can It Be Taught? *Long Range Planning*, *31*(1), 120–129.

Mahoney, J. T., & McGahan, A. M. (2007). The Field of Strategic Management within the Evolving Science of Strategic Organization. *Strategic Organization*, *5*(1), 79–99.

Makadok, R. (2011). Invited Editorial: The Four Theories of Profit and Their Joint Effects. *Journal of Management*, *37*(5), 1316–1334.

Malmendier, U., & Tate, G. (2005). CEO Overconfidence and Corporate Investment. *The Journal of Finance*, *60*(6), 2661–2700.

March, J. G. (2006). Rationality, Foolishness, and Adaptive Intelligence. *Strategic Management Journal*, *27*(3), 201–214.

March, J. G., & Olsen, J. P. (1976). *Ambiguity and Choice in Organizations*. Universitetsforlaget.

Meyer, J. W., & Rowan, B. (1977). Institutionalized Organizations: Formal Structure as Myth and Ceremony. *American Journal of Sociology*, 83(2), 340–363.

Meyer, R. J., & Kunreuther, H. (2017). *The Ostrich Paradox: Why We Underprepare for Disasters*. Wharton Digital Press.

Miller, D. T., & Ross, M. (1975). Self-Serving Biases in the Attribution of Causality: Fact Or Fiction? *Psychological Bulletin*, 82(2), 213–225.

Mintzberg, H., Ahlstrand, B. W., & Lampel, J. (1998). *Strategy Safari: A Guided Tour through the Wilds of Strategic Management*. Free Press.

Moore, D. A., & Healy, P. J. (2008). The Trouble with Overconfidence. *Psychological Review*, *115*(2), 502–517.

Orlikowski, W. J., & Yates, J. (2002). It's About Time: Temporal Structuring in Organizations. *Organization Science*, *13*(6), 684–700.

Pascale, R. T. (1990). *Managing on the Edge: How the Smartest Companies Use Conflict to Stay Ahead*. Simon and Schuster.

Pettigrew, A. M. (1973). *The Politics of Organizational Decision-Making* (1st ed.). Tavistock.

Porter, M.E. (1979). How competitive forces shape strategy. *Harvard Business Review*, *57*, 137–145.

Powell, T. C., Lovallo, D., & Fox, C. R. (2011). Behavioral Strategy. *Strategic Management Journal*, *32*(13), 1369–1386.

Reeves, M., Haanaes, K., & Sinha, J. K. (2015). *Your Strategy Needs a Strategy: How to Choose and Execute the Right Approach*. Harvard Business Review Press.

Reeves, M., Love, C., & Tillmanns, P. (2012). Your Strategy Needs a Strategy. *Harvard Business Review*, 90(9), 76–83.

Rigby, D., Bilodeau, B., & Ronan, K. (2023). *Management Tools & Trends 2023*. Bain & Company, Inc.

Rumelt, R. P. (2011). *Good Strategy Bad Strategy: The Difference and Why it Matters* (1st ed.). Crown Business.

Russo, J. E., & Schoemaker, P. J. H. (1992). Managing Overconfidence. *MIT Sloan Management Review*, 33(2), 7–17.

Sahlin-Andersson, K., & Engwall, L. (2002). *The Expansion of Management Knowledge: Carriers, Flows, and Sources*. Stanford University Press.

Scott, W. R. (2014). *Institutions and Organizations: Ideas, Interests, and Identities* (4th ed.). Sage Publications.

Senge, P. M. (1990). *The Fifth Discipline: The Art & Practice of the Learning Organisation* (1st ed.). Doubleday.

Smith, W. K., & Lewis, M. W. (2011). Toward a Theory of Paradox: A Dynamic Equilibrium Model of Organizing. *Academy of Management Review*, *36*(2), 381–403.

Snowden, D. J., & Boone, M. E. (2007). A Leader's Framework for Decision Making. *Harvard Business Review*, *85*(11), 68–76.

Spee, A. P., & Jarzabkowski, P. (2009). Strategy Tools as Boundary Objects. *Strategic Organization*, *7*(2), 223–232.

Spence, M. (1973). Job Market Signaling. *The Quarterly Journal of Economics*, *87*(3), 355–374.

Staw, B. M. (1981). The Escalation of Commitment to a Course of Action. *Academy of Management Review*, *6*(4), 577–587.

Torraco, R. J. (2005). Writing Integrative Literature Reviews: Guidelines and Examples. *Human Resource Development Review*, *4*(3), 356–367.

Tripsas, M., & Gavetti, G. (2000). Capabilities, Cognition, and Inertia: Evidence from Digital Imaging. *Strategic Management Journal*, *21*(10-11), 1147–1161.

Vaara, E., & Whittington, R. (2012). Strategy-as-Practice: Taking Social Practices Seriously. *Academy of Management Annals*, *6*(1), 285–336.

Vuorinen, T., Hakala, H., Kohtamäki, M., & Uusitalo, K. (2018). Mapping the Landscape of Strategy Tools: A Review on Strategy Tools Published in Leading Journals Within the Past 25 Years. *Long Range Planning*, *51*(4), 586–605.

Worren, N. A., Moore, K., & Elliott, R. (2002). When Theories Become Tools: Toward a Framework for Pragmatic Validity. *Human Relations*, *55*(10), 1227–1250.

Wright, R. P., Paroutis, S. E., & Blettner, D. P. (2013). How Useful Are the Strategic Tools We Teach in Business Schools? *Journal of Management Studies*, *50*(1), 92–125.

2
The 7C Strategy Wheel

2.1 Introduction

The absence of robust integrative frameworks that help navigate the complex and dynamic contours of the strategy landscape and the growing repertoires of strategic postures, strategy development approaches, and methods is challenging. Executives, policymakers, and strategy practitioners who do not want to settle for traditional strategy approaches designed for stable environments will find it difficult to identify and choose among approaches and convince their organizations to adopt them. Therefore, an effective strategy framework should offer strategists a comprehensive strategy toolkit by revealing the many strategy approaches that they could use from diverse disciplines and sectors.

Our answer to these challenges is the 7C Strategy Wheel. This helps organizations navigate the complexities of the strategy landscape and serves as an invaluable strategy toolkit that provides an extensive set of strategy approaches for addressing various strategic contexts and challenges.

2.2 The Characteristics of the Framework

The 7C Strategy Wheel is defined by many key qualities that make it an adaptable and comprehensive instrument for developing strategies in a variety of strategic scenarios. These qualities are intended to assist organizations in overcoming the challenges they encounter when selecting the best strategy approach by addressing the constraints of existing strategy approach selection frameworks. The 7C Strategy Wheel has five primary qualities: it is informed by theory and practice, serves as the most comprehensive strategy toolkit, balances strategic structural factors with strategic agency, adopts a contingency approach, and uses a common language.

DOI: 10.4324/9781003684060-2

2.2.1 Framework Informed by Theory and Practice

As discussed in Chapter 1, Section 1.3, the 7C Strategy Wheel is grounded in a comprehensive integrative review of theoretical, empirical, and practitioner knowledge bases. This approach, as defined by Torraco (2005) and elaborated by Elsbach and van Knippenberg (2020), goes beyond a mere description of the field to generate novel insights and perspectives through critical analysis and synthesis of the existing body of knowledge.

The framework's development draws upon six key sources.

- Extensive catalogue of over 300 strategy tools over the past 100 years.
- In-depth examination of over 25 theoretical perspectives from various disciplines, including strategic management, organization theories, economic theories, sociological theories, public policy theories, future studies, sustainability, and critical management studies.
- Evaluation of over 20 strategy selection frameworks.
- Evaluation of over 15 strategic contextual variables that impact strategy formulation.
- Extensive review of more than 2,000 literature pieces on strategic management, encompassing both peer-reviewed academic research and practitioner-oriented publications spanning decades of strategic management thinking.
- Analytical review of over 200 business and public strategies across different industries, organizational sizes, and geographic regions.

This integrative and interdisciplinary approach positions the 7C Strategy Wheel as a unique contribution to the field of strategic management.

2.2.2 The Most Comprehensive Strategy Toolkit

The 7C Strategy Wheel provides the most comprehensive and integrated toolkit for strategic thinking and decision-making in today's complex and rapidly changing business environment. Unlike most strategy frameworks, which focus on a single level or at most two, the 7C Strategy Wheel offers a detailed three-level architecture that spans from high-level strategic postures and thorough strategy approaches to specific strategy methods.

At the highest level, the framework introduces seven distinct strategic postures: Calculating, Clarifying, Coping, Crafting, Connecting, Conquering, and Challenging. Each posture represents a different way an organization can respond to uncertainty, seize opportunities, and address strategic challenges. By distinguishing these postures, the framework enables organizations to develop a more nuanced understanding of their strategic alternatives and make better-informed choices. In contrast, most frameworks offer only three or four postures. For example, McKinsey's "Strategy Under Uncertainty" framework proposes three postures: adapting, shaping, and reserving the right to play (Courtney, 2001; Courtney et al., 1997). Similarly, the well-known typology by Miles and Snow (1978) identifies four strategy types: Prospector, Defender, Analyzer, and Reactor.

Beyond strategic postures, at the intermediate level of strategy approaches, the 7C Strategy Wheel presents 28 distinct approaches, each logically linked to specific strategic postures. This breadth allows strategists to choose a formulation logic that aligns with their organizational stance and environmental context. In contrast, many popular models rely on simplified 2×2 matrices that typically offer four to five approaches. BCG's Strategy Palette, for instance, includes five approaches: classical, adaptive, shaping, visionary, and renewal (Reeves et al., 2015; Reeves et al., 2012).

At the most operational level, the framework delivers 59 strategy methods that are tied to specific approaches. These methods provide structured guidance for applying strategic thinking in practice. Other frameworks offer far fewer tools at this granular level. The strategy in 3D framework, for example, presents a blend of 15 methods and techniques (Fisher et al., 2020).

This degree of depth and integration of the levels makes the 7C Strategy Wheel a powerful and practical strategy toolkit. Through its extensive three-tier architecture, the framework bridges the gap between high-level strategic stance and operational implementation, providing strategists with unprecedented breadth and depth in their approach to strategy formulation. It also enhances awareness of the implications, biases, and risks associated with different strategic choices, supporting more rigorous and context-sensitive decision-making. Additionally, it serves as a dynamic learning tool, enabling organizations to continuously refine and evolve their strategies as new insights emerge and experience accumulates.

2.2.3 Balances Strategic Structural Factors with Strategic Agency

The 7C Strategy Wheel adeptly navigates the intricate relationship between strategic context, characterized by structural factors such as uncertainty, ambiguity, and complexity, and the strategic agency wielded by individual or collective actors such as CEOs, top management teams, strategists, and politicians. It seeks a middle ground, recognizing the limitations inherent in the extremes of structuralism and intentionalism (Hay, 1995, 2002).

Structuralism advocates the idea that large-scale, systemic factors predominantly dictate strategy approaches and outcomes, as explained by population ecology theory (Hannan & Freeman, 1977) and institutional theory (DiMaggio & Powell, 1983). This often underplays the influence of individual actions and decisions. On the other hand, intentionalism, also known as strategic choice (Child, 1972), champions the notion that the choices and actions of individuals are the primary drivers of strategy outcomes, at times neglecting the impact of larger structures that can either constrain or shape those choices. Both perspectives in their extreme forms fall short of fully encapsulating the nuanced reality of strategy, where individual actions are both influenced by and influential for broader structural contexts.

Our framework underscores the importance of understanding both structural factors and agency. Structural factors encompass elements such as environmental uncertainty, ambiguity, complexity, and institutions. They set the stage for strategy actors, defining the boundaries and providing the resources that either enable or restrict actions. Conversely, strategic agency pertains to the ability of individuals or dominant coalitions (Cyert & March, 1963) to act autonomously and make independent choices. It refers to how individuals and groups interact with, adapt to, and occasionally modify the structural contexts they encounter.

The 7C Strategy Wheel's balanced approach to strategy formulation acknowledges that while individuals are influenced by and operate within broader structures, they also possess the capacity to make decisions and drive change. This perspective offers a more comprehensive understanding of strategy dynamics, enriching both the theoretical depth and practical applicability of strategic analysis.

Adopting a balanced approach yields several benefits. It enables a more holistic and comprehensive analysis, capturing the dynamic interplay between individual actors and the larger systems they function within. This approach sidesteps the determinism of structuralism, where outcomes appear preordained by external factors, as well as the oversimplification of intentionalism, which overstates the role of free will. Furthermore, it amplifies the explanatory power of strategy analysis by recognizing that strategies result from a combination of structural forces and strategic actions.

2.2.4 Uses a Contingency Approach

There are three schools of thought on the strategy approaches for developing strategies. Two of these schools are at the extreme ends of the generalizability continuum. At one end is the universalist school that calls for "one best way" to strategy or universal rules applicable in all situations. At the other extreme is the unique or situational school, which views each organization as unique and requiring its own specific strategy approach, such as conceptualizing strategy as an art of matching the company resources with its environment according to its value (Andrews, 1971). In the middle of the continuum lies the contingency or typological perspective (Hambrick, 1983; Zeithaml et al., 1988), which argues that there is a limited set of strategy approaches that can be used by organizations based on some contingent variables. These contingent variables could be external to the organization, such as environmental uncertainty and volatility, or internal to the organization, such as strategic intent and organizational structure.

The 7C Strategy Wheel uses a contingency approach; but, unlike some frameworks, which use simple 2×2 matrices with two dichotomous variables, the 7C Strategy Framework takes a more thorough approach, integrating seven strategic postures with 28 strategy approaches. This technique introduces more complexity than the simpler 2×2 matrix models. However, this complexity allows for a more exact and accurate identification of relevant strategy approaches and methods, enhancing the efficacy of strategy formulation (Zeithaml et al., 1988).

2.2.5 Common Language

Strategy formulation involves multi-actors engaged in different "games, transactions, debates, or information flows in network" (Hermans & Cunningham, 2018). These multi-actors, whether they are political coalitions (March, 1962) or top management teams (Hambrick & Mason, 1984), share activities, collective cognitions, capabilities, and interactions (Hambrick, 2007). Without having a common strategy vocabulary, this opens the possibility of multiple interpretations of the strategic issues and concepts being discussed (Feldman, 1989; March, 1994; Weick, 1995).

Therefore, having a common vocabulary that is research-informed and utilized in organizations reduces ambiguities, fosters better understanding, and increases alignment between the actors involved in strategy formulation.

2.3 Components of the 7C Strategy Wheel

To achieve the stated functions, the architecture of this framework is illustrated in Figure 2.1. The 7C Strategy Wheel has a three-level architecture represented by three circles. The inner circle is the broadest level and has the 7 strategic postures (7Cs), followed by the middle circle that contains 28 strategy approaches. The outer circle consists of 59 strategy methods.

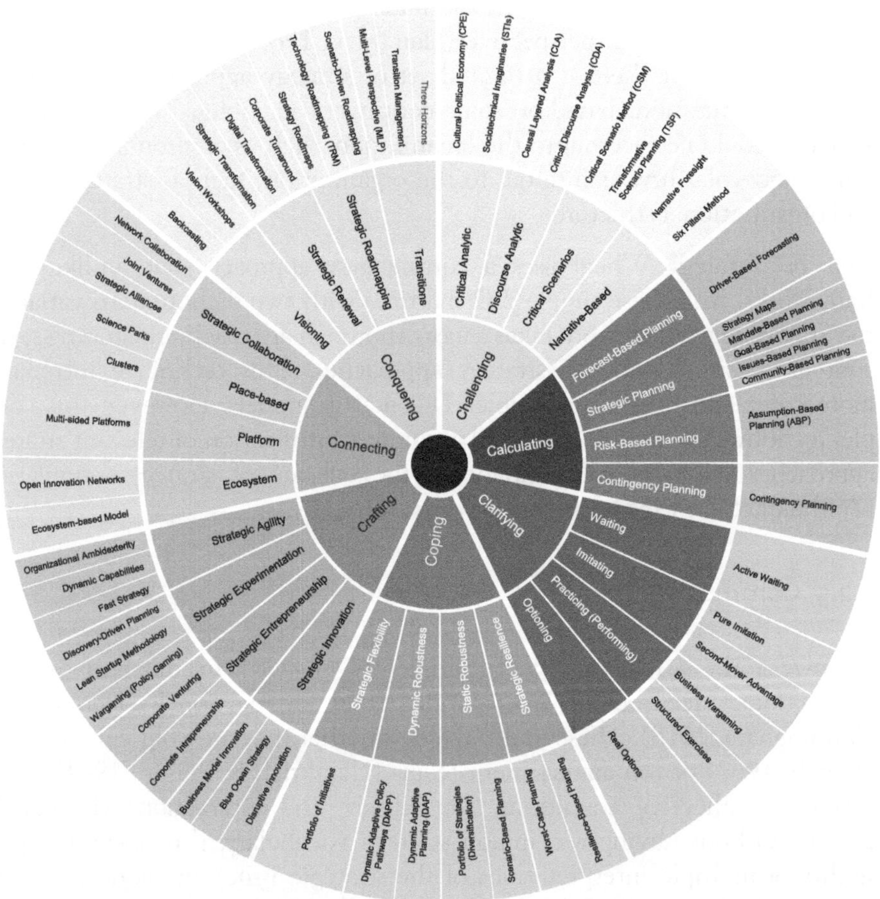

Figure 2.1 7C Strategy Wheel.

2.3.1 The Strategic Postures

Strategic posture refers to the high-level stance an organization intentionally adopts in response to its strategic context, particularly the complexity, uncertainty, and dynamism of its environment, and in response to the challenges triggered by changes in strategic context. It embodies the organization's chosen mode of engagement with the external world and determines how assertively or cautiously it commits, adapts, and influences through strategy formulation and execution.

There are six key elements defining strategic postures.

Overarching orientation: Strategic posture captures the organization's high-level stance toward the external environment. It reflects its philosophy of engagement, whether it seeks to calculate, clarify, cope, craft, connect, conquer, or challenge. This orientation serves as a strategic anchor that shapes how the organization interprets its role in the broader ecosystem, guiding major commitments, resource flows, and leadership behaviors.

Context-sensitive: Strategic posture is not arbitrary or fixed; it is informed by a diagnosis of the external context. This includes the degree of complexity, uncertainty, rate of change, and the perceived malleability of the future. An organization operating in a predictable and controllable environment may adopt a different posture than one facing high volatility or weak predictive signals. The posture thus embeds an environmental interpretation within strategic direction.

Challenge-responsive: Strategic posture reflects an organization's interpretation of the strategic challenges it faces. These challenges, such as digital disruption, innovation fatigue, resilience gaps, or stakeholder misalignment, are often triggered by environmental shifts and contextual turbulence. A posture is, therefore, not just a reflection of the environment, but a targeted response to the specific problems it creates, ensuring the organization's stance is grounded in relevance and purpose.

Guiding logic: Once a posture is chosen, it provides a coherent logic for how strategy should be formulated. It shapes the choice of strategy approaches (e.g., forecasting, waiting, dynamic robustness, strategic flexibility, and strategic experimentation) and informs the selection of appropriate methods. For example, a coping posture may be operationalized through strategic resilience or strategic flexibility, while a conquering posture may rely on visioning or strategic roadmapping.

Variable commitment: Different strategic postures entail different levels and directions of commitment. Some are proactive and assertive (for example, shaping the market or industry), while others are reactive or defensive (for instance, safeguarding core capabilities or preparing for contingencies). This variability reflects how much the organization is willing to invest, risk, or wait in the face of uncertainty. Accordingly, the posture expresses both risk appetite and strategic assertiveness.

Strategic agency: Strategic posture is an expression of strategic agency and the organization's capacity to interpret its environment, make purposeful choices, and commit to action. It reflects the extent to which leaders and strategists can exercise discretion, challenge assumptions, and enact intentional responses within contextual constraints. Strategic agency is what enables an organization to choose its posture rather than passively inherit one.

Our understanding of strategic posture builds on earlier conceptualizations. For example, strategic posture is defined as "the intent of a strategy relative to the current and future state of an industry" (Courtney et al., 1997, p. 8). In the context of competitive strategy, strategy researchers, Galbraith and Schendel, differentiate between a controllable strategy variable that they term strategy type (posture) and an uncontrollable variable that they term environmental variables. They define strategy type as "a consistent pattern or combination of managerial controllable or decision components representing scope, resource deployments, and competitive advantages; and the direction in which these components are shifting over time, which characterize the way businesses tend to compete". This definition of strategic posture captures the interrelationships and the dynamics of the strategy system over time (Galbraith and Schendel, 1983, p. 156).

Furthermore, our conceptualization of strategic posture is closely related to several foundational concepts in strategic management that describe how organizations position themselves in relation to their environment and long-term goals. One such concept is strategic intent, defined by Prahalad and Hamel (1989) as an organization's aspirational vision of future leadership that "envisions a desired leadership position and establishes the criterion the organization will use to chart its progress" (p. 3). While strategic intent focuses on the destination and serves as a motivational force, strategic posture reflects the stance or mode of engagement an organization adopts to navigate the path toward that destination. In this sense, strategic posture operationalizes the organization's intent by shaping its strategic approach considering contextual realities such as uncertainty, complexity, and control.

Strategic posture also builds upon earlier frameworks that categorize systematic differences in how firms respond to their environments. Miles and Snow's (1978) typology of strategy types, including defenders, prospectors, analyzers, and reactors, highlights recurring patterns of adaptation based on how organizations solve the "adaptive problem". These strategy types are early articulations of what can be understood as posture-like positions: broad, coherent patterns of engagement with external conditions.

Similarly, the notion of strategic orientation, as developed by Venkatraman (1989) and later expanded by Zhou, Yim, and Tse (2005), emphasizes the firm's "philosophy of how to conduct business through a deeply rooted set of values and beliefs that guides the firm's attempt to achieve superior performance" (p. 45). Strategic posture can thus be seen as a behavioral manifestation of these orientations, serving not only as a response to the environment, but also as a reflection of the organization's identity, interpretive lens, and strategic agency.

Understanding strategic posture paves the path for creating a typology of postures. The 7C Strategy Wheel offers a meaningful typology of specific stances that an organization may adopt, with such a typology for strategic postures holding great intrinsic value. It has the capacity to distil the multitude of potential phenomena into manageable, holistic categories. This classification not only simplifies the complexity inherent in strategy formulation but also fosters a nuanced, contingency-based perspective of strategy, transcending the limitations of simplistic 2×2 or 3×3 matrices (Hambrick, 1983). Each typological category encapsulates a cohesive set of attributes, offering a configurational view that enriches strategic understanding and application.

For a typology to be well-conceived, it should be underscored by essential elements (Miller, 1996). Far from being arbitrary classifications, effective typologies stem from a profound synthesis of theory and conceptual aesthetics. They are not mere categorizations but are theoretically informed structures that elucidate vital conceptual distinctions and interrelations. Moreover, a robust typology brings to light contrasting elements that not only spur empirical advancement but also resolve enduring debates and contentions. The most impactful typologies, according to Miller, are those where the variables defining each category coalesce thematically, shedding light on significant conceptual, evolutionary, or normative aspects, thereby contributing profoundly to the strategic discourse.

The following are brief descriptions of the seven strategic postures.

Calculating: The calculating strategic posture aims to methodically analyze and plan an organization's strategic direction to optimize outcomes and minimize risks. It focuses on leveraging data, predictive analytics, and structured methodologies to make informed decisions that support the organization's strategic objectives. This posture is characterized by its systematic, analytical, and formal approach to strategy formulation. It values detailed planning, risk assessment, and the use of quantitative methods to forecast and predict the future and guide strategic choices (Chaffee, 1985).

Clarifying: The clarifying strategic posture focuses on adopting a cautious, observant approach that prioritizes understanding over action in environments characterized by high uncertainty, where definitive strategic actions might be premature or risky. This posture emphasizes the importance of buying time to gather more information, observe emerging trends, and understand the evolving landscape before committing to specific strategic directions. Organizations "spend a greater amount of time and resources on environmental scanning... that is directed toward clarifying the administrators' understanding of the probabilities of various events or changes in the environment" (Milliken, 1987, p. 139).

Coping: Adopting the coping strategic posture enables an organization to develop the resilience, robustness, or flexibility to effectively respond to environmental changes and withstand disruptions as they occur (Reeves & Deimler, 2011). This posture focuses on developing plans and capabilities to cope with uncertainty. Unlike the calculating posture, the coping posture does not attempt to predict or control the future. This underscores strategic coping's dynamic, responsive approach to strategy formulation that prioritizes adaptability and learning to produce emergent strategies over long-term planning that produces intended strategies (Mintzberg & Waters, 1985).

Crafting: The forward-thinking, innovative, and entrepreneurial approach to strategy, which characterizes the crafting strategic posture aims to actively change and lead the market through creative destruction and innovation rather than merely survival (Ireland &

Hitt, 1999). This posture requires organizations to be agile, entrepreneurial, and continuously engaged in experimentation and learning. By fostering a culture that embraces change, encourages risk-taking, and values innovation, organizations can navigate the complexities of modern markets, creating new opportunities and achieving a series of transient advantages in an ever-evolving competitive landscape (McGrath, 2013).

Connecting: The connecting posture emphasizes the importance of building and participating in business networks to address complex challenges, exploit opportunities for synergy, and co-create value in innovative ways (Adner, 2017; Jacobides et al., 2018). It recognizes that firms are embedded in complex webs of relationships and interdependencies that shape their ability to create and capture value (Dyer et al., 2018; Iansiti & Levien, 2004). By leveraging the complementary capabilities of diverse actors, firms can enhance their adaptability, resilience, and innovation potential (Adner & Kapoor, 2010; Jacobides et al., 2018).

Conquering: The aim of the conquering posture is to drive radical change and establish new standards, practices, or markets that align with a transformative vision of the future (Hamel & Prahalad, 1994). Like the crafting posture, this posture is rooted in the belief that the future is not to be passively accepted but actively shaped. However, it differs in several key aspects, including the extent of change it perceives as possible, its audacious and transformative vision-based approach, and the higher levels of risk it often involves. It seeks to mobilize resources, stakeholders, and innovative efforts to create entirely new paradigms and disrupt existing systems (Hamel, 2000). Furthermore, the conquering posture views the future as a space for significant, transformative opportunities that can be seized and shaped through deliberate actions today (Godet, 2000).

Challenging: In an increasingly divided and uncertain world riddled with polarized discourse, a growing need emerges for strategic approaches that challenge dominant strategic narratives, question underlying assumptions, and explore alternative futures (Levy et al., 2003; Slaughter, 2004). The challenging strategic posture represents a radical paradigm shift in strategy formulation, emphasizing critical interrogation, examining political interests and dynamics, challenging assumptions, and exploring pluralistic futures (Ezzamel & Willmott, 2010).

To illustrate the seven strategic postures, we can use the analogy of navigating through diverse terrains, each requiring a different mode of transportation tailored to the specific challenges and opportunities of the landscape.

Calculating: This is akin to navigating a well-charted highway in a car, where the path is clear and the focus is on optimizing the car's speed and efficiency based on known parameters.

Clarifying: This is comparable to using a compass and map to find one's way through a dense fog. The goal is to gather further information and wait for visibility to improve before making major moves.

Coping: This resembles off-road driving in a rugged, adaptable vehicle designed to handle uncertain and changing terrain, emphasizing flexibility and resilience.

Crafting: This can be compared to piloting an experimental vehicle, where innovation and creativity lead the way to explore new horizons and possibilities beyond conventional paths.

Connecting: This is similar to coordinating a fleet of cars to navigate through interconnected streets and serve diverse and dispersed clients, leveraging the strength of a network and partnerships for mutual benefit.

Conquering: This is comparable to envisioning a future mobility system where cars travel the skies as well as the road, then mobilizing stakeholders on the journey to shape the future mobility landscape.

Challenging: This is like challenging the status quo and pushing the limits of what is considered possible by asking "do we need vehicles?" and questioning whether we should abandon them for a more equitable public transport system that is accessible for all.

Each mode of transportation and approach to navigation underscores the distinct strategies, adaptabilities, and mindsets needed to traverse different strategic landscapes.

The differences between the seven strategic postures are contrasted in Table 2.1.

2.3.2 The Strategy Approaches

A strategy approach is a coherent and context-sensitive conceptual pathway that guides how strategy should be formulated and executed, given the organization's chosen strategic posture. It represents a structured way of thinking and acting strategically, rooted in assumptions about the environment, causality, time

Table 2.1 Comparing the 7 Strategic Postures

Dimension	Calculating	Clarifying	Coping	Crafting	Connecting	Conquering	Challenging
Aim	Optimize and control outcomes	Buy time and adapt	Adapt and evolve	Innovate and shape the future	Build networks and collaboration	Envision and lead the creation of a desired future	Question and reform the present
Strategic Focus	Planning and prediction	Observation and learning	Flexibility and responsiveness	Innovation and experimentation	Ecosystems and platforms	Visionary transformation	Performative and political implications
Nature of Strategy	Predictive, analytical, planned, and programmed	Imitative and cautious	Adaptative, resilient, robust, and flexible	Innovative and shaping	Collaborative and integrative	Visionary and transformative	Critical and reformative
Value Creation	Efficiency and optimization	Optionality and timing	Resilience and adaptability	Innovation and market-shaping	Synergy and network effects	Future-oriented transformation	Political and social transformation
Strategist as	Engineer	Learner	Steward	Artist	Orchestrator	Conqueror	Rebel
Futures Orientation	Calculating probable futures	Waiting for clarity on plausible multiple futures	Adapting to plausible multiple futures	Opening the future by shaping alternative futures	Building shared plausible futures	Closing the future by creating your own	Challenging and reimagining futures
Approach to Uncertainty	Reduce risk through analysis and hedging	Navigate with strategic patience	Embrace and adapt	Shape and leverage	Leverage interconnectedness	Create your own preferred future	Critically interrogate official accounts and reform them

(Continued)

Table 2.1 (Continued)

Dimension	Calculating	Clarifying	Coping	Crafting	Connecting	Conquering	Challenging
Response to Complexity	Simplify and control	Maintain flexibility	Adapt and co-evolve	Engage and experiment	Connect and synergize	Embrace and direct	Unpack and challenge
Key Theories	Game Theory, Decision Analysis, Industrial Organization (IO), Rational Choice Theory, Market-based View; Stakeholder Theory	Organizational learning (Vicarious), Real Option Theory	Behavioral Theory of the Firm, Complexity Theory, Evolutionary Theory, Institutional Theory, Organizational Ecology, Resource Dependency	Strategic Choice; Schumpeterian Creative Destruction; Transient Advantage; Organizational Ambidexterity; Dynamic Capabilities	Network Theory; Theories of Network Effects; Ecosystem Theory; Stakeholder Theory	Visionary Leadership Theory; Transformational Leadership; Transition	Critical Theory; Post-Structuralism; Institutional Theory; Sociology of the future

horizon, and risk, and serves as a bridge between the overarching strategic stance and specific strategy methods.

Strategy approaches differ from strategy postures in that they do not define the stance itself but rather translate it into a way of engaging with strategy formulation; for example, through strategic flexibility, strategic experimentation, or visioning. They offer internal consistency in logic while allowing for variability in methods and techniques used for implementation (Andiappan & Wan, 2020; Hofler, 1983).

There are five key elements defining strategy approaches.

Conceptual pathway: A strategy approach provides a structured and coherent pathway for how an organization formulates and executes strategy. It operates as a conceptual bridge between the strategic posture and the specific methods used. Unlike ad hoc decision-making, an approach offers an organizing logic that structures strategic thinking.

Context-sensitive: Strategy approaches are selected based on the nature of the strategic context, including environmental complexity, uncertainty, and volatility, and the degree of control the organization has over future outcomes. The appropriateness of an approach depends on how well it aligns with contextual conditions.

Translate posture into practice: While a strategic posture expresses the organization's stance or orientation, a strategy approach translates that stance into action

Supports internal consistency: An effective approach provides a coherent internal logic that helps ensure alignment between diagnosis, goal setting, resource allocation, and implementation. This consistency enhances strategic clarity and reduces fragmentation across teams and functions.

Allows methodological flexibility: While an approach defines the "how" of strategy formulation, it does not prescribe a single method. It allows for multiple methods to be applied depending on organizational capability, urgency, and data availability. For example, as illustrated in Figure 2.2, a strategic innovation approach could entail implementing disruptive innovation, blue ocean strategy, or business innovation methods.

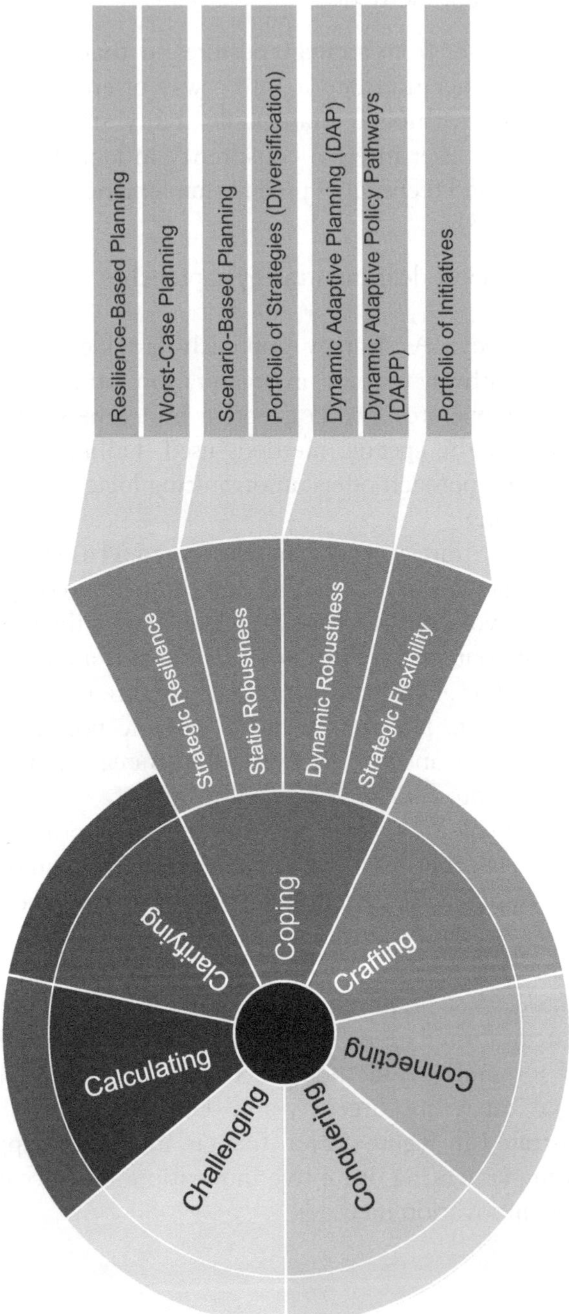

Figure 2.2 Strategic Postures, Strategy Approaches, and Strategy Methods.

2.3.3 The Strategy Methods

A strategy method refers to a structured and repeatable sequence of activities or processes designed to operationalize a given strategy approach. It translates the conceptual orientation of the approach into a systematic procedure for action, often through defined steps, techniques, templates, and analytical tools. Methods guide practitioners through the actual formulation of strategy, meaning what to do, in what order, and often with what data or resources.

Unlike strategy approaches that are broader in scope, strategy methods are pragmatic, replicable, and focused on execution (Hofler, 1983; Andiappan & Wan, 2020). They vary across approaches; for example, backcasting and vision workshops are methods within a visioning approach, and assumption-based planning falls within a risk-based planning approach.

There are four key elements defining strategy methods.

Operational process: A strategy method refers to a structured, repeatable process designed to implement a specific strategy approach. It provides step-by-step guidance for making the chosen approach tangible and executable.

Tied to a specific approach: Each method is logically derived from or aligned with a particular strategy approach, ensuring consistency in logic and execution. For instance, the backcasting method is commonly tied to the visioning approach, while wargaming supports a strategic experimentation approach.

Procedural clarity: Effective strategy methods are characterized by clear procedural steps, defined inputs and outputs, and often visual representations or tools that guide users through a strategic process.

Action-oriented: Methods are designed for execution, not just conceptual framing. They help strategists perform concrete tasks, typically using techniques, templates, or tools.

2.3.4 Comparing Strategic Postures, Strategy Approaches, and Strategy Methods

Table 2.2 highlights the key distinctions between strategic postures, strategy approaches, and strategy methods, the three interconnected layers within the 7C Strategy Wheel. It illustrates how each concept plays a distinct role in guiding strategic thinking and action, from high-level orientation to conceptual logic to practical execution.

Table 2.2 Key Distinctions across the Three Layers of the 7C Strategy Wheel

Dimension	Strategic Posture	Strategy Approach	Strategy Method
Core Function	Defines the organization's overarching stance or orientation toward its external context	Provides a conceptual pathway for how to formulate and execute strategy	Offers a structured, step-by-step process to operationalize the chosen strategy approach
Primary Question	What should our strategic stance be, given our context and challenges?	How should we formulate our strategy, given our stance?	What step-by-step process should we use to implement the approach?
Level of Abstraction	High (philosophical and directional)	Medium (conceptual and integrative)	Low (Procedural and operational)
Basis of Selection	Informed by analysis of strategic context, triggers, and challenges	Aligned with the chosen posture and contextual requirements	Chosen based on the strategy approach and task-specific needs
Role in 7C Strategy Wheel Architecture	Sets the tone and direction for downstream strategic choices	Translates the posture into a coherent logic for strategy formulation	Implements the approach through actionable steps and tools
Degree of Commitment	High; reflects willingness to calculate, clarify, cope, craft, connect, conquer, or challenge based on context	Moderate; reflects strategic logic chosen to fit posture and context	Variable; depends on the design of the method and its degree of iteration
Internal Consistency	Provides a coherent organizational orientation	Ensures logical consistency in how strategy is formulated	Provides procedural consistency in implementation

Variability Allowed	Low; commitment to a particular posture is deliberate and directional	Medium; approaches can vary depending on posture and context	High; multiple methods can be used to implement the same approach depending on capability and preference
Time Horizon	Long-term engagement stance	Medium- to long-term framing of strategy process	Often shorter-term cycles of activity or modules within the process
Adaptability Over Time	May evolve with shifts in context or leadership	Can be adapted to refine or shift strategic logic	Often designed to be iterative or modular to accommodate learning and feedback
End Result or Output	Strategic stance and engagement mode	Strategy formulation logic	Concrete deliverables, insights, visualizations, models, action plans

References

Adner, R. (2017). Ecosystem As Structure: An Actionable Construct for Strategy. *Journal of Management, 43*(1), 39–58.

Adner, R., & Kapoor, R. (2010). Value Creation in Innovation Ecosystems: How the Structure of Technological Interdependence Affects Firm Performance in New Technology Generations. *Strategic Management Journal, 31*(3), 306–333.

Andiappan, V., & Wan, Y. K. (2020). Distinguishing Approach, Methodology, Method, Procedure and Technique in Process Systems Engineering. *Clean Technologies and Environmental Policy, 22*(3), 547–555.

Andrews, K. R. (1971). *The Concept of Corporate Strategy*. Dow Jones-Irwin.

Chaffee, E. E. (1985). Three Models of Strategy. *The Academy of Management Review, 10*(1), 89–98.

Child, J. (1972). Organizational Structure, Environment and Performance: The Role of Strategic Choice. *Sociology*, 6(1), 1–22.

Courtney, H. (2001). *20/20 Foresight: Crafting Strategy in an Uncertain World*. Harvard Business School Press.

Courtney, H., Kirkland, J., & Viguerie, P. (1997). Strategy Under Uncertainty. *Harvard Business Review, 75*(6), 67–79.

Cyert, R. M., & March, J. G. (1963). *A Behavioral Theory of the Firm*. Prentice Hall.

DiMaggio, P. J., & Powell, W. W. (1983). The Iron Cage Revisited: Institutional Isomorphism and Collective Rationality in Organizational Fields. *American Sociological Review*, 48(2), 147–160.

Dyer, J. H., Singh, H., & Hesterly, W. S. (2018). The Relational View Revisited: A Dynamic Perspective on Value Creation and Value Capture. *Strategic Management Journal*, 39(12), 3140–3162.

Elsbach, K. D., & van Knippenberg, D. (2020). Creating High-Impact Literature Reviews: An Argument for 'Integrative Reviews'. *Journal of Management Studies*, 57(6), 1277–1289.

Ezzamel, M., & Willmott, H. (2010). Strategy and Strategizing: A Poststructuralist Perspective. In B. Joel A.C. & J. Lampel (Eds.), *The Globalization of Strategy Research* (Vol. 27, pp. 75–109). Emerald Group Publishing Limited.

Feldman, M. S. (1989). *Order Without Design: Information Production and Policy Making*. Stanford University Press.

Fisher, G., Wisneski, J. E., & Bakker, R. M. (2020). *Strategy in 3D: Essential Tools to Diagnose, Decide, and Deliver* (1st ed.). Oxford University Press.

Galbraith, C., & Schendel, D. (1983). An Empirical Analysis of Strategy Types. *Strategic Management Journal*, 4(2), 153–173.

Godet, M. (2000). The Art of Scenarios and Strategic Planning: Tools and Pitfalls. *Technological Forecasting and Social Change, 65*(1), 3–22.

Hambrick, D. C. (1983). Some Tests of the Effectiveness and Functional Attributes of Miles and Snow's Strategic Types. *Academy of Management Journal, 26*(1), 5–26.

Hambrick, D. C. (2007). Upper Echelons Theory: An Update. *Academy of Management Review, 32*(2), 334–343.

Hambrick, D. C., & Mason, P. A. (1984). Upper Echelons: The Organization as a Reflection of Its Top Managers. *The Academy of Management Review*, 9(2), 193.

Hamel, G. (2000). *Leading the Revolution*. Harvard Business School Press.

Hamel, G., & Prahalad, C. K. (1989). *Strategic Intent. Harvard Business Review*, 67(3), 63–76.

Hamel, G., & Prahalad, C. K. (1994). *Competing for the Future*. Harvard Business School Press.

Hannan, M. T., & Freeman, J. (1977). The Population Ecology of Organizations. *American Journal of Sociology*, 82(5), 929–964.

Hay, C. (1995). Structure and Agency. In D. Marsh & G. Stoker (Eds.), *Theory and Methods in Political Science* (pp. 189–206). Palgrave Macmillan.

Hay, C. (2002). *Political Analysis: A Critical Introduction*. Palgrave Macmillan.

Hermans, L. M., & Cunningham, S. W. (2018). *Actor and Strategy Models: Practical Applications and Step-Wise Approaches* (1st ed.). John Wiley & Sons.

Hofler, D. B. (1983). Approach, Method, Technique a Clarification. *Reading World*, 23(1), 71–72.

Iansiti, M., & Levien, R. (2004). Strategy as Ecology. *Harvard Business Review*, 82(3), 68–78.

Ireland, R. D., & Hitt, M. A. (1999). Achieving and Maintaining Strategic Competitiveness in the 21st Century: The Role of Strategic Leadership. *Academy of Management Perspectives, 13*(1), 43–57.

Jacobides, M. G., Cennamo, C., & Gawer, A. (2018). Towards a Theory of Ecosystems. *Strategic Management Journal*, 39(8), 2255–2276.

Levy, D. L., Alvesson, M., & Willmott, H. (2003). Critical Approaches to Strategic Management. In M. Alvesson & H. Willmott (Eds.), *Studying Management Critically* (pp. 92–110). Sage Publications.

March, J. G. (1962). The Business Firm as a Political Coalition. *The Journal of Politics*, 24(4), 662–678.

March, J. G. (1994). *A Primer on Decision Making: How Decisions Happen*. Free Press.

McGrath, R. (2013). *The End of Competitive Advantage: How to Keep Your Strategy Moving as Fast as Your Business*. Harvard Business Review Press.

Miles, R. E., & Snow, C. C. (1978). *Organizational Strategy, Structure, and Process*. McGraw-Hill.

Miller, D. (1996). Configurations Revisited. *Strategic Management Journal, 17*(7), 505–512.

Milliken, F. J. (1987). Three Types of Perceived Uncertainty About the Environment: State, Effect, and Response Uncertainty. *Academy of Management Review, 12*(1), 133–143.

Mintzberg, H., & Waters, J. A. (1985). Of Strategies, Deliberate and Emergent. *Strategic Management Journal*, 6(3), 257–272.

Reeves, M., & Deimler, M. (2011). Adaptability: The New Competitive Advantage. *Harvard Business Review*, 89(7-8), 134–141.

Reeves, M., Haanaes, K., & Sinha, J. K. (2015). *Your Strategy Needs a Strategy: How to Choose and Execute the Right Approach*. Harvard Business Review Press.

Reeves, M., Love, C., & Tillmanns, P. (2012). Your Strategy Needs a Strategy. *Harvard Business Review*, 90(9), 76–83.

Slaughter, R. (2004). *Futures Beyond Dystopia: Creating Social Foresight*. Routledge.

Torraco, R. J. (2005). Writing Integrative Literature Reviews: Guidelines and Examples. *Human Resource Development Review*, 4(3), 356–367.

Venkatraman, N. (1989). Strategic Orientation of Business Enterprises: The Construct, Dimensionality, and Measurement. *Management Science*, 35(8), 942–962.

Weick, K. E. (1995). *Sensemaking in Organizations*. Sage Publications.

Zeithaml, V. A., "Rajan" Varadarajan, P., & Zeithaml, C. P. (1988). The Contingency Approach: Its Foundations and Relevance to Theory Building and Research in Marketing. *European Journal of Marketing*, 22(7), 37–64.

Zhou, K. Z., Yim, C. K., & Tse, D. K. (2005). The Effects of Strategic Orientations on Technology- and Market-based Breakthrough Innovations. *Journal of Marketing*, 69(2), 42–60.

3 Calculating Strategic Posture

3.1 Overview

3.1.1 Introduction

The calculating strategic posture offers a systematic, analytical, formal approach to strategy formulation designed to navigate today's challenges by leveraging data, predictive models, and structured methodologies to build forecasts and strategic plans. This chapter explores the key characteristics of the calculating posture and its four main strategy approaches: forecast-based planning, strategic planning, risk-based planning, and contingency planning.

3.1.2 Key Characteristics

The aim of the calculating strategic posture is to methodically analyze and plan an organization's strategic direction to optimize outcomes and minimize risks. It focuses on leveraging data, predictive analytics, and structured methodologies to make informed decisions that support the organization's strategic objectives. This posture is characterized by its systematic, analytical, formal approach to strategy formulation. It values detailed planning, risk assessment, and the use of quantitative methods to forecast and predict the future and guide strategic choices (Chaffee, 1985).

The logic underlying the calculating posture is that thorough analysis and planning based on empirical data and predictive modeling can significantly enhance the accuracy of strategic decisions, reduce uncertainty, and improve the organization's competitive positioning (Reeves et al., 2012).

The calculating posture is akin to navigating a well-charted highway in a car, where the path is clear, and the focus is on optimizing speed and efficiency of the car based on known parameters.

DOI: 10.4324/9781003684060-3

The key actors in this posture are the planners and analysts who rely primarily on historical data, statistical models, and traditional decision-making processes to engineer strategies.

3.1.3 Key Theoretical Perspectives

The calculating posture is underpinned by theories and frameworks from strategic management and economics that emphasize analytical rigor. **Game theory** provides a formal framework for analyzing competitive situations and strategic decisions, enabling firms to anticipate competitor behavior and develop optimal strategies (Dixit et al., 2021; Von Neumann & Morgenstern, 1944). **Decision analysis** uses quantitative techniques to assess different strategic options, considering the probabilities and impacts of various outcomes (Keeney & Raiffa, 1993). Furthermore, **Industrial Organization (IO) Economics** offers insights into how firms compete within industries, emphasizing the role of market structure, conduct, and performance (Bain, 1956). The **market-based view** or the positioning school (Mintzberg et al., 1998) builds on the work of IO and offer several strategy tools that form the backbone of this posture. These include the five forces framework (Porter, 1979), generic competitive strategies (Porter, 1980), and the competitive advantage and value chain analysis (Porter, 1985). The calculating posture is also underpinned by **rational choice theory,** which argues that individuals and organizations make decisions by maximizing their utility based on preferences and constraints (Becker, 1976). Also, **stakeholder theory** is an important perspective especially in the public sector that calls for the consideration of all stakeholder interests for long-term success (Freeman, 1984).

3.1.4 Limitations

While the calculating posture provides clarity and direction in predictable settings, it has several limitations, especially in complex, uncertain, or rapidly changing environments. Its reliance on predictive models and data analysis assumes a level of stability and continuity that may not exist in dynamic markets, leading to potential blind spots and strategic missteps (Boulton et al., 2015). Furthermore, the focus on optimization and control can hinder an organization's adaptability and responsiveness, making it difficult to pivot quickly in response to unexpected disruptions or emerging opportunities (Teece et al., 2016). Moreover, the calculating posture's structured approach to planning can become overly rigid, stifling creativity and innovation, and potentially resulting in a bureaucratic mindset that resists necessary changes (Mintzberg, 1994).

3.1.5 Calculating Strategy Approaches

The calculating strategy approaches can be arranged in a matrix consisting of two dimensions: System Model and Future(s), as illustrated in Figure 3.1.

The System Model dimension has two categories. The first is deterministic, which assumes a single, well-understood model of the system that predicts outcomes with a high degree of certainty. The second is probabilistic, assuming multiple possible models of the system and acknowledging that there are various ways the system might behave.

The Future(s) dimension also has two categories: one future which assumes a single, predictable future based on existing trends and data, and one future with several potential contingencies, each requiring different strategies.

As shown in the matrix, there are four key strategy approaches that can be used to achieve the calculating posture:

Forecast-based planning (bottom-left quadrant): This approach uses a single deterministic model to plan for a single, most likely future scenario, assuming that the future can be accurately predicted based

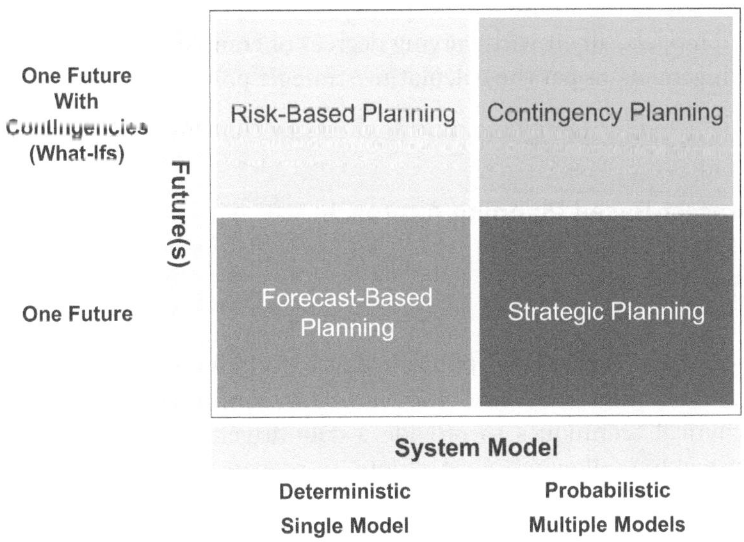

Figure 3.1 The Calculating Strategic Posture Matrix.

on historical data and trends (Saffo, 2007). It is most applicable in stable, predictable environments where the future is expected to resemble the past. However, forecasting struggles in the face of discontinuities, black swans, and other unexpected events (Makridakis et al., 2009).

Strategic planning (bottom-right quadrant): Strategic planning is a systematic process of defining long-term goals, analyzing the internal and external environment, and developing action plans to achieve the desired future state (Bryson, 2018). It is effective in aligning organizational efforts and resources but can be overly rigid and unresponsive to changing circumstances (Mintzberg, 1994).

Risk-based planning (top-left quadrant): Risk-based planning focuses on identifying, assessing, and mitigating potential risks that could impact an organization's objectives (Andersen & Schrøder, 2010). While proactive risk management is crucial, an overemphasis on risk avoidance can stifle innovation and opportunity-seeking (Kaplan & Mikes, 2012).

Contingency planning (top-right quadrant): Contingency planning involves developing contingent plans to prepare the organization to address a limited number of potential high impact and low probability future events or scenarios that could impact their strategy (Wilson, 2003).

All four approaches operate within the same paradigm, sharing the underlying assumption that the future can be predicted and planned for using analytical tools and models, albeit with varying degrees of complexity and consideration for contingencies, as per the calculating strategic posture.

This is depicted further by contrasting their key characteristics in Table 3.1.

3.2 Forecast-Based Planning Approach

3.2.1 Aim

The forecast-based planning approach aims to formulate strategies grounded in predictions of future trends and outcomes. This approach utilizes formal models and analytical techniques to provide a data-driven foundation for strategic decision-making, allowing organizations to prepare for anticipated scenarios (Makridakis, 1990).

Table 3.1 Comparing the Calculating Strategies

Dimension	Forecasting	Strategic Planning	Risk-based Planning	Contingency Planning
Aim	Predict future trends and outcomes using historical data	Define long-term goals and determine actions to achieve them	Identify, assess, and mitigate potential risks	Prepare for unlikely future events or contingencies
Core Logic	The future can be reasonably predicted based on historical data trends	A systematic analysis and planning process can optimize outcomes	Identifying and managing risks reduces their likelihood and impact	Anticipating and planning for unlikely but impactful scenarios
Assumptions	The past patterns will persist into the future	A reasonably accurate understanding of the environment can be achieved and used to craft strategies	By integrating risk management into the strategic planning process, organizations can navigate uncertainty more effectively	Considers contingent futures
System Model	Uses a single coherent model of the system for optimization	Considers single or multiple probable system models	Uses a single model to identify risks	Considers multiple probable system models
Future Perspective	Predicts a single likely future based on continuity from past	Envisions a single desired future state to plan for	Plans for a single future but with contingencies	Prepares for unlikely alternative futures or events
Time Horizon	Short to long-term, depending on system	Typically, long-term strategic direction	Medium to long-term risk outlook	Medium to long-term scenario anticipation

(Continued)

Table 3.1 (Continued)

Dimension	Forecasting	Strategic Planning	Risk-based Planning	Contingency Planning
Strengths	Provides a basis for informed decision-making	Provides direction and coordination	Enhances resilience and adaptability	Improves flexibility and responsiveness
Limitations	Less effective for novel situations; relies on past as predictor of future	Assumes ability to control and shape future; less adaptable to uncertainty	May miss opportunities by focusing only on mitigating risks	Scenarios may not anticipate all possible futures; resource intensive
Methods	• Driver-based forecasting • Forecast-based planning	• Logic maps, strategy maps, success maps, causal maps • Mandate/goal/issues/community-based planning	• Assumption-based planning	• Contingency-based planning

3.2.2 Core Logic

The core logic of the forecast-based planning approach is rooted in the assumption that the dynamics of specific systems can be sufficiently understood to allow for reliable probabilistic forecasting. By analyzing the relationships between key variables, forecasting models predict future states based on past and present data. This approach relies on the continuity principle, which posits that systems will behave in the future as they have in the past, thus making predictions based on historical trends feasible (Poli, 2019).

3.2.3 Key Elements

Formal models and probabilistic forecasting: The approach relies heavily on formal models to predict future trends. These models utilize statistical methods and historical data to generate forecasts (Poli, 2019).

Time windows: Different forecasting models operate over various time windows, including short-term (0–5 years), intermediate (10–50 years), and long-term (100 years or more). The appropriate time window depends on the system being observed and the technical properties of the model (Poli, 2019).

Quantitative and judgmental forecasting: While quantitative models often outperform judgmental forecasts, human judgment remains crucial, especially in novel or complex situations where data is limited (Lawrence et al., 2006).

Optimization: Application of methods to find optimal solutions based on forecasts.

3.2.4 Applications and Examples

Forecast-based planning finds wide application across multiple sectors. In economic forecasting, models predicting inflation, GDP growth, and employment rates assist policymakers and businesses in making informed decisions (Petropoulos et al., 2022). Climate change projections also use models to forecast the impact of CO_2 emissions on global temperatures, ice melt, and sea-level rise, thereby guiding environmental policies and international agreements (Poli, 2019).

3.2.5 Challenges and Limitations

A fundamental assumption of continuity underpins many forecasts, presuming that past patterns will persist into the future (Lewinsohn, 2022). However, this assumption may not hold in rapidly changing or disruptive environments. The effectiveness of forecast-based planning is also limited when dealing with novel or unprecedented scenarios, where historical data may be unavailable or unable to provide reliable guidance. Additionally, optimization based on a single forecast may lead to poor performance in alternative future scenarios not considered in the initial analysis (Makridakis et al., 2009). Selecting an appropriate time window for forecasting can also be challenging, with the chosen horizon significantly impacting the results and their interpretation. Econometric forecasts, for example, are most effective for short time windows ranging from six months to three years and rely on the principle of continuity, which assumes that the system will continue to function in a manner similar to its past behavior (Poli, 2019). In contrast, climate change forecasts adopt longer time windows, spanning up to a century or more, based on the assumption of the constancy of the laws of physics (Poli, 2019). While judgmental forecasting has the benefit of incorporating expert opinions, this can also be a weakness as they may be subject to various cognitive biases, potentially skewing predictions (Hogarth & Makridakis, 1981).

3.2.6 Strategy Methods

Several strategy methods utilize the logic of forecasting, identifying the key factors (drivers) influencing the performance of a business or system, and using them to create accurate and actionable forecasts (Morlidge & Player, 2010).

3.2.6.1 Driver-Based Forecasting

Driver-based forecasting is a method that identifies the key factors (drivers) influencing the performance of a business or system and uses them to create accurate and actionable forecasts (Morlidge & Player, 2010). These value drivers have two characteristics: they have a high impact on value, and they are controllable (L.E.K Consulting, 1998). This approach enables organizations to understand the underlying causes of performance and develop strategies that are based on them.

The process of driver-based forecasting begins with identifying the key drivers that have the most significant impact on business performance. This involves developing a detailed "value driver map" of the business, testing the sensitivity of overall business value to changes in each factor, and determining which potential value drivers are controllable by management (L.E.K Consulting, 1998). Once the key drivers are identified, organizations can develop mathematical, statistical, or judgmental causal models that quantify the relationships between these drivers and the desired outcomes, such as revenue, profitability, or market share (Courtney et al., 2013; Morlidge & Player, 2010). Then by leveraging advanced forecasting techniques, such as time series analysis, regression analysis, and machine learning algorithms, organizations can create more accurate and reliable forecasts that account for various internal and external factors (Hyndman & Athanasopoulos, 2021). These forecasts enable decision-makers to optimize resource allocation and formulate their strategies to be aligned with the predicted future (Makridakis et al., 1998).

There are many applications that use this method. To illustrate, suppose McDonald's decides on new U.S. restaurant locations, it can use driver-based forecasting. The company identifies key success variables, such as local demographics, traffic patterns, real estate prices, and competitor locations. With rich data sources and well-calibrated revenue and cost models, decision-makers can feed this information into discounted cash flow models to predict location performance and make informed go/no-go decisions (Courtney et al., 2013).

However, the accuracy of driver-based forecasting depends on the quality of the data used to develop the models and the ability to identify and quantify the most relevant drivers (Chase, 2013). Additionally, conducting a value driver analysis requires significant time and effort from management, but it provides a foundation for optimizing strategies and decision making around value creation (L.E.K Consulting, 1998).

3.3 Strategic Planning Approach

3.3.1 Aim

The strategic planning approach aims to systematically analyze and plan an organization's strategic direction, optimize outcomes, and minimize risks (Rigby & Bilodeau, 2018). It provides a structured framework for organizations to formulate strategies that align with their mission, vision, and values, ensuring long-term success and sustainability (Vandersmissen & George, 2023).

3.3.2 Core Logic

The strategic planning approach is founded on a calculative and optimizing perspective of strategy formulation, which resonates with managers who favor rational decision-making processes (Mintzberg, 1994). This approach shares fundamental assumptions with analytical reasoning, emphasizing the value of systematic, orderly, and consistent logical thinking in strategy development

(Grant, 2003). It operates on the premise that decision-makers can develop a reasonably accurate understanding of their organizational environment and use this knowledge to craft effective strategies (Wilson, 1998).

3.3.3 Key Elements

Analysis of existing mandates, values, vision, and mission: This foundational step examines the organization's current purpose and guiding principles (Bryson, 2018). It provides a critical understanding of the organization's strategic position and direction (Poister, 2010).

Formulation of updated values, vision, and mission statements: This process involves refining or redefining core organizational elements to guide future strategic efforts (Collins & Porras, 1996). These statements serve as a compass for strategy formulation and actions (Campbell & Yeung, 1991).

Internal and external environment analysis: This typically includes tools such as SWOT analysis to assess organizational capabilities and market context (Andrews, 1971). It provides crucial insights for strategy formulation (Porter, 1980).

Identification of strategic issues: This step involves pinpointing critical challenges and opportunities facing the organization (Bryson, 1988). These strategic issues form the basis for strategy development and prioritization (Dutton & Duncan, 1987).

Formulation of concrete, implementable strategies: This involves developing specific, actionable plans aligned with the organization's mission and vision (Hax & Majluf, 1996).

Strategic objective-setting: This involves establishing clear, specific, and measurable goals for the organization (Drucker, 1954). These objectives provide concrete targets for strategic efforts and performance measurement and evaluation (Kaplan & Norton, 1996, 2008).

Strategy evaluation and operationalization: This involves creating mechanisms to assess strategy effectiveness and translate high-level strategies into operational plans (Rumelt, 1980). It ensures strategies are both effective and practically implemented (Kaplan & Norton, 1996).

3.3.4 Applications and Examples

Strategic planning is widely applied across various sectors, from corporations to nonprofit organizations and government agencies. For instance, multinational corporations use strategic planning to align their global operations with long-term objectives. Nonprofit organizations also employ it to ensure their activities align with their mission and stakeholder expectations. Government agencies use strategic planning to optimize resource allocation and improve public service delivery (Bryson, 2018).

3.3.5 Challenges and Limitations

While strategic planning offers numerous advantages, it also presents several challenges. One major limitation is the assumption of predictability and control in dynamic and complex environments that may not be conducive to setting detailed, concrete strategic plans (Mintzberg, 1994). Relatedly, the approach may lead to rigidity and resistance to change if not implemented with flexibility and adaptability (Bryson & George, 2020) . It also requires significant time and resource investment, which can be a constraint for some organizations (Vandersmissen & George, 2023).

3.3.6 Strategy Methods

Several strategy methods utilize the logic of strategic planning. Strategy maps, success maps, and logic maps are visual tools that represent cause-and-effect relationships between strategic objectives, activities, and outcomes (Kaplan & Norton, 2000; Neely et al., 2002; W.K. Kellogg Foundation, 2004). These tools help organizations clarify their strategic logic, ensure alignment between activities and goals, and effectively communicate their strategy to stakeholders (Bryson et al., 2004). Another approach is mandate-based planning, which concentrates on identifying and addressing legal, political, and social mandates that define an organization's purpose and scope of operation (Bryson, 2018). Goal-based planning centers on setting and achieving specific organizational objectives. Issues-based planning addresses key strategic issues facing the organization, while community-based planning emphasizes stakeholder engagement and collaborative strategy development (Poister et al., 2010).

3.3.6.1 Strategy Maps/Success Maps/Logic Maps

Strategy maps (Kaplan & Norton, 2004) and success maps (Neely et al., 2002) are visual strategy tools used to represent the cause-and-effect relationships between strategic objectives, activities, and outcomes (Bryson et al., 2004; Kaplan & Norton, 2000). These tools help organizations clarify their strategic logic, ensure alignment between their activities and strategic goals, and effectively communicate their strategy to stakeholders (Bryson et al., 2004).

Strategy maps are key component of the Balanced Scorecard framework (Kaplan & Norton, 1996, 2000, 2006, 2008), which integrates financial and nonfinancial performance measures to provide a holistic view of organizational performance.

Success maps are key component of the performance Prism framework (Neely et al., 2002), which also integrates financial and nonfinancial performance measures to strategically link customers, investors, employees, suppliers, alliances, regulators, and communities.

Logic maps (W.K. Kellogg Foundation, 2004) provide a systematic and visual means to present and communicate the relationships between resources, activities, outputs, and outcomes.

3.3.6.2 *Mandate-, Goal-, Issues-, or Community-Based Planning*

Mandate-, goal-, issues-, and community-based planning are specific methods for strategic planning that focus on different aspects of the planning process, enabling organizations to tailor their strategies to their unique contexts and stakeholder needs (Bryson, 2018). By adopting the most suitable planning approach, organizations can enhance the effectiveness and relevance of their strategic plans, leading to improved performance and greater stakeholder satisfaction.

Mandate-based planning focuses on identifying and addressing the legal, political, and social mandates that define an organization's purpose and scope of operation (Bryson, 2018). For example, a government agency responsible for environmental protection might engage in mandate-based planning to ensure that its strategies align with the legislative requirements and public expectations regarding its role in safeguarding natural resources.

Goal-based planning, on the other hand, involves setting specific, measurable, and time-bound goals and developing strategies to achieve them (Poister et al., 2010). This approach is widely used in the private sector, where organizations often have clear financial and market-related objectives (Kaplan & Norton, 1996). A manufacturing company, for instance, might set a goal to increase its market share by 10% within the next three years and develop a comprehensive strategy involving product innovation, marketing campaigns, and capacity expansion to reach this target.

Issues-based planning focuses on identifying and prioritizing the key strategic issues facing the organization and developing strategies to address them

(Bryson, 2018). This approach is particularly useful when organizations face complex, multifaceted challenges that require a more flexible and adaptive response (Eden & Ackermann, 2013). A university, for example, might engage in issues-based planning to tackle declining enrollment, rising costs, and changing student demographics, developing a set of interrelated strategies to address these issues in a coordinated manner.

Finally, community-based planning emphasizes the involvement of stakeholders and the wider community in the planning process to ensure that the resulting strategies are responsive to their needs and priorities (Bryson et al., 2013). This approach is increasingly important in an era of heightened public scrutiny and demand for transparency and accountability (Booher & Innes, 2010). A local government, for instance, may use community-based planning to develop a long-term vision for the city's development, engaging citizens, businesses, and civil society organizations in a participatory process to identify shared goals and co-create strategies for achieving them.

The choice of planning approach depends on various factors, including the organization's mission, stakeholder expectations, and the nature of the challenges it faces. In some cases, organizations might combine elements of different approaches to create a hybrid planning model that best suits their needs (Bryson, 2018). Regardless of the specific approach adopted, the key to successful strategic planning lies in ensuring that the process is formal, participative, evidence-based, and adaptable to changing circumstances.

3.4 Risk-Based Planning Approach

3.4.1 Aim

The aim of the risk-based planning approach is to systematically identify, assess, and mitigate potential strategic risks and uncertainties that could impact an organization's ability to achieve its strategic objectives. This approach seeks to enhance organizational resilience by proactively managing threats and capitalizing on opportunities within uncertain environments (Beasley & Frigo, 2007; Emblemsvåg & Kjølstad, 2002).

3.4.2 Core Logic

The core logic of risk-based planning lies in its structured methodologies, which emphasize data analysis and predictive modeling to inform decision-making and minimize risks. This approach is rooted in the understanding that the future is inherently uncertain, and organizations must plan for potential threats to ensure long-term success (Slywotzky & Drzik, 2005). By integrating risk management into the strategic planning process, organizations can navigate uncertainty more effectively, improving their overall performance and resilience (Sax & Andersen, 2019).

3.4.3 Key Elements

Systematic risk identification and assessment: This involves a comprehensive process to identify potential risks that could impact the organization and assess their likelihood and potential impact (Slywotzky & Drzik, 2005).

Use of data analysis and predictive modeling: Employing data analysis and predictive modeling helps organizations anticipate potential risks and their impacts (Makridakis et al., 2009).

Integration of risk management into strategic planning: Embedding risk management practices within the broader strategic planning process (Frigo & Anderson, 2011; Sax & Andersen, 2019).

Mitigation strategies: Developing and implementing strategies to mitigate identified risks involves creating specific actions designed to reduce the likelihood or impact of potential risks (Hopkin & Thompson, 2022).

Continuous monitoring and evaluation of risks: Ongoing risk monitoring and evaluation ensure that organizations remain aware of emerging risks and the effectiveness of their mitigation strategies (Frigo & Anderson, 2011).

3.4.4 Applications and Examples

Risk-based planning is widely applied in various industries. The LEGO Group has successfully implemented risk-based planning to manage strategic risks and foster growth. They created the Park, Adapt, Prepare, Act (PAPA) model to categorize strategic issues and define the appropriate strategic response (Frigo & Læssøe, 2012; Læssøe, 2015).

3.4.5 Challenges and Limitations

Despite its benefits, the risk-based planning approach faces several challenges. One significant limitation is the difficulty in accurately predicting future risks, particularly in highly volatile environments. There is also the potential for bias in risk assessment, where subjective judgments can influence the identification and evaluation of risks (Frigo & Anderson, 2011). Furthermore, overreliance on risk management can lead to risk aversion, potentially stifling innovation and growth (Beasley & Frigo, 2007). Finally, the approach can be resource-intensive, requiring substantial investments in data analysis and predictive modeling capabilities (Slywotzky & Drzik, 2005).

3.4.6 Strategy Methods

A key strategy method utilizing the logic of risk-based planning is assumptions-based planning. This entails identifying and challenging key assumptions underlying strategic plans, helping organizations prepare for potential risks associated with faulty assumptions (Dewar, 2002).

3.4.6.1 Assumption-Based Planning

Assumption-based planning (ABP) is a methodical approach that was developed by researchers in the RAND Corporation to help organizations prepare for potential changes in their environment that could disrupt their plans (Dewar et al., 1993). ABP operates on the principle that all plans are based on certain assumptions, which are inherently unstable and can be correct, incorrect, or become invalid over time. The goal of ABP is to identify these key assumptions, monitor them closely, and take proactive steps to mitigate the risks associated with their potential failure.

The ABP process involves five key steps (Dewar, 2002). First, critical assumptions (load-bearing) are identified. These assumptions are assertions about the past, present or future that underlie a plan, that are critical to the success of the plan. Second, the vulnerabilities, plausible events or conditions that could invalidate the assumptions, are identified. Third, signposts for the vulnerabilities are identified and monitored to act as an early warning system that a critical assumption is about to be invalidated. Fourth, shaping actions, proactive steps taken to control uncertainty, are identified. These shaping actions aim to steer events in a way that maintains the validity of the assumptions, ensuring that the plan remains intact. Lastly, hedging actions to prepare the organization to cope with an assumption failure by rethinking plans as though the assumption has already failed are identified.

This method has been implemented in various projects with the U.S. military. For example, in the 30 year long term planning of AirLand Battle-Future (ALB-F) concept (Dewar & Levin, 1992).

ABP faces several challenges. It requires an initial strategic plan or strategy, making it a post-planning process and a complementary strategy method. Therefore, it does not concern itself with how effective the plan or the strategy is but with reducing the risks associated with their underlying assumptions (Dewar, 2002). Additionally, ABP tends to produce a portfolio of shaping and hedging actions instead of complete strategies, as it addresses individual assumptions rather than synthesizing an overall comprehensive strategy. Finally, ABP handles threats better than opportunities, focusing more on avoiding risks of failure than promoting opportunities.

3.5 Contingency Planning Approach

3.5.1 Aim

The aim of the contingency planning approach is to prepare organizations for a limited number of potential high impact and low probability future events or scenarios that could impact their strategy and to develop effective response strategies to minimize negative impacts and capitalize on opportunities (Wilson, 2003).

3.5.2 Core Logic

The core logic of contingency planning lies in its proactive approach to identifying and preparing for potential deviations from the expected strategy, ensuring that organizations are equipped to handle unforeseen events effectively (Wilson, 2003). Unlike scenario planning, contingency planning addresses specific uncertainties by developing detailed response plans that are kept in reserve and activated when necessary, focusing on a base case with identified exceptions (Schoemaker, 2022).

3.5.3 Key Elements

Contingencies: They are highly unlikely but highly impactful events or future scenarios that can invalidate the strategy, but they are not planned for in the traditional strategic plans or scenario-based plans (Chakraborty et al., 2011).

Predictable surprise: These are significant negative events that leaders can anticipate based on available information but often fail to prepare for adequately due to psychological (e.g. cognitive biases such as overconfidence) organizational (bureaucracies, lack of accountability), or political barriers (internal politics and conflicts) (Watkins & Bazerman, 2003).

Contingency plans: Unlike strategic planning that produces one strategic plan, contingency planning results in the production of multiple contingency plans corresponding to the contingencies that they address (Schoemaker, 2022).

Continuous monitoring and updating: The contingency plan must be kept up to date through continuous monitoring and appropriately reflect the contingencies that were developed to address (Swanson et al., 2010).

3.5.4 Applications and Examples

Contingency planning is used to cover contingent scenarios that are not addressed in the main strategy. Multinational corporations use contingency planning to prepare for supply chain disruptions. Toyota is well-known for creating robust contingency strategies (Sheffi, 2015). Also, contingent planning in strategies involving critical infrastructure systems such as energy supply systems, water supply systems, telecommunications systems, and food supply chains (Boin & McConnell, 2007). The recent failure in the energy system in Spain highlights the importance of having effective contingency plans.

3.5.5 Challenges and Limitations

Contingency planning is very important in helping organizations to prepare for damaging contingencies. However, it suffers from several challenges and limitation. First, given the uncertainties of the contingencies that the contingency plans are meant to address makes it difficult to anticipate every possible scenario and adequately prepare for them (Eriksson & McConnell, 2011). Furthermore, the development and maintenance of contingency plans is resource-intensive, requiring significant time, money, and personnel, which can put a strain an organization's resources, particularly in smaller entities (Simpkins, 2009). The complexity and scope of comprehensive contingency plans can also be overwhelming, leading to overly complicated strategies that are difficult to implement effectively (Wilson, 2003). Furthermore, the effectiveness of contingency plans depends on their regular updating and the ability of the organization to implement them effectively under pressure, which can be challenging in rapidly evolving crisis situations (Bloom & Menefee, 1994).

3.5.6 Strategy Methods

Contingency planning is a key strategy method to ensure that other plans in place to address contingencies.

3.5.6.1 Contingency Planning

Contingency planning is a strategic method focused on preparing an organization to respond effectively to specific deviations from the assumptions underlying its current strategy. It aims to enhance corporate preparedness by developing targeted responses to potential disruptions, crises, or unanticipated developments (Wilson, 2003). Unlike scenario planning, which explores multiple plausible futures in an open-ended manner, contingency planning typically centers around one or a few well-defined uncertainties and develops actionable strategies to be triggered by specific events (Schoemaker, 2022).

Contingency planning generally involves several sequential steps. First, the organization identifies major contingencies, events, or developments not fully addressed by its core strategy but likely to impact performance if they materialize. These contingencies are often derived from scenario analyses or risk assessments (Wilson, 2003). Next, responsibility is assigned for monitoring relevant indicators and developing plans. A critical step involves identifying precursor events, trends, or signals that may foreshadow a contingency, thereby forming an early warning system. The organization then develops contingent plans, which typically include multiple options and clearly defined trigger points, moments when preprepared actions should be implemented. These plans are incorporated into a broader monitoring and implementation system (Chakraborty et al., 2011).

Toyota developed sophisticated contingency planning system that helped the company recover more quickly than competitors following the 2011 Tōhoku earthquake and tsunami by rapidly activating alternative supply networks (Sheffi, 2015). Another example is the energy sector's planning for regulatory contingencies, such as a sudden ban on fossil fuel expansion, by maintaining ready-to-implement investment plans in renewable infrastructure. However, critics like Clarke (1999) caution that many organizational contingency plans become "fantasy documents", symbolic gestures with little operational value, designed more to inspire confidence than to enable effective action. Clarke (1999) cites the case of the big failure of the Exxon Valdez where contingency plans were greatly infective in addressing the oil spill.

References

Andersen, T. J., & Schrøder, W. P. (2010). *Strategic Risk Management Practice: How to Deal Effectively with Major Corporate Exposures*. Cambridge University Press.

Andrews, K. R. (1971). *The Concept of Corporate Strategy*. Dow Jones-Irwin.

Bain, J. S. (1956). *Barriers to New Competition*. Harvard University Press.

Beasley, M. S., & Frigo, M. L. (2007). Strategic Risk Management: Creating and Protecting Value. *Strategic Finance*, 88(11), 24–31.

Becker, G. S. (1976). *The Economic Approach to Human Behavior*. University of Chicago Press.

Bloom, M. J., & Menefee, M. K. (1994). Scenario Planning and Contingency Planning. *Public Productivity & Management Review*, *17*(3), 223–230.

Boin, A., & McConnell, A. (2007). Preparing for Critical Infrastructure Breakdowns: The Limits of Crisis Management and the Need for Resilience. *Journal of Contingencies and Crisis Management*, *15*(1), 50–59.

Booher, D. E., & Innes, J. E. (2010). *Planning with Complexity: An Introduction to Collaborative Rationality for Public Policy* (1st ed.). Routledge.

Boulton, J. G., Allen, P. M., & Bowman, C. (2015). *Embracing Complexity: Strategic Perspectives for an Age of Turbulence* (1st ed.). Oxford University Press.

Bryson, J., Ackermann, F., Eden, C., & Finn, C. B. (2004). *Visible Thinking: Unlocking Causal Mapping for Practical Business Results* (1st ed.). John Wiley & Sons.

Bryson, J. M. (1988). A Strategic Planning Process for Public and Non-Profit Organizations. *Long Range Planning*, *21*(1), 73–81.

Bryson, J. M. (2018). *Strategic Planning for Public and Nonprofit Organizations: A Guide to Strengthening and Sustaining Organizational Achievement* (5th ed.). John Wiley & Sons.

Bryson, J. M., & George, B. (2020). Strategic Management in Public Administration. In B. G. Peters & I. Thynne (Eds.), *The Oxford Encyclopedia of Public Administration*. Oxford University Press.

Bryson, J. M., Quick, K. S., Slotterback, C. S., & Crosby, B. C. (2013). Designing Public Participation Processes. *Public Administration Review*, *73*(1), 23–34.

Campbell, A., & Yeung, S. (1991). Creating a Sense of Mission. *Long Range Planning*, *24*(4), 10–20.

Chaffee, E. E. (1985). Three Models of Strategy. *The Academy of Management Review*, *10*(1), 89–98.

Chakraborty, A., Kaza, N., Knaap, G.-J., & Deal, B. (2011). Robust Plans and Contingent Plans: Scenario Planning for an Uncertain World. *Journal of the American Planning Association*, *77*(3), 251–266.

Chase, C. W. (2013). *Demand-Driven Forecasting: A Structured Approach to Forecasting* (2nd ed.). John Wiley & Sons.

Clarke, L. (1999). *Mission Improbable: Using Fantasy Documents to Tame Disaster*. University of Chicago Press.

Collins, J., & Porras, J. I. (1996). Building Your Company's Vision. *Harvard Business Review*, *74*(5), 65–77.

Courtney, H., Lovallo, D., & Clarke, C. (2013). Deciding How to Decide. *Harvard Business Review*, *91*(11), 62–70.

Dewar, J. A. (2002). *Assumption-Based Planning: A Tool for Reducing Avoidable Surprises*. Cambridge University Press.

Dewar, J. A., Builder, C. H., Hix, W. M., & Levin, M. (1993). *Assumption-Based Planning: A Planning Tool for Very Uncertain Times*.

Dewar, J. A., & Levin, M. (1992). *Assumption-Based Planning for Army 21* (0-8330-1268-1). R. Corporation.

Dixit, A. K., Skeath, S., & McAdams, D. (2021). *Games of Strategy* (5th ed.). W. W. Norton & Company.

Drucker, P. F. (1954). *The Practice of Management*. Harper & Brothers.

Dutton, J. E., & Duncan, R. B. (1987). The Creation of Momentum for Change Through the Process of Strategic Issue Diagnosis. *Strategic Management Journal*, 8(3), 279–295.

Eden, C., & Ackermann, F. (2013). *Making Strategy: The Journey of Strategic Management*. Sage Publications.

Emblemsvåg, J., & Kjølstad, L. E. (2002). Strategic Risk Analysis – A Field Version. *Management Decision*, 40(9), 842–852.

Eriksson, K., & McConnell, A. (2011). Contingency Planning for Crisis Management: Recipe for Success or Political Fantasy? *Policy and Society*, 30(2), 89–99.

Freeman, R. E. (1984). *Strategic Management: A Stakeholder Approach*. Pitman.

Frigo, M. L., & Anderson, R. J. (2011). Strategic Risk Management: A Foundation for Improving Enterprise Risk Management and Governance. *Journal of Corporate Accounting & Finance*, *22*(3), 81–88.

Frigo, M. L., & Læssøe, H. (2012). Strategic Risk Management at the Lego Group. *Strategic Finance*, 93(8), 27–35.

Grant, R. M. (2003). Strategic Planning in a Turbulent environment: Evidence from the Oil Majors. *Strategic Management Journal, 24*(6), 491–517.

Hax, A. C., & Majluf, N. S. (1996). *The Strategy Concept and Process: A Pragmatic Approach* (2nd ed.). Prentice Hall.

Hogarth, R. M., & Makridakis, S. (1981). Forecasting and Planning: An Evaluation. *Management Science, 27*(2), 115–138.

Hopkin, P., & Thompson, C. (2022). *Fundamentals of Risk Management: Understanding, Evaluating and Implementing Effective Risk Management* (6th ed.). Kogan Page.

Hyndman, R. J., & Athanasopoulos, G. (2021). *Forecasting: Principles and Practice* (3rd ed.). Otexts.

Kaplan, R. S., & Mikes, A. (2012). Managing Risks: A New Framework. *Harvard Business Review*, 90(6), 48–60.

Kaplan, R. S., & Norton, D. P. (1996). *The Balanced Scorecard: Translating Strategy into Action*. Harvard Business School Press.

Kaplan, R. S., & Norton, D. P. (2000). Having Trouble with Your Strategy? Then Map It. *Harvard Business Review*, 49(5), 167–176.

Kaplan, R. S., & Norton, D. P. (2004). *Strategy Maps: Converting Intangible Assets into Tangible Outcomes*. Harvard Business School Press.

Kaplan, R. S., & Norton, D. P. (2006). *Alignment: Using the Balanced Scorecard to Create Corporate Synergies*. Harvard Business School Press.

Kaplan, R. S., & Norton, D. P. (2008). *The Execution Premium: Linking Strategy to Operations for Competitive Advantage*. Harvard Business School Press.

Keeney, R. L., & Raiffa, H. (1993). *Decisions with Multiple Objectives: Preferences and Value Trade-Offs*. Cambridge University Press.

Læssøe, H. (2015). The LEGO Group Implementation of Strategic Risk Management. In T. J. Andersen (Ed.), *The Routledge Companion to Strategic Risk Management*. Routledge.

Lawrence, M., Goodwin, P., O'Connor, M., & Önkal, D. (2006). Judgmental Forecasting: A Review of Progress over the Last 25 Years. *International Journal of Forecasting, 22*(3), 493–518.

L.E.K Consulting. (1998). Identifying and Managing Key Value Drivers. *Executive Insights, 1*(1), 1–5.

Lewinsohn, R. (2022). *Science, Prophecy, and Prediction: Man's Efforts to Foretell the Future, From Babylon to Wall Street*. Forgotten Books.

Makridakis, S., Hogarth, R. M., & Gaba, A. (2009). Forecasting and Uncertainty in the Economic and Business World. *International Journal of Forecasting, 25*(4), 794–812.

Makridakis, S., Wheelwright, S. C., & Hyndman, R. J. (1998). *Forecasting: Methods and Applications* (3rd ed.). John Wiley & Sons.

Makridakis, S. G. (1990). *Forecasting, Planning and Strategy for the 21st Century*. Free Press.

Mintzberg, H. (1994). *The Rise and Fall of Strategic Planning: Reconceiving Roles for Planning, Plans, Planners*. Free Press.

Mintzberg, H., Ahlstrand, B. W., & Lampel, J. (1998). *Strategy Safari: A Guided Tour through the Wilds of Strategic Management*. Free Press.

Morlidge, S., & Player, S. (2010). *Future Ready: How to Master Business Forecasting*. John Wiley & Sons.

Neely, A. D., Adams, C., & Kennerley, M. (2002). *The Performance Prism: The Scorecard for Measuring and Managing Business Success*. Financial Times.

Petropoulos, F., Apiletti, D., Assimakopoulos, V., Babai, M. Z., Barrow, D. K., Ben Taieb, S., Bergmeir, C., Bessa, R. J., Bijak, J., Boylan, J. E., Browell, J., Carnevale, C., Castle, J. L., Cirillo, P., Clements, M. P., Cordeiro, C., Cyrino Oliveira, F. L., De Baets, S., Dokumentov, A., … Ziel, F. (2022). Forecasting: Theory and Practice. *International Journal of Forecasting*, *38*(3), 705–871.

Poister, T. H. (2010). The Future of Strategic Planning in the Public Sector: Linking Strategic Management and Performance. *Public Administration Review*, *70*(1), 246–254.

Poister, T. H., Pitts, D. W., & Hamilton Edwards, L. (2010). Strategic Management Research in the Public Sector: A Review, Synthesis, and Future Directions. *The American Review of Public Administration*, 40(5), 522–545.

Poli, R. (2019). *Working with the Future: Ideas and Tools to Govern Uncertainty* (1st ed.). Bocconi University Press.

Porter, M. E. (1979). How Competitive Forces Shape Strategy. *Harvard Business Review*, *57*(2), 137–145.

Porter, M. E. (1980). *Competitive Strategy: Techniques for Analyzing Industries and Competitors*. Free Press.

Porter, M. E. (1985). *Competitive Advantage: Creating and Sustaining Superior Performance*. Free Press.

Reeves, M., Love, C., & Tillmanns, P. (2012). Your Strategy Needs a Strategy. *Harvard Business Review*, *90*(9), 76–83.

Rigby, D., & Bilodeau, B. (2018). *Management Tools & Trends*. Bain & Company, Inc.

Rumelt, R. (1980). The evaluation of business strategy. In W. F. Glueck (Ed.), *Business Policy and Strategic Management*. McGraw-Hill.

Saffo, P. (2007). Six rules for Effective Forecasting. *Harvard Business Review, 85*(7/8), 122–131.

Sax, J., & Andersen, T. J. (2019). Making Risk Management Strategic: Integrating Enterprise Risk Management with Strategic Planning. *European Management Review, 16*(3), 719–740.

Schoemaker, P. J. H. (2022). *Advanced Introduction to Scenario Planning*. Edward Elgar Publishing.

Sheffi, Y. (2015). *The Power of Resilience: How the Best Companies Manage the Unexpected*. MIT Press.

Simpkins, R. A. (2009). How Great Leaders Avoid Disaster: The Value of Contingency Planning. *Business Strategy Series, 10*(2), 104–108.

Slywotzky, A., & Drzik, J. (2005). Countering the Biggest Risk of All. *Harvard Business Review, 83*(4), 78–88.

Swanson, M. M., Bowen, P., Phillips, A. W., Gallup, D., & Lynes, D. (2010). *Contingency Planning Guide for Federal Information Systems*. NIST Special Publication.

Teece, D., Peteraf, M., & Leih, S. (2016). Dynamic Capabilities and Organizational Agility: Risk, Uncertainty, and Strategy in the Innovation Economy. *California Management Review, 58*(4), 13–35.

Vandersmissen, L., & George, B. (2023). Strategic Planning in Public Organizations: Reviewing 35 Years of Research. *International Public Management Journal, 0*(0), 1–26.

Von Neumann, J., & Morgenstern, O. (1944). *Theory of Games and Economic Behavior*. Princeton University Press.

Watkins, M. D., & Bazerman, M. H. (2003). Predictable Surprises: The Disasters You Should Have Seen Coming. *Harvard Business Review, 81*(3), 72–85.

Wilson, I. (1998). Strategic Planning for the Millennium: Resolving the Dilemma. *Long Range Planning, 31*(4), 507–513.

Wilson, I. (2003). *The Subtle Art of Strategy: Organizational Planning in Uncertain Times*. Praeger.

W.K. Kellogg Foundation. (2004). *Logic Model Development Guide*.

4
Clarifying Strategic Posture

4.1 Overview

4.1.1 Introduction

In today's rapidly changing and unpredictable business landscape, organizations increasingly face high levels of uncertainty and ambiguity (Bennett & Lemoine, 2014). The clarifying strategic posture offers a set of approaches designed to help organizations navigate these challenges by prioritizing understanding, flexibility, and learning (Sull, 2005). This chapter explores the key characteristics of the clarifying posture and its four main strategy approaches: waiting, imitating, practicing, and optioning.

4.1.2 Key Characteristics

The clarifying strategic posture focuses on adopting a cautious, observant approach that prioritizes understanding over action in environments characterized by high uncertainty, where definitive strategic actions might be premature or risky. This posture emphasizes the importance of buying time to gather more information, observe emerging trends, and understand the evolving landscape before committing to specific strategic directions. Organizations "spend a greater amount of time and resources on environmental scanning… that is directed toward clarifying the administrators' understanding of the probabilities of various events or changes in the environment" (Milliken, 1987, p. 139).

The underlying logic of the clarifying posture is that in highly uncertain environments, especially where critical turning points are imminent, the best course of action is often not to commit to or focus on a specific course of action or to pursue flexibility through robust strategies (Ghemawat & del Sol, 1998) but to

DOI: 10.4324/9781003684060-4

wait for clearer signals for how the future might unfold (Wernerfelt & Karnani, 1987). This allows strategies to be made with a better understanding of the landscape, potentially avoiding costly mistakes associated with rushing into uncertain situations (Sull, 2005).

An appropriate analogy for this posture is using a compass and map to find one's way through a dense fog (Day & Schoemaker, 2004). The goal is to gather further information and wait for visibility to improve before making major moves.

Strategists act as scouts. They focus on monitoring strategic uncertainties that "are top management's perception of the contingencies that could threaten or invalidate the assumptions underlying the current strategy of the business" (Simons, 1994, p. 179). They also constantly "scanning and interpreting the periphery" (Day & Schoemaker, 2004, p. 129) to survey the landscape for signs of change and opportunities to act decisively once the path forward becomes clearer (Day & Schoemaker, 2004).

4.1.3 Key Theoretical Perspectives

The clarifying strategic posture is grounded in several key theoretical perspectives that emphasize flexibility, learning, and knowledge transfer. Central to this approach is **real options theory**, which values the ability to make future strategic decisions contingent on unfolding events (Amram & Kulatilaka, 1999; Luehrman, 1998; Trigeorgis, 1996; Trigeorgis & Reuer, 2017). **Vicarious organizational learning** and **knowledge transfer** are also critical components of the clarifying posture. Vicarious learning involves acquiring knowledge and skills by observing the experiences, actions, and outcomes of other organizations (Manz & Sims, 1981). **Knowledge transfer** further complements this by emphasizing the systematic movement of knowledge within and between organizations (Argote & Ingram, 2000). Effective knowledge transfer ensures that insights and best practices are disseminated across the organization, enhancing overall capability and performance.

4.1.4 Limitations

The clarifying posture, while valuable in reducing uncertainty and providing direction, also has its limitations. One significant drawback is that it can lead to excessive caution and missed opportunities. By waiting too long for the "fog to clear", organizations may fail to seize valuable first-mover advantages or fall behind more proactive competitors (Sull, 2005). Moreover, the extended period of gathering and analyzing information associated with this posture can be resource-intensive and time-consuming, potentially delaying critical decisions (Sull, 2005). In some cases, the additional information gained may not significantly reduce uncertainty or provide a clearer path forward (Walker et al., 2013). Finally, the clarifying posture may not be suitable for all contexts, particularly in situations where rapid decision-making and bold action are essential for success (Eisenhardt, 1989).

4.1.5 Clarifying Strategy Approaches

As illustrated in Figure 4.1, the clarifying strategy approaches can be arranged in a matrix consisting of two dimensions: timing and strategy process.

The timing dimension has two categories: now or later. Now means an immediate strategic move is required. The strategy approaches in this quadrant, imitating and practicing, concentrate on timely responses to current events and conditions. Later means delayed action is possible. Waiting and optioning are the strategy approaches in this quadrant, emphasizing the ability to wait and obtain additional information before acting.

The strategy process dimension also has two categories: reactive and proactive. A reactive process refers to strategy approaches (imitating and waiting) that involve responding to changes and developments as they occur rather than

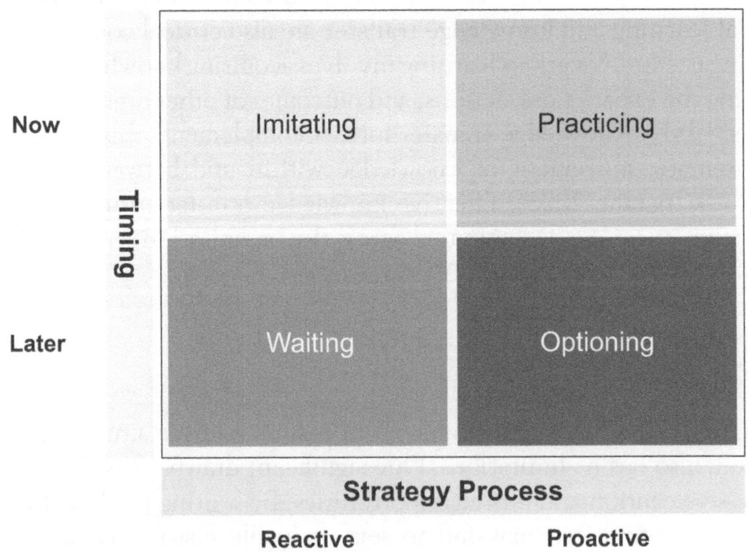

Figure 4.1 The Clarifying Strategic Posture Matrix.

initiating change. Proactive process refers to strategy approaches (practicing and optioning) that involve being ready to take the initiative to respond to changes.

As shown in the matrix, there are four key strategy approaches that can be used to achieve the clarifying posture:

- ***Waiting*** (bottom-left quadrant): Holding off on major decisions until more information becomes available (Sull, 2005). Waiting allows for a methodical gathering of data and assessment of risks before acting.
- ***Imitating*** (top-left quadrant): Observing and potentially following the successful strategies of pioneers, leveraging their learnings while avoiding their mistakes (Lieberman & Asaba, 2006; Posen et al., 2013). This approach saves costs and avoids dead ends by learning from others.
- ***Practicing*** (top-right quadrant): Engaging in simulations and scenario planning to prepare for multiple future possibilities, enhancing preparedness and strategic agility (Anderson, 2010).
- ***Optioning*** (bottom-right quadrant): Utilizing real options thinking to make small, reversible investments that keep future paths open without overcommitting resources (McGrath, 1997; Trigeorgis & Reuer, 2017). This minimizes the risk of overcommitting resources and allows for staged investments over time.

Furthermore, their key characteristics are contrasted in Table 4.1.

4.2 Waiting Approach

4.2.1 Aim

The aim of the waiting approach is to leverage patience strategically in uncertain environments, enabling organizations to make informed decisions and seize opportunities that arise from changing external circumstances (Sull, 2005).

4.2.2 Core Logic

Strategic waiting transcends passive endurance, positioning it as a deliberate and calculated choice to optimize outcomes when future conditions are uncertain

Table 4.1 Comparing the Clarifying Strategies

Dimension	Waiting	Imitating	Practicing	Optioning
Aim	Leverage patience as a means to a desired outcome	Learn from pioneers and avoid their mistakes	Rehearse multiple future possibilities	Keep future paths open reversible commitments
Core Logic	Waiting allows for a methodical gathering of data and assessment of risks before acting	Learn from who has superior information or catch up with rivals	By rehearsing the future, insights and capabilities are developed to deal with it	Using small investments to reserve the right to play in the future
Assumptions	Uncertainty can be reduced through collecting more information	Successful strategies can be copied	Future scenarios can be prepared for through practice	Future flexibility can be maintained through staged investments
Nature	Reactive – delaying irreversible decisions until more information is available	Reactive – observing and potentially following successful strategies of pioneers	Proactive – engaging in simulations and exercises to prepare for multiple futures	Proactive – making small, reversible investments to keep future paths open
Timing of Action	Delayed until clearer signals of how the future may unfold	Can be employed once successful strategies have emerged to imitate	Can be done in advance to tangibly prepare for plausible futures	Involves staged investments over time as new information becomes available

Table 4.1 (Continued)

Dimension	Waiting	Imitating	Practicing	Optioning
Strengths	Reduces the risk of premature decisions	Saves costs and avoids dead ends	Enhances preparedness	Minimizes risk of overcommitting resources
Limitations	May miss out on first-mover advantages	May not be able to imitate due to causal ambiguity	Resource-intensive and time-consuming	May require significant monitoring and management
Methods	• Active waiting	• Pure imitation • Second-mover Advantage	• Business wargaming • Simulations • Structured exercises	• Real options

(Bressler & Bergen, 2015). In volatile markets characterized by rapid and unpredictable changes in technology, customer preferences, and regulations, long-term planning can be unreliable (Sull, 2005). Strategic waiting enables organizations to gather necessary data, assess risks, and explore alternatives before committing to a specific course of action (Clarke & Liesch, 2017).

4.2.3 Key Elements

Strategic patience: It involves carefully balancing the benefits of waiting (reduced uncertainty, more information) against the potential costs (missed opportunities, competitive preemption) (Ghemawat & del Sol, 1998). The key is to maintain flexibility while also being prepared to act decisively when conditions are right (Trigeorgis & Reuer, 2017).

Opportunity capitalization: Waiting can reveal unforeseen opportunities as external circumstances evolve (Bressler & Bergen, 2015).

Situational understanding: Involves a deep understanding of the environment and timing to act at the optimal moment (Sull, 2005).

Informed decision-making: Allows time for gathering data, assessing risks, and exploring alternatives (Clarke & Liesch, 2017).

4.2.4 Applications and Examples

The waiting approach is particularly applicable in industries characterized by rapid technological changes and shifting market demands that create "windows of opportunity". One such industry is the consumer electronics industry. In his well-known book *Good Strategy Bad Strategy*, Richard Rumelt reports on a conversation he had with Apple CEO Steve Jobs, asking him what Apple's strategy was, to which Steve Jobs responded, "to wait for the next big thing" (Rumelt, 2011, p. 14).

The waiting approach is also applicable in industries that are characterized by uncertain regulatory environments such as pharmaceutical and telecommunications industries. Firms operating in these industries might delay entering new markets until regulatory frameworks are more defined. Additionally, this posture is appropriate when firms encounter scenarios awaiting a decision by an external entity, where discrete multiple potential outcomes are possible, and it is unclear which one will materialize. For example, this may arise during the uncertainty surrounding the results of an election.

4.2.5 Challenges and Limitations

Strategic waiting poses several challenges, including the need for significant patience and discipline. The cultural bias to action and the pressure to act quickly and the fear of missing out can drive organizations to abandon a wait-and-see approach prematurely (Bergen & Bressler, 2014). There is also a risk of becoming overly cautious and missing out on window of the opportunity (Ghemawat & del Sol, 1998). Furthermore, identifying the right moment to act requires a clear understanding of the situation and the external environment, which can be difficult to achieve in rapidly changing markets (Bressler & Bergen, 2015).

4.2.6 Strategy Methods

Active waiting is the key strategy method, and it involves continuously monitoring the environment, gathering data, and reassessing risks and opportunities until the optimal moment to act is identified (Clarke & Liesch, 2017).

4.2.6.1 *Active Waiting*

Active waiting is a strategic approach where organizations deliberately choose to delay immediate action while maintaining a state of heightened alertness and preparation (Sull, 2005). Unlike passive waiting, it involves continuous monitoring of the environment, gathering data, assessing risks, and positioning the organization advantageously for future opportunities (Schnaars, 2002). This method is particularly valuable in volatile or uncertain market conditions.

One of the key benefits of active waiting is risk mitigation. In rapidly evolving markets, premature commitment of resources can lead to significant losses if market conditions shift unexpectedly. By employing active waiting, firms can reduce their exposure to such risks while maintaining the flexibility to respond quickly to emerging opportunities (Sull, 2005). This approach aligns with real options theory, emphasizing the value of maintaining strategic flexibility in uncertain environments (McGrath & Nerkar, 2004).

Active waiting also allows organizations to learn from the successes and failures of first movers. For instance, industry leaders with strong competitive skills and financial resources often employ a "watchful waiting" strategy, allowing pioneers to make inevitable mistakes before entering the market themselves (Schnaars, 2002). This can be particularly effective in technology-driven industries where product life cycles are short and the costs of being a first mover can be high (Lieberman & Montgomery, 1998). It is also effective when expanding internationally or being mindful of costly reversals to strategic decisions, instead of expanding or contracting when faced with negative events, "The firm… can adopt a wait-and-see approach if more favorable outcomes are possible in the future" (Reuer & Leiblein, 2000, p. 205).

Successful implementation of active waiting requires a delicate balance between vigilance and action. Firms must remain ready to act on emerging opportunities while avoiding the trap of analysis paralysis (Eisenhardt, 1989). Microsoft's approach to the cloud computing market is a good example illustrating this method. By observing early entrants like Amazon, Microsoft refined its strategy and successfully launched Azure, becoming a major player in the cloud services market (Cusumano et al., 2019).

4.3 Imitating Approach

4.3.1 Aim

The aim of the imitating strategy approach is to leverage the successful elements of competitors' strategies, products, or processes, allowing firms to benefit from the groundwork laid by innovators while avoiding their mistakes and inefficiencies (Lieberman & Asaba, 2006). This strategic approach enables firms to achieve market success through informed decision-making and enhanced competitive positioning.

4.3.2 Core Logic

There are two key theoretical bases for explaining imitation. The information-based theories of imitation posit that organizations pursue imitation strategies because they believe others have superior information, especially in high uncertainty environments (Lieberman & Asaba, 2006). Rivalry-based theories, by contrast, argue that organizations imitate to maintain competitive parity or limit rivalry, particularly when they operate with similar resources in shared competitive spaces (Lieberman & Asaba, 2006). Imitation is rooted in vicarious learning, where organizations learn from the experiences of others rather than through direct trial and error (Levitt & March, 1988). This approach is particularly useful in uncertain or rapidly evolving markets where the costs and risks of innovation can be high (Lieberman & Montgomery, 1998). By observing market responses to pioneers' offerings, imitators can make more informed decisions about product development, market entry timing, and resource allocation, leading to significant cost savings and improved market success (Schnaars, 2002).

4.3.3 Key Elements

Vicarious learning: Organizations learn from the experiences and mistakes of others, which helps in avoiding common pitfalls (Levitt & March, 1988).

Causal ambiguity: A lack of understanding of the causes driving successful strategies or products is a major barrier to imitation as it prevents organizations from accurately replicating the critical elements that generated success (Reed & DeFillippi, 1990).

Benchmarking: This is a "mixes-and-matches" imitation strategy that involves imitating practices from the best-performing firms instead of imitating one single best-performing firm, which would be referred to as "copy-the-best" (Posen et al., 2020). In heterogenous environments, "mixes-and-matches" imitation is typically more effective than "copy-the-best" (Posen et al., 2020).

Policy transfer: In the public policy context, policy transfer commonly occurs, wherein the knowledge of policies, institutions, or administrative arrangements in one time or place is used to develop policies, institutions, or administrative arrangements in another time or place (Dolowitz & Marsh, 1996). This can take the form of voluntary policy transfer, which arises when actors freely exercise the choice to learn and transfer lessons because of dissatisfaction with current policies. Varying degrees of such policy transfer exist, including copying, entailing direct and full transfer (Dolowitz & Marsh, 2000). Policy transfer also encompasses coercive policy transfer, where one government or supranational institution exerts pressure on or obliges a government to adopt a policy.

4.3.4 Applications and Examples

Successfully applied across various industries, the imitating strategy approach has helped achieve competitive advantages. In the airline industry, CEO of Ryanair Holdings Michael O'Leary stated: "All we've done is copy Herb Kelleher's successful model. In fact, we're maybe the only people to copy it successfully and maybe take it beyond where Southwest has gone with it. But other than that it's still Southwest's model" (Shenkar, 2010, p. 86). In addition to Ryanair, imitators of Southwest Airline's model include EasyJet, JetBlue, and WestJet (Shenkar, 2010). Another example of the imitating strategy approach in action is the retail industry, where Walmart is imitated by many firms including Kmart, Best Buys, and Toys R Us.

4.3.5 Challenges and Limitations

Despite its advantages, the imitating strategy approach is not without challenges. One of the key challenges to imitation is causal ambiguity, which refers to ambiguity about the factors, resources, and competencies that cause successful outcomes (Lippman & Rumelt, 1982). Causal ambiguity arises from the tacit nature, complexity, and specificity of a firm's competencies (Reed & DeFillippi, 1990). Relatedly, without adequate attention given to the heterogeneity in socioeconomic and political contexts between different organizations, inappropriate imitation or policy transfer may occur (Dolowitz & Marsh, 2000). Additionally, imitators may incur high costs when attempting to accelerate their imitation efforts, resulting in what is known as time compression diseconomies (Dierickx & Cool, 1989). Inaccurate or inaccurate information about strategies or policies could also produce uninformed transfer or imitation (Wolman, 1992). Imitation requires significant strategic insight and timing to be carried out optimally, and the pressure to innovate continuously can be intense. Additionally, in certain industries where brands are valued, firms risk being perceived as mere copycats if they fail to add unique value beyond replication. They must be wary of legal and ethical issues related to intellectual property rights when adopting imitation strategies (Shenkar, 2010). Furthermore, if imitation leads to industry homogenization, this would reduce differentiation among competitors (DiMaggio & Powell, 1983).

4.3.6 Strategy Methods

Several methods utilize the logic of imitation. In the pure imitation strategy method, organizations directly replicate successful strategies or products of competitors (Schnaars, 2002). The second-mover advantage is another method that benefits from waiting until the first mover has navigated initial uncertainties, allowing the second mover to learn from the first mover's experiences and make more informed decisions (Bressler & Bergen, 2015).

4.3.6.1 Pure Imitation

Pure imitation is a strategic method within the broader imitation strategy approach that involves directly replicating a competitor's successful product, service, or business strategy with minimal alterations (Schnaars, 2002).

Organizations undertake pure imitation for different reasons. They pursue mimetic isomorphism by imitating others perceived as successful in their field to gain legitimacy and reduce uncertainty (DiMaggio & Powell, 1983). This reason is prevalent in public sector organizations that seek to be seen as legitimate by legislators and third-sector organizations that seek to be legitimate in the eyes of their funders. In the private sector, the firms that are subject to regulatory approval and licensing are susceptible to this type of imitation. Another justification for firms utilizing imitation strategies occurs when they are caught off guard by the unexpected success of an innovative offering in the market, compelling them to rapidly respond to maintain their competitive position (Lieberman & Asaba, 2006). Moreover, firms use imitation to mitigate risks, especially in industries characterized by high uncertainty or rapid technological change, where the risks and costs associated with innovation are substantial (Semadeni & Anderson, 2010).

However, firms pursuing pure imitation face some challenges. They may struggle to differentiate themselves from the original innovator, potentially leading to intense price competition and reduced profitability (Porter, 1980). Moreover, legal issues surrounding intellectual property rights can pose significant barriers to pure imitation, particularly in information-based industries such as semiconductors, software, and digital content where several restrictive acts have been legislated (Samuelson & Scotchmer, 2002).

Several examples of pure imitation exist across various industries. In the smartphone market, following the launch of Apple's iPhone in 2007, numerous manufacturers quickly introduced touchscreen smartphones with similar features and designs (West & Mace, 2010). Samsung, in particular, faced legal challenges from Apple due to the perceived similarity of its early Galaxy models to the iPhone (Cusumano, 2013). In streaming services, following Netflix's success in transitioning from a DVD-by-mail service to a streaming platform, numerous competitors, including Amazon Prime Video and Hulu, adopted similar subscription video-on-demand models (Lobato, 2019).

4.3.6.2 *Second-Mover Advantage*

Second-mover advantage is a strategy approach where organizations benefit from entering a market or adopting a technology after the initial innovators or first movers (Lieberman & Montgomery, 1998). This strategy leverages the ability to learn from pioneers' experiences, potentially leading to superior market performance and profitability (Markides & Geroski, 2005).

There are several strengths to adopting the second-mover advantage approach. First, product quality improves as the firm waits and incorporates better technologies or innovations that were not available to the first mover (Hoppe & Lehmann-Grube, 2001). Second, when R&D costs are high, the second mover can gain by entering the market after the first mover, thereby saving money and benefiting from a waiting game rather than a preemption game (Hoppe & Lehmann-Grube, 2001). In a similar vein, first movers often incur substantial costs in educating the market, establishing distribution channels, and developing new technologies. Second movers can leverage these investments, potentially entering the market with lower costs and greater efficiency (Lieberman & Montgomery, 1998). Finally, second movers can also observe the first mover's strategies, market reception, and consumer preferences, allowing them to make more informed decisions and reduce uncertainty (Hoppe & Lehmann-Grube, 2001).

However, successful implementation of second-mover advantage requires more than just waiting and copying. It demands active learning, strategic patience, and the ability to innovate upon existing offerings. This is sometimes called imovation, a combination of imitation and innovation (Shenkar, 2010). For instance, Microsoft entered the web browser market with Internet Explorer after Netscape pioneered the commercial web browser. Microsoft did not simply copy Netscape; instead, it actively learned from Netscape's experiences, observed user preferences, and leveraged its existing strengths and resources to improve upon the original offering. Microsoft's strategic patience and continuous innovation, coupled with its aggressive marketing and distribution strategies, eventually allowed it to overtake Netscape and become the market leader (Cusumano & Yoffie, 1998).

Nevertheless, second movers face challenges. They can find it very difficult to attract customers, even with a superior product, if the first mover has secured a temporary monopoly and established strong brand recognition and customer loyalty (Hoppe & Lehmann-Grube, 2001). This relates to how delaying market entry can result in missed opportunities and reduced market share. If the first mover successfully captures a substantial portion of the market, the second mover may struggle to penetrate and compete effectively, especially if consumer switching costs are high (Hoppe & Lehmann-Grube, 2001).

4.4 Practicing (Performing) Strategy Approach

4.4.1 Aim

The practicing (performing) strategy approach aims to prepare organizations for multiple future possibilities by engaging in simulations, scenario planning, and other immersive techniques that bridge the current moment with envisioned futures (Anderson, 2010)(Anderson, 2010).

4.4.2 Core Logic

This approach is rooted in the belief that actively practicing and simulating potential future scenarios can generate valuable insights and develop organizational capabilities to respond effectively to uncertain events (Oriesek & Schwarz, 2021). It draws from the principles of theatre, drama, and play to create tangible and actionable futures (Anderson, 2010).

4.4.3 Key Elements

Living the future: Living the surprises which we expect in the future before they happen increases our preparedness in dealing with them. Living with the future is done by simulating and practicing it. The logic used here is the logic of risk, focusing on how we can predict, monitor, and deal with the surprise future (Anderson, 2010).

Simulations: Creating realistic models of future scenarios to explore potential outcomes and responses (Morecroft, 1999).

Scenario planning: Developing multiple, plausible scenarios of the future to understand potential challenges and opportunities (Van der Heijden, 2005).

Strategic war games: Engaging in competitive simulations to test strategies and improve decision-making under uncertain conditions (Oriesek & Schwarz, 2008, 2021).

Structured exercises: Using planned activities to practice and refine strategic responses to anticipated future events (Anderson, 2010).

4.4.4 Applications and Examples

Practicing strategies can be applied across various industries to enhance preparedness and strategic agility. For example, in the military, strategic war games are used to simulate combat scenarios and improve tactical decision-making (Oriesek & Schwarz, 2008).

4.4.5 Challenges and Limitations

The practicing strategy approach presents challenges alongside its benefits. One key limitation is the potential for simulations and scenarios to oversimplify complex real-world dynamics, leading to incomplete or misleading insights (Schoemaker, 1995). Additionally, these exercises require substantial time and resources to design and implement effectively, which may not be feasible for all organizations (Anderson, 2010). There is also a risk that participants may not fully engage with the simulations and think of them as just a game, reducing the effectiveness of the practice (Duke & Geurts, 2004).

4.4.6 Strategy Methods

Several strategy methods utilize the logic of practicing. Business wargaming is a method involving competitive simulations to test strategies and improve decision-making under uncertain conditions (Oriesek & Schwarz, 2008). Structured exercises comprise another method where planned activities are designed to practice and refine strategic responses to anticipated future events (Anderson, 2010).

4.4.6.1 Business Wargaming

Wargaming is one of the oldest methods for strategy formulation that has been used in use for the past 200 years (Augier et al., 2018). Adapted from military wargaming techniques, this method involves role-playing different stakeholders to anticipate challenges, understand competitor behavior, and evaluate strategic options in a controlled environment (Oriesek & Schwarz, 2008).

At its core, business wargaming is an experiential learning process that allows organizations to explore complex competitive dynamics and potential future scenarios in a risk-free setting. By engaging participants in realistic simulations of market conditions, business wargaming helps companies identify vulnerabilities, stress-test strategies, and improve strategic agility (Kurtz & Snowden, 2003).

In addition to being used extensively by military organizations, wargaming has been applied within private sector firms. For example, a leading European mobile company uses wargaming for competitive positioning in the new changing strategy landscape (Oriesek & Schwarz, 2021). Another example is its application by an oil company to wargame scenarios for shale oil extraction in Colorado (Herman & Frost, 2008). A large European mobile operator also utilized wargaming to test its market entry strategy (Oriesek & Schwarz, 2008). Public sector organizations have also implemented wargaming, concerning, for instance, the health sector and national security (Oriesek & Schwarz, 2008).

4.4.6.2 Structured Exercises

Structured exercises are designed to simulate specific future scenarios and help organizations develop skills, test plans, and identify areas for improvement (Anderson, 2010). These exercises can take various forms, such as tabletop exercises, role-playing simulations, and crisis management drills (Perry & Lindell, 2003). Structured exercises enable organizations to practice decision-making, communication, and coordination in a controlled environment, enhancing their preparedness for future challenges (Anderson, 2010).

At their core, structured exercises are experiential learning tools that allow participants to engage with potential future scenarios in a hands-on, immersive manner. They bridge the gap between theoretical strategic planning and practical implementation by creating realistic situations that require active problem-solving and decision-making (Kleiboer, 1997).

Examples in the use of structured exercises include the annual airport disaster drill and hazardous materials exercise (Perry, 2004).

4.5 Optioning Approach

4.5.1 Aim

Organizations using the optioning strategy approach aim to keep their options open until they gain more clarity. Indeed, "For some centuries, the intuition of "keeping options open" against the unforeseeable future has motivated the development and use of option contracts in order for individuals to retain the right to future investment choices without being obliged to invest" (Bowman & Hurry, 1993, p. 761).

4.5.2 Core Logic

Organizations make small investments in real assets to position themselves for the future, buying flexibility by doing this instead of immediately making large commitments (Ghemawat & del Sol, 1998). When there is high uncertainty, this approach allows organizations to stage their investments as more information becomes available, make incremental commitments, and avoid the risks associated with big bets, which are large, irreversible investments (Amram & Kulatilaka, 1999; Trigeorgis & Reuer, 2017)(Amram & Kulatilaka, 1999; Trigeorgis & Reuer, 2017). To be more specific, "real options are investments in real assets, as opposed to financial assets, which confer the firm the right, but not the obligation, to undertake certain actions in the future" (Tong & Reuer, 2007, p. 5).

4.5.3 Key Elements

Learning options: Learning options give companies a strategic advantage to invest in the future. They enable delaying commitments until further information or necessary skills are obtained, protecting against losses from premature decisions under uncertainty (Courtney, 2001).

Staged investments (time to build options): Stage investments involve making small, incremental commitments rather than large, irreversible ones (Luehrman, 1998). This approach enables organizations to learn and gather information over time, reducing uncertainty and the risk of costly mistakes (McGrath, 1997), and creating the option to abandon plans when the information is unfavorable (Trigeorgis, 1996).

Options to defer: They allow firms to delay making a strategic investment or decision until more information is accessible or until conditions become more favorable (Trigeorgis, 1996).

4.5.4 Applications and Examples

In practice, optioning is used in various industries. For instance, pharmaceutical companies often invest in multiple drug development projects simultaneously, treating each as a real option. This approach allows them to pursue promising candidates while maintaining the flexibility to abandon less successful projects (McGrath & Nerkar, 2004). Timing and switching real options are also used in the energy sector to stage the investments (Nadarajah & Secomandi, 2023).

4.5.5 Challenges and Limitations

Despite its advantages, the optioning strategy approach has limitations. Developing a real options mindset requires a significant shift from traditional, static planning to a more dynamic, flexible approach (McGrath, 1997). There is also the potential risk of over-reliance on flexibility, which can lead to indecisiveness or delayed actions (MacMillan & Putten, 2004). Moreover, decision-makers making real option investments are prone to overconfidence cognitive bias. Recent research has shown that overconfident CEOs are likely to invest less in real options compared to their non-overconfident counterparts due to their overly optimistic assessment of their own performance, as well as their underestimation of uncertainties (Lee et al., 2023). This tendency becomes even more pronounced in environments with higher market uncertainty. Lastly, the complex and resource-intensive process of accurately identifying, valuing, and managing real options may limit its use (Copeland & Tufano, 2004).

4.5.6 Strategy Methods

In the context of the clarifying strategic posture, real-options portfolio is a strategy method that utilizes the logic of optioning to answer the question of now or later in terms of strategic investments (Courtney, 2001).

4.5.6.1 *Real Options*

Real options provide organizations with the right, but not the obligation, to invest or divest in the future as the company's information set changes

(Luehrman, 1998). Real options manage risk by limiting downside losses while maintaining upside returns. They are valuable in uncertain situations because they allow decision-makers to re-optimize over time without incurring substantial sunk costs (Courtney, 2001). Stage investments allow organizations to implement the real options method by making small, incremental commitments rather than large, irreversible ones (Luehrman, 1998). This approach enables organizations to learn and gather information over time, reducing uncertainty and the risk of costly mistakes (McGrath, 1997). By staging investments, organizations can create a portfolio of strategic opportunities that they can pursue or abandon as circumstances change (Luehrman, 1998).

References

Amram, M., & Kulatilaka, N. (1999). *Real Options: Managing Strategic Investment in an Uncertain World*. Harvard Business School Press.

Anderson, B. (2010). Preemption, Precaution, Preparedness: Anticipatory Action and Future Geographies. *Progress in Human Geography*, *34*(6), 777–798.

Argote, L., & Ingram, P. (2000). Knowledge Transfer: A Basis for Competitive Advantage in Firms. *Organizational Behavior and Human Decision Processes*, *82*(1), 150–169.

Augier, M., Dew, N., Knudsen, T., & Stieglitz, N. (2018). Organizational Persistence in the Use of War Gaming and Scenario Planning. *Long Range Planning*, *51*(4), 511–525.

Bennett, N., & Lemoine, G. J. (2014). What a Difference a Word Makes: Understanding Threats to Performance in a VUCA World. *Business Horizons*, *57*(3), 311–317.

Bergen, C. W. V., & Bressler, M. (2014). Active Waiting Revisited: Learning from Lions International. *International Journal of Strategic Management*, *14*(1), 89–102.

Bowman, E. H., & Hurry, D. (1993). Strategy Through the Option Lens: An Integrated View of Resource Investments and the Incremental-Choice Process. *The Academy of Management Review*, *18*(4), 760–782.

Bressler, M., & Bergen, C. W. V. (2015). Active Waiting As Business Strategy: Learning From The Serengeti Plains. *Journal of Business Strategies*, *32*(1), 21–40.

Clarke, J. E., & Liesch, P. W. (2017). Wait-And-See Strategy: Risk Management in the Internationalization Process Model. *Journal of International Business Studies*, *48*(8), 923–940.

Copeland, T., & Tufano, P. (2004). A Real-World Way to Manage Real Options. *Harvard Business Review*, *82*(3), 90–99.

Courtney, H. (2001). *20/20 Foresight: Crafting Strategy in an Uncertain World*. Harvard Business School Press.

Cusumano, M. A. (2013). The Apple-Samsung Lawsuits. *Communications of the ACM*, 56(1), 28–31.

Cusumano, M. A., Gawer, A., & Yoffie, D. B. (2019). *The Business of Platforms: Strategy in the Age of Digital Competition, Innovation, and Power* (1st ed.). Harper Business.

Cusumano, M. A., & Yoffie, D. B. (1998). *Competing on Internet Time: Lessons from Netscape and Its Battle with Microsoft*. Free Press.

Day, G. S., & Schoemaker, P. J. H. (2004). Driving Through the Fog: Managing at the Edge. *Long Range Planning*, *37*(2), 127–142.

Dierickx, I., & Cool, K. (1989). Asset Stock Accumulation and Sustainability of Competitive Advantage. *Management Science*, *35*(12), 1504–1511.

DiMaggio, P. J., & Powell, W. W. (1983). The Iron Cage Revisited: Institutional Isomorphism and Collective Rationality in Organizational Fields. *American Sociological Review*, *48*(2), 147–160.

Dolowitz, D. P., & Marsh, D. (1996). Who Learns What from Whom: A Review of the Policy Transfer Literature. *Political Studies*, *44*(2), 343–357.

Dolowitz, D. P., & Marsh, D. (2000). Learning from Abroad: The Role of Policy Transfer in Contemporary Policy-Making. *Governance*, *13*(1), 5–23.

Duke, R. D., & Geurts, J. L. A. (2004). *Policy Games for Strategic Management: Pathways into the unknown*. Dutch University Press.

Eisenhardt, K. M. (1989). Making Fast Strategic Decisions in High-Velocity Environments. *The Academy of Management Journal*, *32*(3), 543–576.

Ghemawat, P., & del Sol, P. (1998). Commitment Versus Flexibility? *California Management Review*, *40*(4), 26–42.

Herman, M. L., & Frost, M. D. (2008). *Wargaming for leaders: Strategic decision making from the battlefield to the boardroom*. McGraw-Hill.

Hoppe, H. C., & Lehmann-Grube, U. (2001). Second-Mover Advantages in Dynamic Quality Competition. *Journal of Economics & Management Strategy*, *10*(3), 419–433.

Kleiboer, M. (1997). Simulation Methodology for Crisis Management Support. *Journal of Contingencies and Crisis Management*, *5*(4), 198–206.

Kurtz, C. F., & Snowden, D. J. (2003). The New Dynamics of Strategy: Sense-Making in a Complex and Complicated World. *IBM Systems Journal*, *42*(3), 462–483.

Lee, J. M., Park, J. C., & Chen, G. (2023). A cognitive perspective on real options investment: CEO overconfidence. *Strategic Management Journal*, *44*(4), 1084–1110.

Levitt, B., & March, J. G. (1988). Organizational Learning. *Annual Review of Sociology*, *14*(1), 319–338.

Lieberman, M. B., & Asaba, S. (2006). Why Do Firms Imitate Each Other? *Academy of Management Review*, *31*(2), 366–385.

Lieberman, M. B., & Montgomery, D. B. (1998). First-Mover (dis) advantages: Retrospective and Link with the Resource-Based View. *Strategic Management Journal*, *19*(12), 1111–1125.

Lippman, S. A., & Rumelt, R. P. (1982). Uncertain Imitability: An Analysis of Interfirm Differences in Efficiency Under Competition. *The Bell Journal of Economics*, *13*(2), 418–438.

Lobato, R. (2019). *Netflix Nations: The Geography of Digital Distribution*. New York University Press.

Luehrman, T. A. (1998). Strategy As a Portfolio of Real Options. *Harvard Business Review*, *76*(5), 89–99.

MacMillan, I., & Putten, A. v. (2004). Making Real Options Really Work. *Harvard Business Review*, *812*(12), 134–141.

Manz, C. C., & Sims, H. P. (1981). Vicarious Learning: The Influence of Modeling on Organizational Behavior. *Academy of Management Review*, *6*(1), 105–113.

Markides, C., & Geroski, P. A. (2005). *Fast Second: How Smart Companies Bypass Radical Innovation to Enter and Dominate New Markets* (1st ed.). Jossey-Bass.

McGrath, R., & Nerkar, A. (2004). Real Options Reasoning and a New Look at the R&D Investment Strategies of Pharmaceutical Firms. *Strategic Management Journal*, *25*(1), 1–21.

McGrath, R. G. (1997). A Real Options Logic for Initiating Technology Positioning Investments. *The Academy of Management Review*, *22*(4), 974–996.

Milliken, F. J. (1987). Three Types of Perceived Uncertainty About the Environment: State, Effect, and Response Uncertainty. *Academy of Management Review*, *12*(1), 133–143.

Morecroft, J. (1999). Visualising and Rehearsing Strategy. *Business Strategy Review*, *10*(3), 17–32.

Nadarajah, S., & Secomandi, N. (2023). A Review of the Operations Literature on Real Options in Energy. *European Journal of Operational Research*, 309(2), 469–487.

Oriesek, D. F., & Schwarz, J. O. (2008). *Business Wargaming: Securing Corporate Value*. Gower.

Oriesek, D. F., & Schwarz, J. O. (2021). *Winning the Uncertainty Game: Turning Strategic Intent into Results with Wargaming* (1st ed.). Routledge.

Perry, R. W. (2004). Disaster Exercise Outcomes for Professional Emergency Personnel and Citizen Volunteers. *Journal of Contingencies and Crisis Management, 12*(2), 64–75.

Perry, R. W., & Lindell, M. K. (2003). Preparedness for Emergency Response: Guidelines for the Emergency Planning Process. *Disasters, 27*(4), 336–350.

Porter, M. E. (1980). *Competitive Strategy: Techniques for Analyzing Industries and Competitors*. Free Press.

Posen, H. E., Lee, J., & Yi, S. (2013). The Power of Imperfect Imitation. *Strategic Management Journal, 34*(2), 149–164.

Posen, H. E., Yi, S., & Lee, J. (2020). A Contingency Perspective on Imitation Strategies: When Is "Benchmarking" Ineffective? *Strategic Management Journal, 41*(2), 198–221.

Reed, R., & DeFillippi, R. J. (1990). Causal Ambiguity, Barriers to Imitation, and Sustainable Competitive Advantage. *Academy of Management Review, 15*(1), 88–102.

Reuer, J. J., & Leiblein, M. J. (2000). Downside Risk Implications of Multinationality and International Joint Ventures. *The Academy of Management Journal, 43*(2), 203–214.

Rumelt, R. P. (2011). *Good Strategy Bad Strategy: The Difference and Why it Matters* (1st ed.). Crown Business.

Samuelson, P., & Scotchmer, S. (2002). The Law and Economics of Reverse Engineering. *The Yale Law Journal, 111*(7), 1575–1663.

Schnaars, S. P. (2002). *Managing Imitation Strategies: How Later Entrants Seize Markets from Pioneers*. Free Press.

Schoemaker, P. J. H. (1995). Scenario Planning: A Tool for Strategic Thinking. *MIT Sloan Management Review, 36*(2), 25–40.

Semadeni, M., & Anderson, B. S. (2010). The Follower's Dilemma: Innovation and Imitation in the Professional Services Industry. *Academy of Management Journal, 53*(5), 1175–1193.

Shenkar, O. (2010). *Copycats: How Smart Companies Use Imitation to Gain a Strategic Edge*. Harvard Business Press.

Simons, R. (1994). *Levers of Control: How Managers Use Innovative Control Systems to Drive Strategic Renewal*. Harvard Business School Press.

Sull, D. N. (2005). Strategy as Active Waiting. *Harvard Business Review, 83*(9), 120–129.

Tong, T. W., & Reuer, J. J. (2007). Real Options in Strategic Management. In J. J. Reuer & T. W. Tong (Eds.), *Real Options Theory* (Vol. 24, pp. 3–28). Emerald Group Publishing Limited.

Trigeorgis, L. (1996). *Real Options: Managerial Flexibility and Strategy in Resource Allocation*. MIT Press.

Trigeorgis, L., & Reuer, J. J. (2017). Real Options Theory in Strategic Management. *Strategic Management Journal*, *38*(1), 42–63.

Van der Heijden, K. (2005). *Scenarios: The Art of Strategic Conversation* (2nd ed.). John Wiley & Sons.

Walker, W. E., Marchau, V. A. W. J., & Kwakkel, J. H. (2013). Uncertainty in the Framework of Policy Analysis. In W. A. H. Thissen & W. E. Walker (Eds.), *Public Policy Analysis: New Developments* (pp. 215–261). Springer.

Wernerfelt, B., & Karnani, A. (1987). Competitive Strategy Under Uncertainty. *Strategic Management Journal*, *8*(2), 187–194.

West, J., & Mace, M. (2010). Browsing As the Killer App: Explaining the Rapid Success of Apple's iPhone. *Telecommunications Policy*, *34*(5), 270–286.

Wolman, H. (1992). Understanding Cross National Policy Transfers: The Case of Britain and the US. *Governance*, *5*(1), 27–45.

5
Coping Strategic Posture

5.1 Overview

5.1.1 Introduction

The coping strategic posture aims to enhance an organization's ability to withstand disruptions and adapt to change by building resilience and flexibility into its operations, culture, and strategic outlook (Evans, 1991). This chapter explores the key characteristics of the coping posture and its four main strategy approaches: strategic resilience, static robustness, dynamic robustness, and strategic flexibility.

5.1.2 Key Characteristics

Adopting the coping strategic posture enables an organization to develop the resilience, robustness, or flexibility to effectively respond to environmental changes and withstand disruptions as they occur (Reeves & Deimler, 2011). This posture focuses on developing plans and capabilities to cope with uncertainty. Unlike the calculating posture, the coping posture does not attempt to predict or control the future. This underscores strategic coping's dynamic, responsive approach to strategy formulation that prioritizes adaptability and learning to produce emergent strategies over long-term planning that produces intended strategies (Mintzberg & Waters, 1985).

The logic behind the coping posture is that in environments characterized by uncertainty and rapid change, the ability to quickly adapt to new changes and conditions is more valuable than trying to predict the future (Evans, 1991) or to shape it (Courtney et al., 1997).

DOI: 10.4324/9781003684060-5

An appropriate analogy for this posture is off-road driving in a rugged vehicle designed to handle uncertain road conditions ahead, necessitating flexibility and resilience.

Strategists act as navigators, constantly assessing the environment for changes and guiding the organization to respond swiftly and effectively.

5.1.3 Key Theoretical Perspectives

The coping strategic posture integrates several key theoretical perspectives that help organizations cope with complexities, uncertainties, and future developments. Central to this approach is the **behavioral theory of the firm**, initially articulated by Barnard (1938), and later expanded by Cyert and March (1963). This theory emphasizes the bounded rationality of decision-makers and the importance of organizational routines and processes in shaping firm behavior. It highlights how firms cope with environmental uncertainty through satisficing, a process of settling for satisfactory rather than optimal decisions, and through the development of standard operating procedures. Another foundational perspective is the **resource-based view (RBV)**, which emphasizes the importance of internal resources and capabilities in navigating competitive landscapes and achieving and sustaining competitive advantage (Barney, 1991; Penrose, 1959). The concept of **dynamic capabilities**, developed by Teece et al. (1997), extends the RBV by emphasizing the firm's ability to continuously integrate, build, and reconfigure internal and external competences to address rapidly changing environments. Firms cope with **resource dependency** by managing relationships and negotiating with external actors to secure critical resources, thereby reducing uncertainty and enhancing their strategic position (Pfeffer & Salancik, 1978). The **evolutionary theory** of the firm highlights how firms cope with changes by developing and refining routines that guide their actions, thereby ensuring survival and gradual improvement over time (Nelson & Winter, 1982). Lastly, the **complexity perspective**, as discussed by Boulton et al. (2015), frames organizations as complex adaptive systems. This perspective underscores the importance of nonlinear interactions, emergence, and self-organization in coping with complex and unpredictable environments. It suggests that firms need to embrace complexity and foster adaptive capacities to effectively navigate and thrive amidst uncertainty. This complexity perspective is relevant to all other postures. Therefore, its description will not be repeated in the following chapters.

5.1.4 Limitations

While the coping strategic posture offers a pragmatic approach to embracing complexity and navigating uncertainty and change, it has its limitations. By focusing primarily on resilience, adaptability, robustness, and flexibility, organizations may miss opportunities to shape their environment and proactively influence their future (Courtney, 2001). The emphasis on short-to-medium term challenges and maintaining stability can lead to a reactive stance, where organizations are constantly responding to external pressures rather than driving innovation and growth (Hamel & Välikangas, 2003). Furthermore, the coping posture may not be sufficient for organizations facing disruptive, transformative changes that require a fundamental shift in strategy and business models (Christensen et al., 2015). In such cases, a more proactive, future-oriented approach may be necessary to ensure long-term success (McGrath, 2013). Finally, the coping posture's focus on managing risks and uncertainties can sometimes lead to a risk-averse culture that stifles creativity and experimentation, which are essential for staying competitive in today's fast-paced business environment (Teece et al., 2016).

5.1.5 Coping Strategy Approaches

There are several strategy approaches stressing the coping posture. These include resistance, resilience, static robustness, dynamic robustness, strategic flexibility, and strategic agility. These approaches differ in two major dimensions: their adaptive capacity and responsiveness to changes and disruptions. Adaptive capacity refers to the extent of its ability to respond to change while responsiveness refers to its speed to respond.

In our framework, we exclude resistance because it is a special case of resilience. The resistance approach is meant to resist change and therefore is the least responsive and adaptive. The strategic agility approach is characterized by high levels of responsiveness and adaptability. However, it goes beyond the coping posture to include capitalizing on opportunities, which entails shaping the strategic context in which it is situated. Therefore, we exclude from the coping posture and discuss in the craft posture chapter (Figure 5.1).

To produce a better understanding of what differentiates them, the coping strategy approaches are arranged in a matrix consisting of two dimensions: the output of the strategy and the strategy process.

The vertical output of the strategy dimension, referring to strategy outputs, has two categories: plan and capability. For the capability output, the strategy

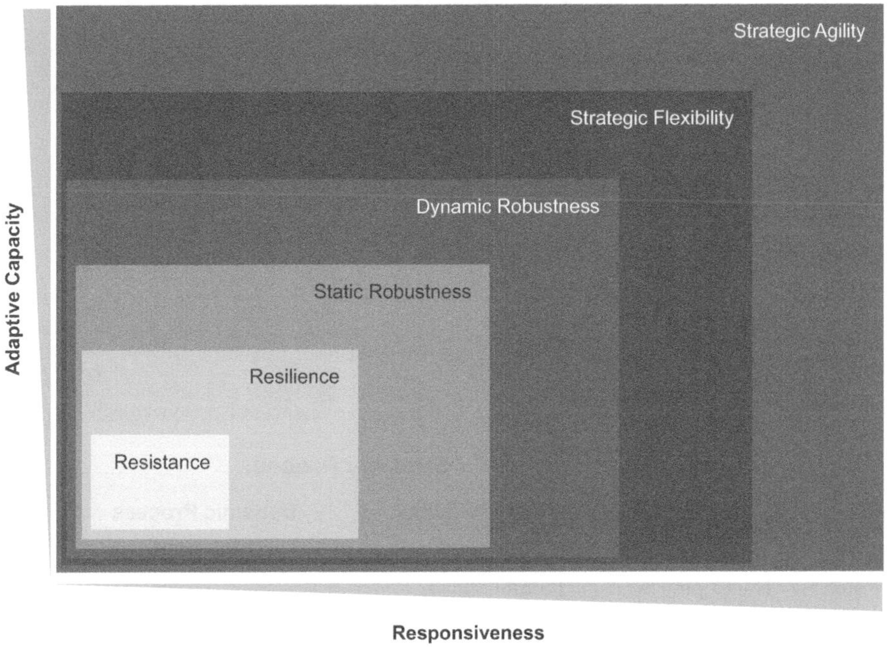

Figure 5.1 The Coping Strategy Approaches.

approaches focus on building internal capacities to adapt and respond to changes (Barney, 1991). These approaches emphasize developing the skills, resources, and processes necessary for resilience and adaptability. The plan category refers to strategy approaches that create detailed plans to address potential scenarios (Wilson & Ralston, 2006). These strategy approaches tend to use formal and structured strategy processes to create robust plans.

The horizontal strategy process dimension also has two categories: static process (intended) and dynamic process (emergent) (Mintzberg & Waters, 1985). Strategy approaches using the static solution (intended) formulate strategies once and design them to be stable over time, intending for them to maintain robustness and performance without frequent adjustments. Static strategies are characterized by a focus on stability and resilience within a predetermined framework. In contrast, strategies formulated using dynamic process (emergent) are continually updated in response to changes and learning. They are adaptive and evolve based on new information and changing conditions. Dynamic processes emphasize strategic flexibility and responsiveness (Figure 5.2).

As shown in the matrix, four key strategy approaches that can be drawn upon to achieve the coping posture:

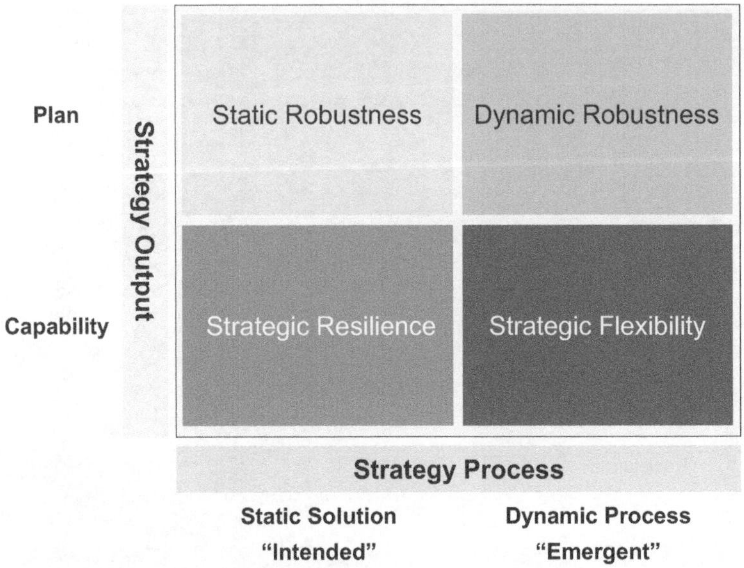

Figure 5.2 The Coping Strategic Posture Matrix.

Strategic resilience (bottom-left quadrant): This strategy approach involves developing capacities to resist and recover from unexpected disruptions, building resilient systems that can withstand and bounce back from adverse events (Hamel & Välikangas, 2003). Focusing on anticipating and preparing for potential disruptions to ensure ongoing stability and recovery is crucial (Annarelli & Nonino, 2016). The approach assumes a static strategy process, where capabilities are built then remain relatively constant over time.

Static robustness (top-left quadrant): This strategy approach is designed to maintain satisfactory performance across a wide range of potential future scenarios (Rosenhead et al., 1972). It prioritizes stability and security over optimizing performance for a specific predicted future, often sacrificing potential high pay-offs for robustness (Lempert et al., 2003). It also assumes a static strategy process, where a plan is formulated once and is intended to be robust in various strategic contexts.

Dynamic robustness (top-right quadrant): This strategy approach involves implementing short-term measures and setting up monitoring criteria to keep track of developments that might require policy adjustments (Walker et al., 2013). Recognizing that complex dynamics will inevitably unfold differently than anticipated, it calls

Table 5.1 Comparing the Coping Strategies

Dimension	Strategic Resilience	Static Robustness	Dynamic Robustness	Strategic Flexibility
Aim	Develop capacities to resist and recover from unexpected disruptions	Maintain satisfactory performance across a wide range of potential future scenarios	Perform well in all scenarios while being responsive to both anticipated changes and unforeseen events	Respond effectively to both anticipated and unanticipated changes
Core Logic	Resilience focuses on bouncing back and maintaining function	Static robustness focuses on robustness across multiple futures over optimization for a single future	Same as static robustness but adds preparing for expected and unexpected deviations from the plan	Strategic flexibility focuses on adaptability and responsiveness to both expected and unexpected changes
Assumptions	Disruptions are inevitable and need to be managed	Future conditions can be anticipated and planned for	System dynamics will unfold differently than anticipated	Unforeseen issues and changes will arise
Output	Capability	Plan	Plan with triggers	Dynamic capabilities to maintain flexibility
Timing of Action	Anticipatory	Anticipatory	Anticipatory and concurrent	Anticipatory and concurrent
Time Horizon	Short to medium term	Medium to long term	Medium to long-term	Medium to long-term
Strengths	Ensures continuity and quick recovery from disruptions	Ensures stability and performance across various conditions	Ensures continued effectiveness by responding to changes	Ensures adaptability and responsiveness to changing conditions

(*Continued*)

Table 5.1 (Continued)

Dimension	Strategic Resilience	Static Robustness	Dynamic Robustness	Strategic Flexibility
Limitations	May require significant investment in preparedness	Sacrifices optimal performance for robustness	Requires continuous monitoring and adaptation	May lead to overemphasis on flexibility at the expense of stability
Methods	• Resilience-Based Planning • Worst-Case Planning	• Scenario-Based Planning • Portfolio of Strategies (Diversification)	• Dynamic Adaptive Planning • Dynamic Adaptive Policy Pathways	• Portfolio of Initiatives

for a predesigned ability to deal with changing conditions or sudden shocks (McCray et al., 2010). This approach assumes a dynamic strategy process, where the plan is updated in response to changes and learning, leading to an emergent strategy.

Strategic flexibility (bottom-left quadrant): This strategy approach refers to the capacity of a strategy to adapt to both anticipated and unanticipated conditions (Bahrami, 1992; Evans, 1991). It emphasizes the ability to initiate deliberate changes, adapt to unexpected changes, and manage the consequences of predictable changes (Shimizu & Hitt, 2004; Volberda, 1996). Strategic flexibility assumes a dynamic strategy process and focuses on developing dynamic capabilities (Teece et al., 1997) that enable the organization to respond effectively to changing circumstances. This stands in contrast to the strategic resilience approach that builds capabilities to maintain its position in the face of changes.

The key characteristics of these approaches are contrasted in Table 5.1.

5.2 Strategic Resilience Approach

5.2.1 Aim

The strategic resilience approach aims to develop organizational capabilities that enable anticipation, resistance, response, and adaptation to unexpected disruptions and environmental shocks, ensuring long-term sustainability and performance (Annarelli & Nonino, 2016).

5.2.2 Core Logic

Unlike resistance strategies that focus on not reacting to disturbances, resilience involves rebounding and adapting to maintain organizational integrity (Duchek, 2020). This approach is grounded in the belief that while disruptions are inevitable, their negative impacts can be minimized through proactive planning and dynamic response capabilities (Annarelli & Nonino, 2016).

Unlike the risk-based planning approach, which centers on identifying risks and reducing vulnerability to external disturbances, a resilience approach emphasizes developing capabilities and capacities that "create or retain resources (cognitive, emotional, relational, or structural) in a form sufficiently flexible, storable, convertible, and malleable give rise to resilience and allow organizations, their units and members to avert maladaptive tendencies and positively cope with the unexpected" (Sutcliffe & Vogus, 2003, p. 95). Moreover, resilient organizations may go a step further and become antifragile when not only recover but experience positive gains from the learning from responding to external shocks and disturbances (Taleb, 2012).

5.2.3 Key Elements

- *Anticipation capabilities:* The ability to observe internal and external developments, identify critical developments and potential threats, and prepare for unexpected events (Duchek, 2020).
- *Coping capabilities:* The ability to accept problems and develop/implement solutions when facing unexpected events. This involves sensemaking, improvisation, coordination, and quick implementation (Duchek, 2020; Linnenluecke, 2017).
- *Adaptation capabilities:* The ability to reflect on and learn from crisis situations, as well as implement organizational changes based on those learnings. This involves reflection, learning, and change management capabilities (Duchek, 2020).
- *Adaptive capacity:* This involves learning from crises, reconfiguring resources, and innovating to create new opportunities from adversity and emerge stronger from crises (Burnard & Bhamra, 2011; Taleb, 2012).
- *Resilience thinking:* This element emphasizes embedding resilience thinking into all aspects of planning and operations, ensuring that systems and people are better prepared to withstand and adapt to disruptions across the organization (Snape & Weeks, 2022).
- *Flexible resources:* This involves creating multipurpose capabilities and resources that can be quickly repurposed or redeployed in different crisis situations (van der Vegt et al., 2015).

5.2.4 Applications and Examples

The strategic resilience approach has been successfully applied in various contexts. For example, during the COVID-19 pandemic, organizations with resilience strategies were able to quickly pivot to remote work, adapt supply chains, and meet changing customer needs (Rapaccini et al., 2020). Toyota's supply chain resilience practices also allowed the company to swiftly recover from the 2011 earthquake and tsunami in Japan by diversifying its supply base and implementing flexible manufacturing systems (Matsuo, 2015).

5.2.5 Challenges and Limitations

Implementing a strategic resilience approach is not without challenges. Developing a resilience mindset requires significant cultural, structural, relational, and operational changes within an organization (Sutcliffe & Vogus, 2003). It can be also resource-intensive because most resilience strategies requiring duplicating resources and having spare capacity (slack). Additionally, while resilience can mitigate the impact of disruptions, it cannot eliminate risks, and overreliance on resilience planning might lead to complacency (Duchek, 2020).

5.2.6 Strategy Methods

Several strategy methods utilize the logic of resilience. Resilience-based planning involves preparing for potential disruptions by developing detailed plans that outline specific responses to identified risks. This proactive planning helps ensure that the organization can maintain operations during and after a disruption. Worst-case planning is another method that focuses on preparing for the most severe potential disruptions. By planning for worst-case scenarios, organizations can develop robust strategies that ensure they are prepared for any eventuality, thereby enhancing their overall resilience (Sheffi, 2005).

5.2.6.1 *Resilience-Based Planning*

Resilience-based planning focuses on developing organizational capabilities to withstand, recover from, and adapt to disruptions. This method emphasizes building resilience into the organization's structures, processes, and culture to ensure continuity and sustainability in the face of unexpected challenges (Hamel & Välikangas, 2003). It involves identifying potential vulnerabilities, eliminating redundancies in critical systems, and fostering a culture of adaptability and learning (Bhamra et al., 2011). These resilience-based planning activities enhance an organization's ability to maintain core functions under adverse conditions, while also positioning it to capitalize on new opportunities that may arise from disruptions (Weick & Sutcliffe, 2015).

5.2.6.2 *Worst-Case Planning*

Worst-case planning is a strategic method that involves preparing for the most severe and unlikely scenarios to ensure that the organization is capable of handling extreme disruptions and minimizing their impact (Boin & McConnell, 2007). This approach encourages organizations to imagine and plan for the most catastrophic events that could affect their operations, even if these events are highly improbable (Taleb, 2007). By doing so, organizations can build stronger resilience capabilities, develop robust response strategies, and allocate resources more effectively to mitigate potential disruptions (Boin et al., 2010).

5.3 Static Robustness Approach

5.3.1 Aim

The static robustness approach aims to formulate strategies that ensure satisfactory performance across various potential future scenarios, thereby giving priority to stability and security over optimizing for a single predicted future (Mason, 1994; Wulf et al., 2013).

5.3.2 Core Logic

The core logic of the static robustness approach is based on the need to create strategies that are robust and applicable to various anticipated futures, rather than optimized for only one predicted future. This approach acknowledges the inherent difficulty in accurately forecasting the future and instead focuses on ensuring consistent performance across multiple possible future scenarios (Van der Heijden, 2005).

5.3.3 Key Elements

Scenario planning: Developing multiple plausible future scenarios to understand potential risks and opportunities is critical (Van der Heijden, 2005).

Strategy evaluation: Evaluating the impact of different strategies on organizational performance to identify robust strategies is a significant component of adopting a static robustness approach (Lempert et al., 2003; Wilson, 2000).

Strategic Uncertainties: These are the unpredictable strategic factors that could unfold differently across scenarios, compared to elements that are predictable and consistent across multiple scenarios. These are called predetermineds (Van der Heijden, 2005).

Plausibility: This is a key criterion for effectiveness in both the construction and utilization of scenarios. For scenarios to be considered plausible, they must be specific, logically consistent, and contain coherent narratives that broaden participants' perspectives, preparing them for future events (Walton et al., 2019).

5.3.4 Applications and Examples

Static robustness strategies have been successfully applied in various industries. For example, the Shell Oil Company has used scenario planning since the 1970s to anticipate and prepare for major shifts in the global energy landscape, allowing the company to navigate uncertain market conditions effectively (Wack, 1985). In the pharmaceutical industries, companies maintain diverse R&D portfolios to build a robust strategy (Hartmann & Hassan, 2006).

5.3.5 Challenges and Limitations

While static robustness strategies offer significant benefits in terms of robustness, they also come with limitations. One major challenge is the potential trade-off between robustness and high pay-offs, as these strategies prioritize stability over optimizing performance (Lempert et al., 2003). Additionally, in highly dynamic environments, static robustness may lead to organizational inertia, making it difficult for organizations to adapt quickly to emerging opportunities or threats (Teece et al., 1997).

5.3.6 Strategy Methods

Several strategy methods utilize the logic of static robustness. Scenario-based planning involves developing and analyzing multiple plausible future scenarios to identify robust strategies (Schwartz, 1996). The portfolio of strategies method entails maintaining a diversified portfolio of strategies to buffer against specific risks and uncertainties, ensuring stable performance across different scenarios (Beinhocker, 1997).

5.3.6.1 *Scenario-Based Planning*

Scenario-based planning is a strategic method that encompasses identifying key drivers of change, creating detailed and plausible scenarios to anticipate future conditions, and developing strategies that are resilient and effective across these scenarios (De Ruijter, 2014; Schoemaker, 2022; Wulf et al., 2013). This method focuses on building robust strategies that can maintain satisfactory performance across a wide range of potential future (Wulf et al., 2013).

5.3.6.2 *Portfolio of Strategies (Diversification)*

This method involves running multiple strategies in parallel to ensure that at least some will succeed regardless of how future conditions unfold (Beinhocker, 1997; Raynor, 2007). This strategy method is referred to as robust adaptive strategies (Beinhocker, 1999). They are also diversification strategies and more specifically called defensive external diversification strategies (Ansoff, 1965). They involve participating in multiple product markets and technologies ensuring that at least one of them will succeed (Aaker & Mascarenhas, 1984). For example, Sony's strategy of diversifying into various electronics, gaming, and entertainment products helps it maintain stability and absorb shocks from declining divisions (Aaker & Mascarenhas, 1984). By employing a portfolio approach, organizations can hedge against the failure of any one strategy.

The essence of the portfolio of strategies lies in its emphasis on diversification and flexibility. Instead of relying on a single, focused strategy, organizations cultivate and manage a range of strategic options that evolve over time. Recognizing that in complex and uncertain environments, relying on a single strategy can be risky, organizations develop and maintain multiple strategies concurrently (Beinhocker, 1999). Markides and Charitou (2004) discuss how some companies successfully compete with dual business models. For instance, they describe how Charles Schwab maintained both a traditional brokerage business and a discount online brokerage, effectively hedging against uncertainty in the evolution of the brokerage industry.

Implementing a portfolio of strategies requires a dynamic and adaptive management approach. Organizations must continuously monitor the performance of each strategy, reallocating resources as needed to support the most promising initiatives. This iterative process allows businesses to respond quickly to changes in the environment, ensuring that their strategic portfolio remains aligned with long-term objectives.

This is illustrated by the COVID-19 pandemic, where public sector organizations made major investments in multiple vaccine technologies (e.g. mRNA, Adenoviral vector, inactivated virus) to ensure that they have a robust strategy for developing an effective vaccine (Lalani et al., 2023).

5.4 Dynamic Robustness Approach

5.4.1 Aim

The dynamic robustness approach aims to develop strategies that perform well across multiple scenarios while remaining adaptable to both anticipated changes and unforeseen events (Walker et al., 2013). While it shares similarities with the static robustness approach in terms of seeking satisficing outcomes, it does not limit itself to a fixed plan that is applied across all strategic contexts; instead incorporating the flexibility to update plans.

5.4.2 Core Logic

The dynamic robustness approach operates on the principle that while a plan must perform well across various scenarios, it must also be capable of adaptation in response to new information and unexpected changes. This approach involves implementing robust strategies with predefined triggers for adjustments, enabling organizations to remain resilient and responsive over time (Walker et al., 2013).

5.4.3 Key Elements

In addition to all the key elements for robust static approach, it has the following additional elements:

Signposts and triggers or tipping points: Dynamic robustness should allow for strategy adjustments as future developments occur that necessitated change in the robust strategy. In addition to the monitoring for any changes that could impact the strategy, there is a need to monitor for specific certain indicators that track specific strategic uncertainties, events, or developments that might impact the strategy. These indicators are called signposts and their critical values that once reached call for a change in strategy are called triggers or tipping points (Swanson et al., 2010).

Strategy adjustments: In the event the critical value of a signpost is reached, this will trigger a strategy adjustment. This will be accomplished through one of three ways. First, when the triggering condition and the strategy adjustments are clearly defined, fully automatic response can be activated. Second, when the triggering conditions are clearly defined but the strategy adjustments cannot be predesigned, a semi-automatic response is warranted. Third, when there is ambiguity about the triggering and the strategy adjustment, a manual response is needed (Swanson et al., 2010).

Continuous monitoring: Implementing robust monitoring systems to track changes and gather new information for informed decision-making is key to the dynamic robustness approach (Swanson et al., 2010).

5.4.4 Applications and Examples

Dynamic robustness strategies have been successfully applied in various domains. For instance, the Dutch Delta Programme utilizes adaptive delta management, combining long-term planning with flexible short-term measures to manage flood risks and sea-level rise. This approach involves continuous monitoring and predefined trigger points for policy adjustments (Bloemen et al., 2018).

5.4.5 Challenges and Limitations

While dynamic robustness strategies enhance adaptability under deep uncertainty, they present several challenges. Designing and maintaining monitoring systems capable of tracking multiple signposts and triggers is complex and resource-intensive, requiring significant investment in data collection, analytical capacity, and decision-support infrastructure (Kwakkel et al., 2010; Haasnoot et al., 2013). Defining triggers and thresholds also demands careful calibration: overly sensitive triggers can lead to frequent adjustments and organizational instability, whereas overly conservative ones may delay necessary responses and reduce effectiveness (Swanson et al., 2010).

Another limitation concerns path dependency and lock-in effects. Even with predefined adjustment mechanisms, organizations may become constrained by established pathways and fail to adapt when environmental shifts exceed anticipated bounds (Walker et al., 2013). Furthermore, the reliance on predetermined options can narrow managerial attention and reduce openness to novel or unconventional responses outside the designed pathways (Bloemen et al., 2018).

5.4.6 Strategy Methods

Several strategy methods utilize the logic of dynamic robustness. Dynamic Adaptive Planning (DAP) focuses on creating flexible plans that can be adjusted over time as new information becomes available (Walker et al., 2013). Dynamic Adaptive Policy Pathways (DAPP) combines adaptive planning with robust decision-making, allowing for multiple predefined pathways and adjustment points to handle uncertainty and change (Haasnoot et al., 2013).

5.4.6.1 *Dynamic Adaptive Planning*

DAP is a strategy method that focuses on creating robust plans with built-in mechanisms for monitoring, learning, and adjustment that can dynamically adjust based on new information and changing conditions (Walker et al., 2001).

One of the critical aspects of DAP is the use of signposts and triggers. Signposts are indicators that are monitored to determine when adjustment to the robust plan may be necessary, while triggers are specific thresholds that, when crossed, initiate adjustment actions (Kwakkel et al., 2010). This system transforms robust static plans to dynamic robust plans.

DAP was used in long term planning of the expansion of Amsterdam's Schiphol Airport where the planners needed to consider multiple uncertain factors, such as future demand for air travel, technological advancements, and environmental regulations, and develop a flexible strategy that could adapt to various scenarios (Kwakkel et al., 2010).

5.4.6.2 Dynamic Adaptive Policy Pathways

DAPP involves creating adaptive pathways that provide flexibility to adjust policies over time in response to new developments and changing conditions (Haasnoot et al., 2013). This approach recognizes the inherent uncertainty in future conditions and aims to build resilience by designing policies that can adapt to a wide range of possible futures.

At its core, DAPP combines two complementary approaches: adaptive policymaking and adaptation pathways (Haasnoot et al., 2013). This integration allows for the development of flexible strategies that can be adjusted over time as new information becomes available or as conditions change. The DAPP approach is particularly valuable in situations where long-term decisions need to be made in the face of deep uncertainty, such as climate change adaptation or infrastructure planning.

One of the critical aspects of DAPP is the concept of adaptation tipping points. These are points at which the current strategy will no longer be able to meet the specified objectives, necessitating a change in course (Kwadijk et al., 2010). By identifying these tipping points in advance, policymakers can prepare alternative strategies and define clear triggers for when to switch between pathways.

DAPP has been applied to the Dutch Delta Programme, which aims to protect the Netherlands from flooding and ensure freshwater supply in the face of climate change. DAPP allowed planners to develop flexible strategies that could adapt to various sea-level rise scenarios and changing socioeconomic conditions (Bloemen et al., 2018). Instead of committing to a single large-scale infrastructure project, the program identified a series of potential interventions that could be implemented sequentially as needed, based on observed changes in sea level and other relevant factors.

5.5 Strategic Flexibility Approach

5.5.1 Aim

The aim of the strategic flexibility approach is to equip organizations with the capability to adapt swiftly and effectively to both anticipated and unanticipated changes in their external and internal environments (Bahrami & Evans, 2005). It seeks to build the capacity enabling effective responses to unforeseen issues and dynamic contexts and hence promoting sustained success in unpredictable markets (Shimizu & Hitt, 2004).

5.5.2 Core Logic

Strategic flexibility is grounded in the recognition that the boundary between anticipated and unanticipated changes can shift rapidly (Evans, 1991). Unlike traditional robustness strategies, which prepare for foreseen conditions, strategic flexibility focuses on the capacity to adapt to unforeseen changes as well (Hitt et al., 1998). This approach emphasizes a holistic understanding of system complexity, performance, and dynamics, ensuring organizations can respond to unexpected challenges and opportunities (Bahrami & Evans, 2005; Shimizu & Hitt, 2004; Bahrami & Evans, 2005; Shimizu & Hitt, 2004).

5.5.3 Key Elements

Strategic adjustment: Strategic flexibility can be defined as a firm's ability to change its current strategies to avoid being stuck in obsolete strategies. It represents an organization's ability to align its strategies with the business environment. Strategic adjustment allows firms to change their business strategies in a timely manner to meet new business conditions.

Strategic options: Strategic flexibility can also be defined as a firm's ability to generate and keep options and alternatives, thus providing the firm with readily available options to react instantly by realigning and readjusting plans and strategies (Brozovic, 2018). Having a diverse portfolio of strategic options allows firms to leverage them to act, either proactively or reactively, to identified environmental opportunities and threats (Herhausen et al., 2021).

Dynamic capability: Strategic flexibility is considered a prominent dynamic capability that enables a firm to reconfigure resources and act quickly to changing competitive conditions, thus achieving competitive advantage. As a dynamic capability, strategic flexibility depends on both the inherent flexibilities of a firm's resources (resource flexibility) and the firm's ability to apply those resources to alternative courses of action (coordination flexibility).

Resource flexibility: Resource flexibility refers to the inherent flexibility of a firm's resources that enables the firm to make necessary internal changes in response to new external developments. It emphasizes the range of alternative uses of the firm's resources and the cost of switching from one resource to another. Resource flexibility allows firms to more efficiently and innovatively combine internal and external resources to pursue new opportunities.

5.5.4 Applications and Examples

One example of strategic flexibility is Genentech's Medical Unit, facing challenges from program terminations, developed a flexible business model by cross-training experts, strategically allocating resources based on a drug's phase and probability of success, and redefining roles throughout the development life cycle, resulting in a more agile and resilient team culture.

5.5.5 Challenges and Limitations

While strategic flexibility offers significant advantages, it also presents challenges. Developing and maintaining flexibility requires substantial investment in managerial capabilities and infrastructure. Organizations must balance the need for stability with the ability to adapt, which can sometimes lead to conflicting priorities. Crucially, excessive flexibility can result in a lack of strategic focus, potentially leading to inefficiencies and missed opportunities (Hitt et al., 1998; Sanchez, 1995).

5.5.6 Strategy Methods

One of the key strategy methods that utilizes the logic of strategic flexibility is the Portfolio of Initiatives (POI). By maintaining a diverse portfolio of strategic initiatives, organizations can spread risk and remain adaptable. This approach allows firms to pivot quickly in response to changing conditions, ensuring that they can capitalize on emerging opportunities while mitigating potential downsides (Luehrman, 1998; McGrath, 1997).

5.5.6.1 *Portfolio of Initiatives*

The POI method developed by McKinsey concentrates on managing a collection of diverse initiatives to navigate uncertainty and achieve long-term value creation (Bryan, 2002). POI involves actively searching for and nurturing a variety of opportunities that leverage a company's existing strengths while continuously exploring "no regrets" options, making staged investments, and adapting based on learnings. This approach emphasizes flexibility and adaptability, allowing organizations to shift resources and efforts toward initiatives with the highest potential for value creation as circumstances evolve (Bryan, 2002).

POI requires active management involvement, ensuring that initiatives are regularly assessed and adjusted based on real-time data and insights, fostering a culture of continuous learning and improvement. A notable example is Amazon's portfolio, which spans e-commerce, cloud computing, artificial intelligence, and media, allowing the company to adapt and thrive in a rapidly changing business environment.

By balancing short-term priorities with long-term strategic goals, the POI method helps companies create a sustainable competitive advantage, ensuring they are well-positioned to seize emerging opportunities and navigate future challenges effectively (Bryan, 2002).

References

Aaker, D. A., & Mascarenhas, B. (1984). The Need for Strategic Flexibility. *Journal of Business Strategy*, 5(2), 74–82.

Annarelli, A., & Nonino, F. (2016). Strategic and Operational Management of Organizational Resilience: Current State of Research and Future Directions. *Omega*, 62, 1–18.

Ansoff, H. I. (1965). *Corporate Strategy: an Analytic Approach to Business Policy for Growth and Expansion*. McGraw-Hill.

Bahrami, H. (1992). The Emerging Flexible Organization: Perspectives from Silicon Valley. *California Management Review*, 34(4), 33–52.

Bahrami, H., & Evans, S. (2005). *Super-Flexibility for Knowledge Enterprises: A Toolkit for Dynamic Adaptation* (1st ed.). Springer.

Barnard, C. I. (1938). *The Functions of the Executive*. Harvard University Press.

Barney, J. (1991). Firm Resources and Sustained Competitive Advantage. *Journal of Management*, 17(1), 99–120.

Beinhocker, E. D. (1997). Strategy at the Edge of Chaos. *McKinsey Quarterly*, (1), 24–39.

Beinhocker, E. D. (1999). Robust Adaptive Strategies. *MIT Sloan Management Review*, *40*(3), 95–106.

Bhamra, R., Dani, S., & Burnard, K. (2011). Resilience: The Concept, A Literature Review and Future Directions. *International Journal of Production Research*, *49*(18), 5375–5393.

Bloemen, P., Reeder, T., Zevenbergen, C., Rijke, J., & Kingsborough, A. (2018). Lessons Learned from Applying Adaptation Pathways in Flood Risk Management and Challenges for the Further Development of This Approach. *Mitigation and Adaptation Strategies for Global Change*, *23*(7), 1083–1108.

Boin, A., Comfort, L. K., & Demchak, C. C. (2010). The Rise of Resilience. In L. K. Comfort, A. Boin, & C. C. Demchak (Eds.), *Designing Resilience: Preparing for Extreme Events* (pp. 1–12). University of Pittsburgh Press.

Boin, A., & McConnell, A. (2007). Preparing for Critical Infrastructure Breakdowns: The Limits of Crisis Management and the Need for Resilience. *Journal of Contingencies and Crisis Management*, *15*(1), 50–59.

Boulton, J. G., Allen, P. M., & Bowman, C. (2015). *Embracing Complexity: Strategic Perspectives for an Age of Turbulence* (1st ed.). Oxford University Press.

Brozovic, D. (2018). Strategic Flexibility: A Review of the Literature. *International Journal of Management Reviews*, *20*(1), 3–31.

Bryan, L. L. (2002). Just-in-Time Strategy for a Turbulent World. *The McKinsey Quarterly*, 17–28.

Burnard, K., & Bhamra, R. (2011). Organisational Resilience: Development of a Conceptual Framework for Organisational Responses. *International Journal of Production Research*, *49*(18), 5581–5599.

Christensen, C. M., Raynor, M. E., & McDonald, R. (2015). What Is Disruptive Innovation? *Harvard Business Review*.

Courtney, H. (2001). *20/20 Foresight: Crafting Strategy in an Uncertain World*. Harvard Business School Press.

Courtney, H., Kirkland, J., & Viguerie, P. (1997). Strategy Under Uncertainty. *Harvard Business Review*, *75*(6), 67–79.

Cyert, R. M., & March, J. G. (1963). *A Behavioral Theory of the Firm*. Prentice Hall.

De Ruijter, P. (2014). *Scenario Based Strategy: Navigate the Future*. Gower.

Duchek, S. (2020). Organizational Resilience: A Capability-Based Conceptualization. *Business Research*, *13*(1), 215–246.

Evans, J. S. (1991). Strategic Flexibility for High Technology Manoeuvres: A Conceptual Framework. *Journal of Management Studies*, *28*(1), 69–89.

Haasnoot, M., Kwakkel, J. H., Walker, W. E., & Ter Maat, J. (2013). Dynamic Adaptive Policy Pathways: A Method for Crafting Robust Decisions for a Deeply Uncertain World. *Global Environmental Change*, *23*(2), 485–498.

Hamel, G., & Välikangas, L. (2003). The Quest for Resilience. *Harvard Business Review, 81*(9), 52–63.

Hartmann, M., & Hassan, A. (2006). Application of Real Options Analysis for Pharmaceutical R&D Project Valuation—Empirical Results from a Survey. *Research Policy, 35*(3), 343–354.

Herhausen, D., Morgan, R. E., Brozović, D., & Volberda, H. W. (2021). Re-Examining Strategic Flexibility: A Meta-Analysis of its Antecedents, Consequences and Contingencies. *British Journal of Management, 32*(2), 435–455.

Hitt, M. A., Keats, B. W., & DeMarie, S. M. (1998). Navigating in the New Competitive Landscape: Building Strategic Flexibility and Competitive Advantage in the 21st Century. *Academy of Management Perspectives, 12*(4), 22–42.

Kwadijk, J. C. J., Haasnoot, M., Mulder, J. P. M., Hoogvliet, M. M. C., Jeuken, A. B. M., van der Krogt, R. A. A., van Oostrom, N. G. C., Schelfhout, H. A., van Velzen, E. H., van Waveren, H., & de Wit, M. J. M. (2010). Using Adaptation Tipping Points to Prepare for Climate Change and Sea Level Rise: A Case Study in the Netherlands. *WIREs Climate Change, 1*(5), 729–740.

Kwakkel, J. H., Walker, W. E., & Marchau, V. A. W. J. (2010). Adaptive Airport Strategic Planning. *European Journal of Transport and Infrastructure Research, 10*(3).

Lalani, H. S., Nagar, S., Sarpatwari, A., Barenie, R. E., Avorn, J., Rome, B. N., & Kesselheim, A. S. (2023). US Public Investment in Development of mRNA Covid-19 Vaccines: Retrospective Cohort Study. *BMJ, 380*, e073747.

Lempert, R. J., Popper, S. W., & Bankes, S. C. (2003). *Shaping the Next One Hundred Years: New Methods for Quantitative, Long-Term Policy Analysis*. RAND Corporation.

Linnenluecke, M. K. (2017). Resilience in Business and Management Research: A Review of Influential Publications and a Research Agenda. *International Journal of Management Reviews, 19*(1), 4–30.

Luehrman, T. A. (1998). Strategy as a Portfolio of Real Options. *Harvard Business Review, 76*(5), 89–99.

Markides, C., & Charitou, C. D. (2004). Competing with Dual Business Models: A Contingency Approach. *Academy of Management Perspectives, 18*(3), 22–36.

Mason, D. H. (1994). Scenario-Based Planning: Decision Model for the Learning Organization. *Planning Review, 22*(2), 6–11.

Matsuo, H. (2015). Implications of the Tohoku Earthquake for Toyota's Coordination Mechanism: Supply Chain Disruption of Automotive Semiconductors. *International Journal of Production Economics, 161*, 217–227.

McCray, L. E., Oye, K. A., & Petersen, A. C. (2010). Planned Adaptation in Risk Regulation: An Initial Survey of US Environmental, Health, and Safety Regulation. *Technological Forecasting and Social Change, 77*(6), 951–959.

McGrath, R. (2013). *The End of Competitive Advantage: How to Keep Your Strategy Moving as Fast as Your Business*. Harvard Business Review Press.

McGrath, R. G. (1997). A Real Options Logic for Initiating Technology Positioning Investments. *The Academy of Management Review*, *22*(4), 974–996.

Mintzberg, H., & Waters, J. A. (1985). Of Strategies, Deliberate and Emergent. *Strategic Management Journal*, 6(3), 257–272.

Nelson, R. R., & Winter, S. G. (1982). The Schumpeterian Tradeoff Revisited. *The American Economic Review*, *72*(1), 114–132.

Penrose, E. T. (1959). *The Theory of the Growth of the Firm*. Basil Blackwell.

Pfeffer, J., & Salancik, G. R. (1978). *The External Control of Organizations: A Resource Dependence Perspective*. Harper & Row.

Rapaccini, M., Saccani, N., Kowalkowski, C., Paiola, M., & Adrodegari, F. (2020). Navigating Disruptive Crises Through Service-Led Growth: The Impact of COVID-19 on Italian Manufacturing Firms. *Industrial Marketing Management*, 88, 225–237.

Raynor, M. E. (2007). *The Strategy Paradox: Why Committing to Success Leads to Failure and What to Do About It*. Crown Business.

Reeves, M., & Deimler, M. (2011). Adaptability: The New Competitive Advantage. *Harvard Business Review*, *89*(7-8), 134–141.

Rosenhead, J., Elton, M., & Gupta, S. K. (1972). Robustness and Optimality as Criteria for Strategic Decisions. *Journal of the Operational Research Society*, *23*(4), 413–431.

Sanchez, R. (1995). Strategic Flexibility in Product Competition. *Strategic Management Journal*, *16*(S1), 135–159.

Schoemaker, P. J. H. (2022). *Advanced Introduction to Scenario Planning*. Edward Elgar Publishing.

Schwartz, P. (1996). *The Art of the Long View: Paths to Strategic Insight for Yourself and Your Company* (1st ed.). Crown Business.

Sheffi, Y. (2005). *The Resilient Enterprise: Overcoming Vulnerability for Competitive Advantage*. MIT Press.

Shimizu, K., & Hitt, M. A. (2004). Strategic Flexibility: Organizational Preparedness to Reverse Ineffective Strategic Decisions. *Academy of Management Perspectives*, *18*(4), 44–59.

Snape, I., & Weeks, M. (2022). *Resilience by Design: How to Survive and Thrive in a Complex and Turbulent World*. John Wiley & Sons.

Sutcliffe, K. M., & Vogus, T. J. (2003). Organizing for Resilience. In K. S. Cameron, J. E. Dutton, & R. E. Quinn (Eds.), *Positive Organizational Scholarship: Foundations of a New Discipline* (pp. 94–110). Berrett-Koehler.

Swanson, D., Barg, S., Tyler, S., Venema, H., Tomar, S., Bhadwal, S., Nair, S., Roy, D., & Drexhage, J. (2010). Seven Tools for Creating Adaptive Policies. *Technological Forecasting and Social Change*, *77*(6), 924–939.

Taleb, N. N. (2007). *The Black Swan: The Impact of the Highly Improbable* (2nd ed.). Random House.

Taleb, N. N. (2012). *Antifragile: How to Live in a World We Don't Understand*. Allen Lane.

Teece, D., Peteraf, M., & Leih, S. (2016). Dynamic Capabilities and Organizational Agility: Risk, Uncertainty, and Strategy in the Innovation Economy. *California Management Review*, *58*(4), 13–35.

Teece, D. J., Pisano, G., & Shuen, A. (1997). Dynamic Capabilities and Strategic Management. *Strategic Management Journal*, *18*(7), 509–533.

Van der Heijden, K. (2005). *Scenarios: The Art of Strategic Conversation* (2nd ed.). John Wiley & Sons.

van der Vegt, G. S., Essens, P., Wahlström, M., & George, G. (2015). From the Editors: Managing Risk and Resilience. *The Academy of Management Journal*, *58*(4), 971–980.

Volberda, H. W. (1996). Toward the Flexible Form: How to Remain Vital in Hypercompetitive Environments. *Organization Science*, *7*(4), 359–374.

Wack, P. (1985). Scenarios: Shooting the Rapids. *Harvard Business Review*, *63*(6), 139–150.

Walker, W. E., Haasnoot, M., & Kwakkel, J. H. (2013). Adapt or Perish: A Review of Planning Approaches for Adaptation Under Deep Uncertainty. *Sustainability*, *5*(3), 955–979.

Walker, W. E., Rahman, S. A., & Cave, J. (2001). Adaptive Policies, Policy analysis, and Policy-Making. *European Journal of Operational Research*, *128*(2), 282–289.

Walton, S., O'Kane, P., & Ruwhiu, D. (2019). Developing a Theory of Plausibility in Scenario Building: Designing Plausible Scenarios. *Futures*, *111*, 42–56.

Weick, K. E., & Sutcliffe, K. M. (2015). *Managing the Unexpected: Sustained Performance in a Complex World* (3rd ed.). John Wiley & Sons.

Wilson, I. (2000). From Scenario Thinking to Strategic Action. *Technological Forecasting and Social Change*, *65*(1), 23–29.

Wilson, I., & Ralston, W. (2006). *Scenario Planning Handbook: Developing Strategies in Uncertain Times*. Thomson South-Western.

Wulf, T., Meissner, P., Brands, C., & Stubner, S. (2013). Scenario-Based Strategic Planning: A New Approach to Coping with Uncertainty. In B. Schwenker & T. Wulf (Eds.), *Scenario-based Strategic Planning: Developing Strategies in an Uncertain World* (pp. 43–66). Springer Fachmedien Wiesbaden.

6 Crafting Strategic Posture

6.1 Overview

6.1.1 Introduction

The aim of posture is to move beyond coping and adapting to rapidly changing and highly competitive business environments to actively seeking to shape their environments (Rindova & Courtney, 2020). The crafting strategic posture encompasses proactive approach, emphasizing innovation, entrepreneurship, and experimentation as key drivers of growth and competitive differentiation (Hitt et al., 2001). This chapter explores the key characteristics of the crafting posture and its four main strategy approaches: strategic innovation, strategic entrepreneurship, strategic experimentation, and strategic agility.

6.1.2 Key Characteristics

The forward thinking, innovative, and entrepreneurial approach to strategy that characterizes the crafting strategic posture aims to actively change and lead the market through creative destruction and innovation, rather than merely surviving (Ireland & Hitt, 1999).

This posture requires organizations to be agile, entrepreneurial, and continuously engaged in experimentation and learning. By fostering a culture that embraces change, encourages risk-taking, and values innovation, organizations can navigate the complexities of modern markets, creating new opportunities and achieving a series of transient advantages in an ever-evolving competitive landscape (McGrath, 2013a).

The core logic is that sustainable success in today's fast-paced markets requires more than adaptation; it necessitates active engagement with and creation of the future. It avoids the Red Queen effect (RQE), where continuous

DOI: 10.4324/9781003684060-6

improvement and incremental innovation are necessary just to maintain competitive parity but not to advance (Barnett & Hansen, 1996). This posture goes beyond adaptation and exploitation and seeks to redefine the playing field, leveraging novelty and exploration to drive growth and competitive differentiation (March, 1991). This posture thrives on the principles of Schumpeterian creative destruction and the pursuit of transient advantages, promoting the evolution of businesses through disruption existing markets and the creation of new ones (Schumpeter, 1934).

This can be compared to piloting an experimental vehicle, where innovation and creativity lead the way to explore new horizons and possibilities beyond the conventional paths.

Key actors include innovators and entrepreneurs who are comfortable with uncertainty and adept at navigating and shaping the future marketplace.

6.1.3 Key Theoretical Perspectives

The crafting of a strategic posture leverages several key theoretical perspectives to shape complex and dynamic environments. Central to this approach is **Schumpeterian creative destruction** that posits that economic prosperity is driven by the continuous process of innovation, where new products and processes replace outdated ones, thereby disrupting market structures and creating new opportunities (Schumpeter, 1934). In rapidly changing environments, the concept of **transient advantage** becomes crucial, where the sources of competitive advantage are no longer sustainable over long periods (McGrath, 2013b). Instead, organizations must constantly innovate and adapt to maintain their competitive edge. Another perspective is the **RQE**, which highlights that organizations must constantly adapt and evolve not just for incremental gains but to maintain their current position relative to competitors (Voelpel et al., 2004). The crafting posture also integrates **evolutionary and ecological theories** to explain dynamic competitive interactions and coevolution among firms. Firms operate within ecosystems where they coevolve with other entities, influencing and being influenced by their competitive and cooperative interactions (Barnett & Hansen, 1996; Derfus et al., 2008). **Organizational ambidexterity** is another critical perspective in this posture, which highlights the need for organizations to pursue both exploitation and exploration simultaneously (March, 1991; Raisch et al., 2009).

6.1.4 Limitations

While the crafting of a strategic posture offers numerous advantages, such as fostering innovation, creativity, and competitive advantage, it also has its limitations. One significant challenge is the inherent risk and uncertainty associated with continuous experimentation and disruptive innovation (Christensen, 1997). Without having innovation processes and systems that ensure a steady pipeline of innovations, many firms risk falling into the sporadic innovation trap where innovation is sporadic (McGrath, 2013b). In addition to the systems, you need to have the right managerial skills of sensing, seizing, and reconfiguring to pursue this strategic posture that may not be always available in firms and need to be developed (Teece, 2007). Furthermore, having the right processes, systems, and managerial skills can be costly and time-consuming to develop and maintain (Teece, 2007). Finally, the effectiveness of this posture may be limited in stable or slow-moving industries, where the benefits of continuous innovation and adaptation may not outweigh the costs (Birkinshaw et al., 2016).

6.1.5 Crafting Strategy Approaches

As illustrated in Figure 6.1, the crafting strategy approaches can be arranged in a matrix consisting of two dimensions: responsiveness and level of control. The vertical level of the control dimension has two categories: high and low. High is reserved for strategy approaches that involve a higher degree of control over strategic changes. These approaches are more structured and planned, providing greater predictability in their implementation. Low is reserved for strategy approaches that involve a lower degree of control over strategic

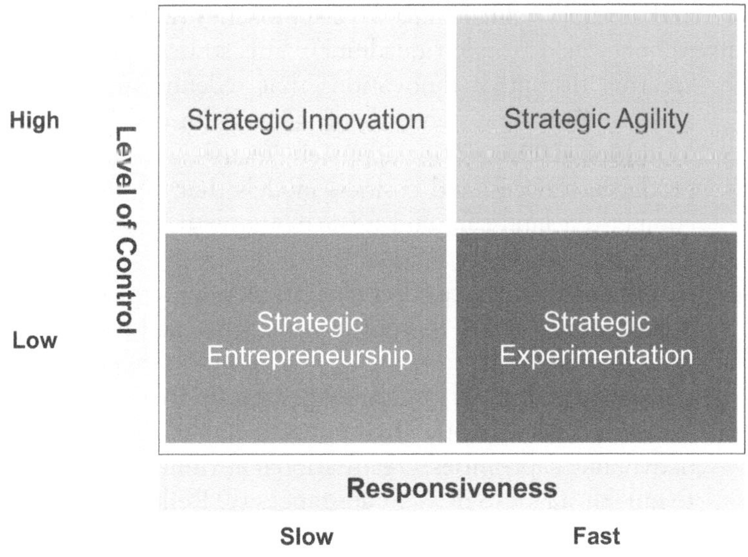

Figure 6.1 The Crafting Strategic Posture Matrix.

changes. These approaches often rely on external factors and less predictable outcomes.

The horizontal responsiveness dimension has two categories: slow and fast. The slow category refers to the strategy approaches that produce strategies that take time to develop and implement. The fast category refers to the strategy approaches that produce strategies that require quick responses to changes in the environment. These approaches emphasize agility and the ability to adapt rapidly.

As shown in the matrix, there are four key strategy approaches that can be used to achieve the crafting posture:

Strategic entrepreneurship (bottom-left quadrant): This approach aims to create and sustain competitive advantage by integrating entrepreneurial opportunity-seeking with strategic advantage-seeking behaviors (Hitt et al., 2001; Ireland et al., 2003). It balances innovation and strategic alignment, seeking to identify and exploit new opportunities while ensuring long-term success through effective resource management (Covin & Miles, 1999; Sarasvathy, 2001).

Strategic experimentation (bottom-right quadrant): This strategy approach involves systematically testing various strategic approaches through trial and error to identify the most effective ways to compete in the market (Andries et al., 2013; Nicholls-Nixon et al., 2000). It relies on experiential and vicarious learning to iteratively refine strategies and develop viable competitive approaches (Levinthal, 1997).

Strategic innovation (top-left quadrant): This strategy approach involves creating disruptive innovations that redefine market boundaries and establish new standards of value (Kim & Mauborgne, 1997; Markides, 1997). This approach focuses on generating novel products, services, and business models that significantly alter the competitive landscape and create new growth opportunities (Hamel, 1998; Johnson et al., 2008).

Strategic agility (top-right quadrant): This strategy approach refers to an organization's ability to continuously sense and respond rapidly to changing environments, thereby sustaining competitive advantage through constant adaptation and renewal (Doz & Kosonen, 2010; Weber & Tarba, 2014). This approach emphasizes the development of dynamic capabilities, organizational flexibility, and ambidexterity to quickly adapt to new circumstances (O'Reilly & Tushman, 2013; Teece et al., 2016).

Table 6.1 Comparing the Creating Strategies

Dimension	Strategic Innovation	Strategic Entrepreneurship	Strategic Experimentation	Strategic Agility
Aim	Create disruptive innovations that redefine market boundaries and establish new standards of value	Integrate entrepreneurial activities with strategic objectives	Discover and validate effective strategic options through systematic trial and error	Enable continuous sensing and rapid response to changing environments
Core Logic	Continuous innovation is necessary to remain competitive	Strategic entrepreneurship aligns innovation with long-term goals	Strategic experimentation focuses on adaptive learning and risk management	Strategic agility balances responsiveness with strategic coherence
Assumptions	Innovation can create new value and market spaces	Innovation and strategic goals can be integrated	Systematic experimentation will identify the most effective strategies	Continuous sensing and responding to changes are crucial for success
Nature	Radical and disruptive	Opportunity-focused and venturesome	Adaptive and iterative	Responsive and nimble
Time Horizon	Short to medium term	Long-term with short-term milestones	Short to medium term	Balances both short-term responsiveness and long-term adaptability

(*Continued*)

Table 6.1 (Continued)

Dimension	Strategic Innovation	Strategic Entrepreneurship	Strategic Experimentation	Strategic Agility
Strengths	Redefines market boundaries, creates high growth opportunities	Balances innovation with strategic alignment	Generates new insights, validates strategic options, ensures rapid iteration and refinement	Ensures constant adaptation and renewal, maintains competitive advantage
Limitations	Requires significant investment and risk-taking	Current business may suffer if entrepreneurial activities are not balanced	Outcomes can be uncertain and vary widely	May lead to overemphasis on exploration over exploitation
Methods	• Disruptive Innovation • Blue Ocean Strategy • Business Model Innovation	• Corporate Intrapreneurship • Corporate Venturing	• Wargaming (Policy Gaming) • Lean Startup Methodology • Discovery-Driven Planning	• Fast Method • Dynamic Capabilities • Organizational Ambidexterity

Furthermore, their key characteristics are contrasted in Table 6.1.

6.2 Strategic Innovation Approach

6.2.1 Aim

The strategic innovation approach aims to fundamentally change business models and competitive landscapes by creating disruptive innovations that redefine market boundaries and establish new standards of value (Christensen, 1997; Kim & Mauborgne, 1997; Markides, 1997).

6.2.2 Core Logic

One of the underlying ideas of this strategy approach is to rethink current industry structures to create new value for customers, outmaneuver competitors, and generate wealth for all stakeholders (Hamel, 1998). Another idea focuses on making competition irrelevant by offering superior buyer value in existing markets and creating new markets through quantum leaps in value proposition (Kim & Mauborgne, 1997). Another idea revolves around thinking in terms of arenas and not industries where arenas are defined as the combination of customer segments and product offering and place (McGrath, 2013b).

6.2.3 Key Elements

- *Disruptive innovation:* Introducing novel products, services, or business models that significantly alter existing market dynamics and create new market spaces (Christensen, 1997).
- *Value innovation:* Creating new value for customers by enhancing product or service offerings in ways that differentiate from competitors (Kim & Mauborgne, 1997).
- *Dynamic capabilities:* Developing the ability to sense, seize, and transform opportunities and threats in the market, requiring organizational flexibility and agility (Teece, 2007).
- *Short- and long-term focus:* Balancing rapid prototyping and iterative testing of new ideas in the short term with the aim of establishing sustainable competitive advantages through continuous innovation and strategic foresight in the long term (Afuah, 2009).

6.2.4 Applications and Examples

Strategic innovation has been observed in many successful firms. Apple, for example, has consistently reformulated market limits with devices such as the iPhone and iPad, establishing totally new product categories and industry standards (Yoffie & Rossano, 2012). Furthermore, Tesla's approach to electric automobiles and renewable energy solutions illustrates strategic innovation by disrupting established automotive and energy industries while setting new standards for sustainable technology (Valentin, 2019).

6.2.5 Challenges and Limitations

While strategic innovation offers significant growth opportunities, it also presents several challenges. Implementing disruptive innovations often involves high levels of risk and uncertainty, requiring substantial investment and commitment. Organizations must balance the need for stability with the pursuit of radical change, which can strain resources and management focus. Additionally, fostering an innovative culture requires overcoming resistance to change and ensuring that all levels of the organization are aligned with the innovation strategy (Tushman & O'Reilly, 2002).

6.2.6 Strategy Methods

Several strategy methods utilize the logic of strategic innovation. Disruptive innovation focuses on creating products or services that disrupt existing markets and establish new ones, often by targeting underserved segments or offering more accessible solutions (Christensen, 1997). Another method is Blue Ocean Strategy, which emphasizes creating uncontested market spaces and making the competition irrelevant by offering unique value propositions (Kim & Mauborgne, 2005). Lastly, business model innovation (BMI) rethinks and redesigns how a company creates, delivers, and captures value (Teece, 2010).

6.2.6.1 Disruptive Innovation

Disruptive innovation is a strategy method that describes how new entrants can enter a market by initially targeting underserved or nonconsumer segments with simpler, more affordable, or more convenient solutions compared to established offerings. These solutions are usually seen as inferior to current offerings and do not appeal to mainstream customers (Christensen & Raynor,

2003; Christensen, 1997). Over time, as the disruptive innovation evolves and improves, it moves upmarket, attracting mainstream customers and eventually challenging the dominant players in the industry (Christensen et al., 2018). For example, in the case of higher education, online courses began as an accessible and affordable solution to underserved or nonconsumer segments of society, although less comprehensive than attending in-person courses at a university. They then increasingly evolved and improved into more comprehensive online-only universities that competed with established incumbents (Christensen & Eyring, 2011). The COVID-19 pandemic has only accelerated the trend towards online higher education, with revenue from university online education estimated to show an annual growth rate of 10.06% from 2024 to 2029 (Statista, 2024). This pattern can also be observed in the personal computer industry, where affordable, user-friendly Personal Computers (PCs) disrupted the market for mainframe computers and minicomputers (Christensen, 1997). Established firms often struggle to respond effectively to disruptive innovations because they focus on serving their existing customer base and are constrained by their current business models and organizational structures. Kodak, for example, was slow to embrace digital photography due to its focus on the profitable film business, ultimately leading to its decline as digital cameras disrupted the market (Lucas & Goh, 2009).

6.2.6.2 *Blue Ocean Strategy*

Blue Ocean Strategy offers a systematic method to creating new, uncontested market spaces (blue oceans) rather than competing in existing, crowded markets (red oceans) (Kim & Mauborgne, 2005). The goal is to pursue value innovation (Kim & Mauborgne, 1997) – differentiation and low cost simultaneously by identifying and exploiting untapped market opportunities and creating unique value propositions that align with customers' needs and preferences (Kim & Mauborgne, 2015). A well-cited example of a Blue Ocean Strategy is Cirque du Soleil, which reinvented the circus industry by eliminating animal acts and focusing on artistic performance, thereby creating a new market space that appealed to a different audience (Kim & Mauborgne, 2005). The Blue Ocean Strategy framework consists of several analytical tools, such as the Strategy Canvas, Four Actions Framework, and Six Paths Framework, which help organizations systematically explore and create new market spaces (Kim & Mauborgne, 2002, 2015). By focusing on value innovation, organizations can break the value-cost trade-off and create a leap in value for both buyers and the company (Kim & Mauborgne, 2017). This is demonstrated by the case of Nintendo's Wii console, which targeted nontraditional gamers by introducing motion-controlled gaming, thus creating a new market space in the video game industry (Kim & Mauborgne, 2015). Overall, successful implementation of the Blue Ocean Strategy requires a shift in strategic thinking, a willingness to challenge industry boundaries, and the ability to align the organization's value, profit, and people propositions (Kim & Mauborgne, 2015).

6.2.6.3 Business Model Innovation

BMI is a strategic approach that involves fundamentally redesigning the way a company creates, delivers, and captures value (Zott & Amit, 2010). This method enables firms to differentiate themselves and gain a competitive advantage in their industries by developing novel business models that better meet customer needs and capitalize on untapped market opportunities (Chesbrough, 2010). BMI goes beyond product or process innovation, focusing instead on the holistic reconfiguration of a company's value proposition, target customer segments, revenue streams, and cost structure (Johnson et al., 2008). An example of BMI is Netflix, which disrupted the traditional video rental industry by transitioning from a DVD-by-mail service to a subscription-based streaming platform, fundamentally altering how consumers access and enjoy media content (Johnson et al., 2008). Other examples include Airbnb, which revolutionized the hospitality industry by connecting travellers with local hosts, and Uber, which transformed the transportation sector by leveraging mobile technology and a sharing economy model (Gassmann et al., 2014).

6.3 Strategic Entrepreneurship Approach

6.3.1 Aim

The strategic entrepreneurship approach seeks to create and sustain competitive advantage by merging entrepreneurial opportunity-seeking behaviors with strategic advantage-seeking perspectives, focusing on wealth creation through innovation and strategic alignment (Hitt et al., 2001; Ireland et al., 2003). This approach aims to achieve an optimal balance between entrepreneurial initiatives and strategic objectives to ensure long-term success and market leadership.

6.3.2 Core Logic

Strategic entrepreneurship combines the explorative nature of entrepreneurship that entails the pursuit of new business opportunities with the exploitative focus of strategic management on achieving strategic objectives (Hitt et al., 2001). This dual focus emphasizes a balanced approach to opportunity-seeking and advantage-seeking behaviors, allowing organizations to innovate and create value while maintaining a strategic framework that supports sustainable growth (Kuratko & Audretsch, 2009). The approach is designed to anticipate future trends and market shifts, enabling organizations to stay ahead of the competition while adapting quickly to emerging opportunities and challenges (Ketchen Jr. et al., 2007).

6.3.3 Key Elements

Opportunity-seeking: Identifying and pursuing new business ventures, markets, or products that can drive growth and create value (Hitt et al., 2001).

Advantage-seeking: Ensuring that entrepreneurial activities are strategically aligned with the organization's goals to build and sustain competitive advantage (Ireland & Webb, 2007).

Long-term vision: Maintaining a forward-looking perspective to anticipate and respond to future market trends and shifts (Ketchen Jr. et al., 2007).

Iterative learning: Emphasizing quick adaptation and learning to respond to immediate opportunities and challenges effectively (Eisenhardt & Brown, 1998).

Balanced risk-taking: Encouraging experimentation and innovation while maintaining control over outputs through strategic intent and resource management (Covin & Miles, 1999; Sarasvathy, 2001).

6.3.4 Applications and Examples

Strategic entrepreneurship can be observed in companies such as IBM, Google, and 3M. To illustrate, Google's "20% time" policy allows employees to spend 20% of their work time on self-directed projects, fostering innovation and entrepreneurial culture (Steiber & Alänge, 2013). Similarly, 3M's innovation program, which permits employees to devote 15% of their time to personal projects, encourages intrapreneurship and new product development (Garud et al., 2011).

6.3.5 Challenges and Limitations

While strategic entrepreneurship offers significant growth opportunities, it also presents challenges. By allowing employees to pursue their own projects, they may be distracted them from carrying their regular work. Moreover, managing entrepreneurial activities and ongoing business activities may distract managers from carrying out their responsibilities. Additionally, fostering an entrepreneurial culture requires alignment with other organizational systems including the performance management and reward systems (Ketchen Jr. et al., 2007).

6.3.6 Strategy Methods

Numerous methods can be employed to formulate strategies using the strategic entrepreneurship approach, including corporate intrapreneurship and corporate venturing. Corporate intrapreneurship entails encouraging employees to act like entrepreneurs within the organization, fostering innovation and new business ventures (Antoncic & Hisrich, 2001). On the other hand, corporate venturing involves investing in new business ventures or startups, either internally or through partnerships, to explore new markets and technologies (Covin & Miles, 2007; Narayanan et al., 2009).

6.3.6.1 Corporate Intrapreneurship

Corporate intrapreneurship empowers employees to innovate and develop new products, services, or processes within the company. It involves promoting a culture that values risk-taking, experimentation, and creative problem-solving (Antoncic & Hisrich, 2003). Providing resources such as funding, time, and access to knowledge enables companies to tap into their workforce's creative potential, driving growth, generating new revenue streams, and sustaining competitive advantage (Kuratko et al., 1990).

Management support is important to facilitate the entrepreneurial efforts (Hornsby et al., 1993). Furthermore, corporate intrapreneurship hinges on recognizing and rewarding successful intrapreneurial efforts, which motivates employees to adopt an entrepreneurial mindset and aligns their creativity with the organization's strategic goals (Hornsby et al., 1993). For example, 3M's policy of allowing employees to spend 15% of their time on self-chosen projects has led to innovations such as Post-it Notes, highlighting the benefits of an intrapreneurial culture (Fry, 1987). Establishing cross-functional teams to facilitate this enhances idea generation and implementation by combining diverse skills and perspectives, fostering rapid prototyping and adaptation to market feedback and technological advancements (Covin & Miles, 1999).

6.3.6.2 *Corporate Venturing*

Corporate venturing involves established firms investing in or creating new ventures, often in the form of startups, to explore emerging opportunities, drive innovation, and capture value outside their core operations (Narayanan et al., 2009). Through various mechanisms such as corporate venture capital, incubators, or accelerators, organizations can support high-potential startups by providing financial resources, strategic guidance, and access to networks and markets (Dushnitsky & Lenox, 2005). Corporate venturing allows firms to diversify their portfolio, gain exposure to disruptive technologies, and enter new markets by leveraging the agility and innovative capacity of entrepreneurial ventures while mitigating the risks associated with internal development (Chesbrough, 2002). Successful corporate venturing requires a delicate balance between providing sufficient autonomy to the ventures to foster entrepreneurial spirit and ensuring strategic alignment with the parent firm's objectives (Kuratko et al., 2009). One way to achieve this balance is through structural ambidexterity where the new venture is structurally separated from the established business and ensures alignment through top management team (O'Reilly & Tushman, 2004). An example of corporate venturing is Intel Capital, the venture capital arm of Intel Corporation, which has invested in numerous successful startups across various sectors, enabling Intel to stay at the forefront of technological innovation and tap into new growth opportunities (Dushnitsky & Lenox, 2005). This is also exemplified by Google Ventures (now GV), which has invested in and supported a wide range of startups such as Uber and Nest, helping Google to diversify its portfolio and stay ahead of emerging trends (Sahaym et al., 2016).

6.4 Strategic Experimentation Approach

6.4.1 Aim

The strategic experimentation approach aims mainly to systematically test and validate various strategic options usually through controlled trial-and-error processes, seeking to discover effective competitive strategies that align with organizational goals (Nicholls-Nixon et al., 2000). But it can also be used to develop solutions through iterative experimentation (Ansell & Bartenberger, 2016).

6.4.2 Core Logic

Experimental perspective stems from the view that strategies and policies are set of hypotheses. In the realm of policies, the American philosopher, Jon Dewey, called for

> policies and proposals for social action be treated as working hypotheses, not as programs to be rigidly adhered to and executed. They will be experimental in the sense that they will be entertained subject to constant and well-equipped observation of the consequences they entail when acted upon, and subject to ready and flexible revision in the light of observed consequences.
>
> (Dewey, 1927, p. 202)

In the field of strategy, Kaplan and Norton state that "[a] strategy is a set of hypotheses about cause and effect" (Kaplan & Norton, 1996, p. 65). Instead of conceptualizing strategies as stable plans, they should be thought of as dynamic consisting of hypotheses to be tested and modified through experiments (Edmondson & Verdin, 2017). Strategic experimentation relies heavily on experiential learning, where organizations learn from direct experience through systematic and purposeful actions (Huber, 1991). There are three logics for experimentation based on their purposes: controlled experimentation isolates causal relationships through rigorous testing of hypotheses; Darwinian experimentation generates variety through multiple trials to select successful outcomes; and generative experimentation involves iterative refinement of solutions based on continuous feedback (Ansell & Bartenberger, 2016). Experimentation may serve one or more of these logics (Ansell & Bartenberger, 2016). Another way to evaluate the logic of experimentation is by understanding how it is carried out. There are generally two approaches that can be pursued depending on the strategic context: local or distant search (Levinthal, 1997). Local search is conducted through small-scale experiments by making incremental changes to strategic choices and observing the outcomes while distant search involves making significant changes to multiple components simultaneously to explore entirely new strategic configurations (Levinthal, 1997). A related but different concept is improvisation. Experimentation involves a planned, systematic approach to testing hypotheses and learning through controlled environments over time, while improvisation is a spontaneous, flexible response to immediate, unforeseen circumstances in real time (Miner et al., 2001).

6.4.3 Key Elements

Controlled experimentation: Controlled experimentation aims to isolate causal relationships through carefully designed interventions.

It typically involves randomized controlled trials or laboratory experiments with tightly managed conditions to minimize confounding factors. But it can also use natural or quasi-experiments that do not deliberately use control group (Cook & Campbell, 1979). This approach is deductive, focusing on testing specific hypotheses and establishing clear cause-effect relationships. It emphasizes internal validity and replicability but may sacrifice external validity. Controlled experimentation is particularly useful for testing precise hypotheses and evaluating specific interventions (Ansell & Bartenberger, 2016).

Darwinian experimentation: Darwinian experimentation focuses on generating variety through multiple parallel or sequential trials. This approach embraces the power of large numbers to increase the likelihood of discovering successful innovations. It is inductive, allowing for the selection of successful variants through a process akin to natural selection. Darwinian experimentation is particularly useful for exploring a wide range of possibilities and identifying best practices in complex or uncertain environments (Ansell & Bartenberger, 2016).

Generative experimentation: Generative experimentation involves the iterative refinement of a solution concept based on continuous feedback, often in real-world contexts. This approach is abductive, focusing on developing and improving responses to specific problems through learning and adaptation. It emphasizes the creation of novel solutions and is particularly useful for addressing complex, context-specific challenges. Generative experimentation often involves stakeholders in the process and allows for flexible adaptation to emerging insights (Ansell & Bartenberger, 2016).

Local (incremental, neighborhood, refinement, exploitative) search: Local search involves making small, incremental changes to an organization's current position or strategy. It focuses on refining and improving existing competencies, technologies, and paradigms. This type of search is characterized by experimenting with stepwise changes, often altering only one component at a time. It leads to more reliable performance and immediate returns but can result in organizations becoming trapped in suboptimal positions. Local search is associated with exploitation, efficiency, and incremental innovation (Levinthal, 1997; March, 1991).

Distant (innovative, explorative, long jump) search: Distant search involves making significant changes to multiple components of an organization's strategy or structure simultaneously. It focuses on exploring new possibilities, experimenting with novel alternatives, and seeking radical innovations. This type of search is characterized by "long jumps" in the fitness landscape, potentially leading to the discovery of superior positions. While riskier and less predictable than local search, distant search is crucial for maintaining adaptability in changing environments and avoiding competency traps (Levinthal, 1997; March, 1991).

6.4.4 Applications and Examples

Strategic experimentation can be seen in various industries where rapid adaptation and learning are critical. For instance, companies in the technology sector often engage in strategic experimentation to stay ahead of market trends. Google, for example, uses A/B testing extensively to experiment with new features and optimize user experiences (Ghosh et al., 2020). Another example is Amazon, which employs strategic experimentation in its product development and logistics processes to enhance efficiency and customer satisfaction (Andries et al., 2013).

6.4.5 Challenges and Limitations

While strategic experimentation provides significant insights and flexibility, it also presents challenges. One major limitation is the potential for incremental improvements that may not lead to breakthrough innovations unless combined with broader explorative search processes (March, 1991). Additionally, the outcomes of experiments are often uncertain and can vary widely, making it difficult to predict success (Miner et al., 2001).

6.4.6 Strategy Methods

Several methods can be employed to formulate strategies using the strategic experimentation approach. Wargaming involves simulating competitive scenarios to test strategic responses and improve decision-making under uncertainty (Schwarz, 2011). Furthermore, the Lean Startup methodology involves implementing a build-measure-learn feedback loop to develop and refine business models rapidly (Ries, 2011). Finally, discovery-driven planning focuses on learning and adaptability by setting up experiments to test assumptions and adjust plans based on feedback (McGrath & MacMillan, 1995).

6.4.6.1 *Wargaming (Policy Gaming)*

Business wargaming simulates competitive market scenarios to test and refine strategies. This method involves role-playing various stakeholders, such as competitors, customers, and regulators, allowing organizations to anticipate challenges and understand stakeholder behaviors in a controlled environment (Gilad, 2009). It relies on creating detailed scenarios based on real-world data and trends, then executing these scenarios to observe outcomes and refine strategies accordingly. This enhances decision-making by providing a safe space to explore the consequences of different strategic choices and to practice responses to unforeseen events (Oriesek & Schwarz, 2008).

Companies, including Shell, have employed wargaming to navigate complex market conditions and geopolitical risks. By simulating oil price fluctuations and regulatory changes, Shell has been able to develop more resilient strategies (Wack, 1985).

6.4.6.2 *Lean Startup Methodology*

The Lean Startup methodology emphasizes the development of businesses and products through iterative testing, validated learning, and the creation of minimal viable products (MVPs) (Ries, 2011). Central to the Lean Startup approach is the continuous loop of Build-Measure-Learn and the concept of building an MVP, a simplified version of a product that allows the organization to collect the maximum amount of validated learning about customers with the least effort (Ries, 2011). This methodology is designed to reduce product development cycles by rapidly determining market viability, allowing for more efficient resource allocation and faster responses to market feedback (Blank, 2013). It is particularly effective in environments of high uncertainty, where traditional market research and product development methods may be too slow or imprecise (Ries, 2011).

An example of the Lean Startup methodology in action is Dropbox, which used a simple explainer video as an MVP to gauge interest before investing in full-scale development. This approach validated market demand and gathered valuable user feedback, leading to significant growth and success (Thiel & Masters, 2014). Another example is Zappos, which tested its online shoe retail concept by initially listing a few products online and purchasing them from local stores as orders were placed. This MVP approach allowed Zappos to validate its business model with minimal upfront investment (Blank, 2013).

6.4.6.3 *Discovery-Driven Planning*

Discovery-driven planning is a method of managing strategic initiatives in uncertain environments by systematically testing assumptions and adjusting plans based on new information (McGrath & MacMillan, 1995). This approach involves identifying key assumptions underlying the strategy, defining checkpoints and milestones, and collecting data to validate or invalidate the assumptions. Discovery-driven planning allows organizations to manage risk, learn from failures, and adapt their strategies as they gain new insights (McGrath, 2010).

A key aspect of discovery-driven planning is the development of a reverse income statement, which starts with the desired outcome and works backward to identify the necessary assumptions and actions required to achieve that goal (McGrath & MacMillan, 1995).

Fashion retail company Rent the Runway serves as an example of discovery-driven planning. The founders initially assumed that women would primarily rent dresses for special occasions, but through systematic testing and data collection, they discovered that customers also wanted to rent everyday clothing items (McGrath, 2010). By validating and invalidating their assumptions, Rent the Runway was able to pivot their strategy and expand their offerings to better meet customer needs.

6.5 Strategic Agility Approach

6.5.1 Aim

The strategic agility approach aims to enable organizations to continuously sense and rapidly respond to changing environments, sustaining competitive advantage through constant innovation and adaptation (Weber & Tarba, 2014).

6.5.2 Core Logic

Strategic agility encompasses management's ability to swiftly perceive and respond to changes in the environment by making intentional strategic moves and adapting organizational configurations for successful implementation (Weber & Tarba, 2014). It moves beyond traditional static strategies by emphasizing the creation of new business models and categories rather than merely adjusting existing ones (Doz & Kosonen, 2010). This approach leverages dynamic capabilities, such as continuous innovation, rapid responsiveness, and organizational flexibility, to navigate the complexities of modern markets (Teece et al., 2016).

6.5.3 Key Elements

Continuous innovation: Developing new products, services, and business models to stay ahead of competitors (Teece, 2007).

Rapid responsiveness: Quickly sensing and reacting to market changes to seize opportunities and mitigate risks (Doz & Kosonen, 2010).

Organizational flexibility: Maintaining a flexible organizational structure that allows for swift adaptation to new circumstances (O'Reilly & Tushman, 2013).

Dynamic capabilities: Building capabilities that enable the organization to integrate, build, and reconfigure internal and external competencies to address rapidly changing environments (Teece et al., 1997).

Ambidexterity: Balancing exploration of new opportunities with the exploitation of existing capabilities (O'Reilly & Tushman, 2013).

6.5.4 Applications and Examples

Strategic agility has been applied successfully in various industries. For instance, IBM's transformation from a hardware company to a leader in services and cloud computing exemplifies strategic agility. Facing declining hardware sales in the 1990s, IBM strategically shifted its business model to focus on consulting services and cloud computing, demonstrating its ability to adapt to changing market conditions and emerging technologies (Harreld et al., 2007). Another example is Zara's fast-fashion business model, enabling quick response to market trends (Ferdows et al., 2004).

6.5.5 Challenges and Limitations

Implementing strategic agility presents several challenges. One major challenge is maintaining a balance between flexibility and control. While organizations need to be responsive and adaptable, they must also ensure that their actions align with long-term strategic goals (Doz & Kosonen, 2010). Moreover, fostering an agile culture requires significant changes in organizational structure and processes, which can be met with resistance from employees accustomed to traditional ways of working (Teece, 2007). Another limitation is the potential for strategic drift, where the focus on rapid responses and continuous change can lead to a loss of strategic coherence (Weber & Tarba, 2014).

6.5.6 Strategy Methods

Multiple methods can be employed to formulate strategies utilizing strategic agility. Fast Strategy is one such strategy method designed to achieve strategic agility in rapidly changing business environments (Doz & Kosonen, 2008). Dynamic capabilities is another approach to building and leveraging capabilities that enables organizations to integrate, build, and reconfigure competencies to address rapidly changing environments (Teece, 2007). Ambidexterity works by developing the ability to balance the exploration of new opportunities with the exploitation of existing capabilities to ensure long-term success (O'Reilly & Tushman, 2013).

6.5.6.1 Fast Strategy

The Fast Strategy approach provides a framework for achieving strategic agility in fast-changing business environments (Doz & Kosonen, 2008). This approach emphasizes the development of three key dimensions: strategic sensitivity, resource fluidity, and collective commitment.

Strategic sensitivity is the ability to detect and interpret weak signals of change in the external environment, helping organizations identify emerging opportunities and threats (Doz & Kosonen, 2008). It requires alertness, open-mindedness, and rapid information processing Companies with strong strategic sensitivity anticipate shifts in customer needs, technological advancements, and competitive dynamics, enabling proactive strategy adaptation (Doz & Kosonen, 2010).

Resource fluidity is the capacity to swiftly reconfigure organizational resources in response to changing circumstances (Doz & Kosonen, 2008). This involves a flexible structure, modular processes, and efficient resource reallocation. Resource fluidity allows organizations to seize new opportunities and mitigate threats by quickly redeploying assets, adjusting business models, and forming strategic partnerships (Doz & Kosonen, 2010).

Collective commitment emphasizes securing stakeholder alignment for strategic initiatives (Doz & Kosonen, 2008). It involves fostering a shared purpose, engaging employees in strategic dialogues, and building a culture of trust and collaboration (Doz & Kosonen, 2010). This commitment enables organizations to make bold decisions, take calculated risks, and implement strategic changes with full support.

Nokia exemplified the Fast Strategy approach in the early 2000s by moving its focus from the declining mobile phone market to the emerging smartphone industry (Doz & Kosonen, 2008). Utilizing strategic sensitivity, resource fluidity, and collective commitment, Nokia introduced innovative products, adapted its business model, and maintained a competitive edge in a rapidly evolving market (Doz & Kosonen, 2010).

6.5.6.2 *Dynamic Capabilities*

The Dynamic Capabilities Framework is a strategic approach that focuses on an organization's ability to sense, seize, and transform opportunities and threats in a rapidly changing business environment (Teece et al., 1997). This framework emphasizes the importance of developing and leveraging a firm's dynamic capabilities, which are defined as "the firm's ability to integrate, build, and reconfigure internal and external competences to address rapidly changing environments" (Teece, 2007, p. 516). Dynamic capabilities enable firms to continuously adapt and innovate, ensuring their long-term competitive advantage (Eisenhardt & Martin, 2000).

The Dynamic Capabilities Framework consists of three key components: sensing, seizing, and transforming. First, the sensing element involves the ability to identify and assess opportunities and threats in the business environment. It requires a deep understanding of market trends, customer needs, and emerging technologies (Teece, 2007). Firms with strong sensing capabilities can quickly spot and interpret weak signals, allowing them to anticipate and prepare for future changes (Helfat & Peteraf, 2015). Second, once opportunities are identified, the seizing component requires making timely and effective decisions to capitalize on them. This may include investing in new resources, forming strategic alliances, or adapting business models (Teece, 2007). Seizing capabilities enable firms to quickly mobilize resources and execute strategic moves to capture value from emerging opportunities (Helfat & Winter, 2011). Third, the transforming component involves the continuous reconfiguration and renewal of a firm's assets, structures, and processes to maintain competitiveness in a dynamic environment (Teece, 2007). In order for this framework to be effective, it requires a culture of innovation, organizational agility, and the ability to manage complex change processes (Teece et al., 2016).

An example of a company, which has successfully leveraged its dynamic capabilities, is Amazon. Amazon has consistently demonstrated its ability to sense and seize opportunities in the rapidly evolving e-commerce and technology sectors, while continuously transforming its business model and operations. From its origins as an online bookstore, Amazon has expanded into various domains, including cloud computing (Amazon Web Services), artificial intelligence (Alexa), and entertainment (Amazon Prime Video) (Ritala et al., 2016).

6.5.6.3 Organizational Ambidexterity

Ambidexterity is a strategic approach that enables organizations to simultaneously pursue exploratory and exploitative activities, balancing the need for innovation and efficiency (O'Reilly & Tushman, 2013). Exploratory activities involve searching for new opportunities, experimenting with novel ideas, and developing radical innovations, while exploitative activities focus on refining existing capabilities, optimizing processes, and driving incremental improvements (March, 1991).

There are two main approaches to creating ambidexterity: structural (simultaneous) and contextual. Structural ambidexterity involves creating distinct separate subunits, each with its own processes, cultures, and metrics tailored to their specific focus, which would be either exploration or exploitation (O'Reilly & Tushman, 2004). IBM's shift from hardware to a services-oriented company included forming new business units to explore emerging technologies, while the traditional units continued to enhance their hardware products (Harreld et al., 2007). Contextual ambidexterity is achieved at the individual level within the same organizational units and employees are encouraged to engage in both explorative and exploitative activities. Central to this approach is developing a supportive organizational context that fosters both alignment and adaptability. The organizational culture at companies like 3M promotes this balance, encouraging employees to spend a portion of their time on innovative projects while meeting their routine responsibilities (Gibson & Birkinshaw, 2004). There is another type of structural ambidexterity referred to as sequential ambidexterity where firms alternate between exploitative structures and explorative structures (O'Reilly & Tushman, 2013).

References

Afuah, A. (2009). *Strategic Innovation: New Game Strategies for Competitive Advantage.* Routledge.

Andries, P., Debackere, K., & Van Looy, B. (2013). Simultaneous Experimentation as a Learning Strategy: Business Model Development Under Uncertainty. *Strategic Entrepreneurship Journal, 7*(4), 288–310.

Ansell, C. K., & Bartenberger, M. (2016). Varieties of Experimentalism. *Ecological Economics*, *130*, 64–73.

Antoncic, B., & Hisrich, R. D. (2001). Intrapreneurship: Construct Refinement and Cross-Cultural Validation. *Journal of Business Venturing*, *16*(5), 495–527.

Antoncic, B., & Hisrich, R. D. (2003). Clarifying the Intrapreneurship Concept. *Journal of Small Business and Enterprise Development*, *10*(1), 7–24.

Barnett, W. P., & Hansen, M. T. (1996). The Red Queen in Organizational Evolution. *Strategic Management Journal*, *17*(S1), 139–157.

Birkinshaw, J., Zimmermann, A., & Raisch, S. (2016). How Do Firms Adapt to Discontinuous Change? Bridging the Dynamic Capabilities and Ambidexterity Perspectives. *California Management Review*, *58*(4), 36–58.

Blank, S. (2013). Why the Lean Start-Up Changes Everything. *Harvard Business Review*, *91*(5), 63–72.

Chesbrough, H. W. (2002). Making Sense of Corporate Venture Capital. *Harvard Business Review*, *80*(3), 90–99.

Chesbrough, H. W. (2010). Business Model Innovation: Opportunities and Barriers. *Long Range Planning*, *43*(2), 354–363.

Christensen, C. M., & Eyring, H. J. (2011). *The Innovative University: Changing the DNA of Higher Education from the Inside Out* (1st ed.). Jossey-Bass.

Christensen, C. M., McDonald, R., Altman, E. J., & Palmer, J. E. (2018). Disruptive Innovation: An Intellectual History and Directions for Future Research. *Journal of Management Studies*, *55*(7), 1043–1078.

Christensen, C. M., & Raynor, M. E. (2003). *The Innovator's Solution: Creating and Sustaining Successful Growth*. Harvard Business School Press.

Christensen, C. R. (1997). *The Innovator's Dilemma: When New Technologies Cause Great Firms to Fail*. Harvard Business School Press.

Cook, T. D., & Campbell, D. T. (1979). *Quasi-Experimentation: Design and Analysis Issues for Field Settings*. Houghton Mifflin.

Covin, J. G., & Miles, M. P. (1999). Corporate Entrepreneurship and the Pursuit of Competitive Advantage. *Entrepreneurship Theory and Practice*, *23*(3), 47–63.

Covin, J. G., & Miles, M. P. (2007). Strategic Use of Corporate Venturing. *Entrepreneurship Theory and Practice*, *31*(2), 183–207.

Derfus, P. J., Maggitti, P. G., Grimm, C. M., & Smith, K. G. (2008). The Red Queen Effect: Competitive Actions and Firm Performance. *Academy of Management Journal*, *51*(1), 61–80.

Dewey, J. (1927). *The Public and Its Problems*. Henry Holt and Company.

Doz, Y. L., & Kosonen, M. (2008). *Fast Strategy: How Strategic Agility Will Help You Stay Ahead of the Game* (1st ed.). Wharton School Publishing.

Doz, Y. L., & Kosonen, M. (2010). Embedding Strategic Agility: A Leadership Agenda for Accelerating Business Model Renewal. *Long Range Planning*, *43*(2–3), 370–382.

Dushnitsky, G., & Lenox, M. J. (2005). When Do Incumbents Learn from Entrepreneurial Ventures?: Corporate Venture Capital and Investing Firm Innovation Rates. *Research Policy*, *34*(5), 615–639.

Edmondson, A. C., & Verdin, P. J. (2017). Your Strategy Should Be a Hypothesis You Constantly Adjust. *Harvard Business Review Digital Article*, November 09. Available at: https://hbr.org/ 2017/11/ your-strategy-should-be-a-hypothesis-you-constantly-adjust

Eisenhardt, K. M., & Brown, S. L. (1998). Time Pacing: Competing in Markets That Won't Stand Still. *Harvard Business Review*, *76*(2), 59–70.

Eisenhardt, K. M., & Martin, J. A. (2000). Dynamic Capabilities: What Are They? *Strategic Management Journal*, *21*(10-11), 1105–1121.

Ferdows, K., Lewis, M. A., & Machuca, J. A. D. (2004). Rapid-Fire Fulfillment. *Harvard Business Review*, *82*(11), 104–117.

Fry, A. (1987). The Post-it® Note: An Intrapreneurial Success. *SAM Advanced Management Journal*, *52*(3), 4.

Garud, R., Gehman, J., & Kumaraswamy, A. (2011). Complexity Arrangements for Sustained Innovation: Lessons from 3M Corporation. *Organization Studies*, *32*(6), 737–767.

Gassmann, O., Frankenberger, K., & Csik, M. (2014). *The Business Model Navigator: 55 Models That Will Revolutionise Your Business*. Pearson.

Ghosh, S., Thomke, S., & Pourkhalkhali, H. (2020). The Effects of Hierarchy on Learning and Performance in Business Experimentation. *Academy of Management Proceedings*, *2020*(1), 20500.

Gibson, C. B., & Birkinshaw, J. (2004). The Antecedents, Consequences, and Mediating Role of Organizational Ambidexterity. *Academy of Management Journal*, *47*(2), 209–226.

Gilad, B. (2009). *Business War Games: How Large, Small, and New Companies Can Vastly Improve Their Strategies and Outmaneuver the Competition*. Career Press.

Hamel, G. (1998). Strategy Innovation and the Quest for Value. *MIT Sloan Management Review*, *39*(2), 7–14.

Harreld, J. B., O'Reilly, C. A., & Tushman, M. L. (2007). Dynamic Capabilities at IBM: Driving Strategy into Action. *California Management Review*, *49*(4), 21–43.

Helfat, C. E., & Peteraf, M. A. (2015). Managerial Cognitive Capabilities and the Microfoundations of Dynamic Capabilities. *Strategic Management Journal*, *36*(6), 831–850.

Helfat, C. E., & Winter, S. G. (2011). Untangling Dynamic and Operational Capabilities: Strategy for the (N)ever-Changing World. *Strategic Management Journal*, *32*(11), 1243–1250.

Hitt, M. A., Ireland, R. D., Camp, S. M., & Sexton, D. L. (2001). Strategic Entrepreneurship: Entrepreneurial Strategies for Wealth Creation. *Strategic Management Journal*, *22*(6-7), 479–491.

Hornsby, J. S., Naffziger, D. W., Kuratko, D. F., & Montagno, R. V. (1993). An Interactive Model of the Corporate Entrepreneurship Process. *Entrepreneurship Theory and Practice*, *17*(2), 29–37.

Huber, G. P. (1991). Organizational Learning: The Contributing Processes and the Literatures. *Organization Science*, *2*(1), 88–115.

Ireland, R. D., & Hitt, M. A. (1999). Achieving and Maintaining Strategic Competitiveness in the 21st Century: The role of Strategic Leadership. *Academy of Management Perspectives*, *13*(1), 43–57.

Ireland, R. D., Hitt, M. A., & Sirmon, D. G. (2003). A Model of Strategic Entrepreneurship: The Construct and its Dimensions. *Journal of Management*, *29*(6), 963–989.

Ireland, R. D., & Webb, J. W. (2007). Strategic Entrepreneurship: Creating Competitive Advantage Through Streams of Innovation. *Business Horizons*, *50*(1), 49–59.

Johnson, M. W., Christensen, C. M., & Kagermann, H. (2008). Reinventing Your Business Model. *Harvard Business Review*, *86*(12), 50–59.

Kaplan, R. S., & Norton, D. P. (1996). *The Balanced Scorecard: Translating Strategy into Action*. Harvard Business School Press.

Ketchen Jr., D. J., Ireland, R. D., & Snow, C. C. (2007). Strategic Entrepreneurship, Collaborative Innovation, and Wealth Creation. *Strategic Entrepreneurship Journal*, *1*(3-4), 371–385.

Kim, W. C., & Mauborgne, R. (1997). Value Innovation: The Strategic Logic of High Growth. *Harvard Business Review*, *75*(1), 102–112.

Kim, W. C., & Mauborgne, R. (2002). Charting Your Company's Future. *Harvard Business Review*, *80*(6), 76–85.

Kim, W. C., & Mauborgne, R. (2005). *Blue Ocean Strategy: How to Create Uncontested Market Space and Make the Competition Irrelevant*. Harvard Business School Press.

Kim, W. C., & Mauborgne, R. (2015). *Blue Ocean Strategy: How to Create Uncontested Market Space and Make the Competition Irrelevant* (Expanded ed.). Harvard Business Review Press.

Kim, W. C., & Mauborgne, R. (2017). *Blue Ocean Shift: Beyond Competing – Proven Steps to Inspire Confidence and Seize New Growth* (1st ed.). Hachette Books.

Kuratko, D. F., & Audretsch, D. B. (2009). Strategic Entrepreneurship: Exploring Different Perspectives of an Emerging Concept. *Entrepreneurship Theory and Practice*, *33*(1), 1–17.

Kuratko, D. F., Covin, J. G., & Garrett, R. P. (2009). Corporate Venturing: Insights from actual Performance. *Business Horizons*, *52*(5), 459–467.

Kuratko, D. F., Montagno, R. V., & Hornsby, J. S. (1990). Developing an Intrapreneurial Assessment Instrument for an Effective Corporate Entrepreneurial Environment. *Strategic Management Journal*, *11*, 49–58.

Levinthal, D. A. (1997). Adaptation on Rugged Landscapes. *Management Science*, *43*(7), 934–950.

Lucas, H. C., & Goh, J. M. (2009). Disruptive Technology: How Kodak Missed the Digital Photography Revolution. *The Journal of Strategic Information Systems*, *18*(1), 46–55.

March, J. G. (1991). Exploration and Exploitation in Organizational Learning. *Organization Science*, *2*(1), 71–87.

Markides, C. (1997). Strategic Innovation. *MIT Sloan Management Review*, *38*(3), 9–23.

McGrath, R. (2013a). *The End of Competitive Advantage: How to Keep Your Strategy Moving as Fast as Your Business*. Harvard Business Review Press.

McGrath, R. (2013b). Transient Advantage. *Harvard Business Review*, *91*(6), 62–70.

McGrath, R., & MacMillan, I. (1995). Discovery-Driven Planning. *Harvard Business Review*, *73*(4), 44–54.

McGrath, R. G. (2010). Business Models: A Discovery Driven Approach. *Long Range Planning*, *43*(2), 247–261.

Miner, A. S., Bassof, P., & Moorman, C. (2001). Organizational Improvisation and Learning: A Field Study. *Administrative Science Quarterly*, *46*(2), 304–337.

Narayanan, V. K., Yang, Y., & Zahra, S. A. (2009). Corporate Venturing and Value Creation: A Review and Proposed Framework. *Research Policy*, *38*(1), 58–76.

Nicholls-Nixon, C. L., Cooper, A. C., & Woo, C. Y. (2000). Strategic Experimentation: Understanding Change and Performance in New Ventures. *Journal of Business Venturing*, *15*(5), 493–521.

O'Reilly, C. A., & Tushman, M. (2004). The Ambidextrous Organization. *Harvard Business Review*, *82*(4), 74–83.

O'Reilly, C. A., & Tushman, M. L. (2013). Organizational Ambidexterity: Past, Present, and Future. *Academy of Management Perspectives*, *27*(4), 324–338.

Oriesek, D. F., & Schwarz, J. O. (2008). *Business Wargaming: Securing Corporate Value*. Gower.

Raisch, S., Birkinshaw, J., Probst, G., & Tushman, M. L. (2009). Organizational Ambidexterity: Balancing Exploitation and Exploration for Sustained Performance. *Organization Science*, *20*(4), 685–695.

Ries, E. (2011). *The Lean Startup: How Today's Entrepreneurs Use Continuous Innovation to Create Radically Successful Businesses* (1st ed.). Crown Business.

Rindova, V., & Courtney, H. (2020). To Shape or Adapt: Knowledge Problems, Epistemologies, and Strategic Postures under Knightian Uncertainty. *Academy of Management Review*, *45*(4), 787–807.

Ritala, P., Heiman, B., & Hurmelinna-Laukkanen, P. (2016). The Need for Speed—Unfamiliar Problems, Capability Rigidity, and Ad Hoc Processes in Organizations. *Industrial and Corporate Change*, *25*(5), 757–777.

Sahaym, A., Cho, S. Y., Kim, S. K., & Mousa, F.-T. (2016). Mixed Blessings: How Top Management Team Heterogeneity and Governance Structure Influence the Use of Corporate Venture Capital by Post-IPO Firms. *Journal of Business Research*, *69*(3), 1208–1218.

Sarasvathy, S. D. (2001). Causation and Effectuation: Toward a Theoretical Shift from Economic Inevitability to Entrepreneurial Contingency. *Academy of Management Review*, *26*(2), 243–263.

Schumpeter, J. A. (1934). *The Theory of Economic Development: An Inquiry into Profits, Capital, Credit, Interest, and the Business Cycle*. Harvard University Press.

Schwarz, J. O. (2011). Ex ante Strategy Evaluation: The Case for Business Wargaming. *Business Strategy Series*, *12*(3), 122–135.

Statista. (2024). *Online University Education – Worldwide*.

Steiber, A., & Alänge, S. (2013). A Corporate System for Continuous Innovation: The Case of Google Inc. *European Journal of Innovation Management*, *16*(2), 243–264.

Teece, D., Peteraf, M., & Leih, S. (2016). Dynamic Capabilities and Organizational Agility: Risk, Uncertainty, and Strategy in the Innovation Economy. *California Management Review*, *58*(4), 13–35.

Teece, D. J. (2007). Explicating Dynamic Capabilities: The Nature and Microfoundations of (Sustainable) Enterprise Performance. *Strategic Management Journal*, *28*(13), 1319–1350.

Teece, D. J. (2010). Business Models, Business Strategy and Innovation. *Long Range Planning*, *43*(2), 172–194.

Teece, D. J., Pisano, G., & Shuen, A. (1997). Dynamic Capabilities and Strategic Management. *Strategic Management Journal*, *18*(7), 509–533.

Thiel, P. A., & Masters, B. (2014). *Zero to One: Notes on Startups, or How to Build the Future* (1st ed.). Crown Business.

Tushman, M., & O'Reilly, C. A. (2002). *Winning Through Innovation: A Practical Guide to Leading Organizational Change and Renewal.* Harvard Business School Press.

Valentin, M. (2019). *The Tesla Way: The Disruptive Strategies and Models of Teslismn.* Kogan Page.

Voelpel, S. C., Leibold, M., & Tekie, E. B. (2004). The Wheel of Business Model Reinvention: How to Reshape Your Business Model to Leapfrog Competitors. *Journal of Change Management*, 4(3), 259–276.

Wack, P. (1985). Scenarios: Shooting the Rapids. *Harvard Business Review*, 63(6), 139–150.

Weber, Y., & Tarba, S. Y. (2014). Strategic Agility: A State of the Art Introduction to the Special Section on Strategic Agility. *California Management Review*, 56(3), 5–12.

Yoffie, D. B., & Rossano, P. (2012). *Apple Inc. in 2012.*

Zott, C., & Amit, R. (2010). Business Model Design: An Activity System Perspective. *Long Range Planning*, 43(2), 216–226.

7 Connecting Strategic Posture

7.1 Overview

7.1.1 Introduction

In today's interconnected and rapidly changing business landscape, organizations increasingly recognize the importance of collaboration, networks, and ecosystems in navigating complexity and uncertainty (Adner, 2017; Jacobides et al., 2018). The connecting strategic posture advocates for a shift from traditional, competitive strategies to a more integrated, collaborative approach that leverages the collective strengths of multiple actors to drive innovation and create shared value (Dyer et al., 2018; Gulati et al., 2000). This chapter explores the key characteristics of the connecting posture and its four main strategy approaches: ecosystem-based approach, platform-based approach, place-based approach, and strategic collaboration approach.

7.1.2 Key Characteristics

The connecting posture emphasizes the importance of building and participating in business networks to address complex challenges, exploit opportunities for synergy, and cocreate value in innovative ways (Adner, 2017; Jacobides et al., 2018). It recognizes that firms are embedded in complex webs of relationships and interdependencies that shape their ability to create and capture value (Dyer et al., 2018; Iansiti & Levien, 2004). By leveraging the complementary capabilities of diverse actors, firms can enhance their adaptability, resilience, and innovation potential (Adner & Kapoor, 2010; Jacobides et al., 2018).

The logic behind the connecting posture is that in an increasingly complex and uncertain world, success often requires collaboration, resource sharing, and

DOI: 10.4324/9781003684060-7

collective action (Dyer et al., 2018; Gulati et al., 2000). Collaborative and integrative, this posture thrives on the principle that the whole is greater than the sum of its parts (Dyer & Singh, 1998; Lavie, 2006). It seeks to build bridges between diverse entities, facilitating the flow of ideas, resources, and capabilities across organizational boundaries to achieve shared goals (Chesbrough, 2003; Powell et al., 1996).

This strategic posture can be likened to an ecosystem in nature, where diverse organisms coexist, interact, and support each other's growth, demonstrating resilience and adaptability through collaboration (Iansiti & Levien, 2004; Moore, 1993). Therefore, this posture underscores the importance of platforms, ecosystems, strategic alliances, and networks in achieving sustainable competitive advantages in today's interconnected and rapidly changing business landscape (Gulati et al., 2000; Lavie, 2006). Organizations are encouraged to embrace coopetition (Brandenburger & Nalebuff, 1996), strategic collaboration (Dyer & Singh, 1998), ecosystem thinking (Iansiti & Levien, 2004; Moore, 1993), and platform strategies (Gawer & Cusumano, 2014; Parker et al., 2016) to navigate complexity, uncertainty, and the evolving futures of global markets.

An appropriate analogy for the collaborative posture is like coordinating a fleet of cars to navigate through interconnected streets and serve diverse and dispersed clients, leveraging the strength of a network and partnerships for mutual benefit.

Key actors act as orchestrators, connectors, and facilitators, identifying potential synergies, fostering strategic alliances, and nurturing relationships and networks that underpin collaborative ecosystems (Dhanaraj & Parkhe, 2006).

7.1.3 Key Theoretical Perspectives

The connecting strategic posture is grounded in several interrelated theoretical frameworks that emphasize the importance of networks, ecosystems, platforms, locations, and collaborative efforts in driving innovation and competitive advantage. **Network theory** is fundamental to this posture, highlighting the importance of social networks in facilitating information flow and resource access (Burt, 1992; Granovetter, 1973). **Theories of network effects** further support this posture by explaining how the value of a product or service increases as more people use it (Katz & Shapiro, 1985; Shapiro & Varian, 1999). The **concept of business ecosystems** elaborates on the interconnected nature of modern businesses, where firms interact within a complex web of relationships to cocreate value (Iansiti & Levien, 2004; Moore, 1993). **Open**

innovation is another critical component, advocating for the integration of external ideas and technologies into the innovation process (Chesbrough, 2003). **Resource dependency theory** (Pfeffer & Salancik, 1978) also plays a crucial role in the coping posture. This theory posits that organizations depend on external resources, which makes them vulnerable to the actions of other entities that control those resources. Lastly, the **relational view framework** highlights how firms can achieve superior performance by working together (Dyer & Singh, 1998; Dyer et al., 2018).

7.1.4 Limitations

Despite its potential benefits from collaboration, networks, and ecosystems, the connecting strategic posture has several limitations. First, the complexity of managing and coordinating diverse actors within networks can lead to high transaction costs and potential conflicts (Gulati et al., 2012). Second, the reliance on external partners may expose firms to risks such as knowledge leakage, opportunistic behavior, and loss of control over key resources and capabilities (Dyer et al., 2018). Third, the dynamics of collaboration and competition in ecosystems can create tensions and instability, requiring careful management of coopetitive relationships (Raza-Ullah et al., 2014). Fourth, the connecting posture may not be suitable for all industries or contexts, particularly those with low interdependence or high appropriability regimes (Pisano & Teece, 2007). Finally, the emphasis on collaboration and shared value creation may sometimes come at the expense of individual firm profitability and competitive advantage (Ritala & Hurmelinna-Laukkanen, 2013).

7.1.5 Connecting Strategy Approaches

As illustrated in Figure 7.1, the connecting strategy approaches can be arranged in a matrix consisting of two dimensions: solution and coordination.

The vertical solution type dimension has two categories: broad and specific. Strategy approaches produce broad solutions that address a variety of issues and can be applied across different contexts and scenarios. In contrast to strategy approaches that produce specific solutions that address particular problems or opportunities within a specific context.

The horizontal coordination dimension also has two categories: loose and tight. Strategy approaches requiring loose coordination refer to a flexible and less structured approach to managing relationships and interactions among various entities in the network. It allows for greater autonomy and less formal collaboration.

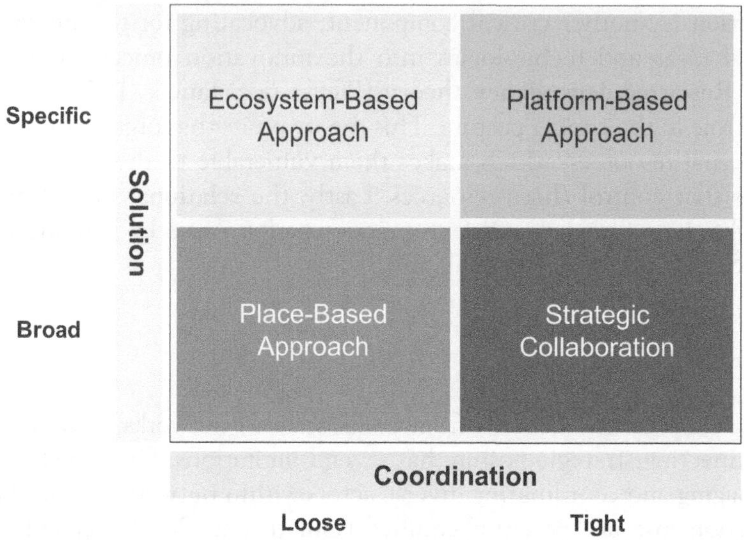

Figure 7.1 The Connecting Strategic Posture Matrix.

In contrast to strategy approaches that require tight coordination, where managing interactions is more structured and formalized to ensure alignment among network actors, those that require loose coordination offer a more flexible and informal way to manage relationships, allowing for greater autonomy.

As shown in the matrix, there are four key strategy approaches that can be used to achieve the connect posture:

Ecosystem-based approach (top-left quadrant): Focuses on creating and nurturing a network of interdependent actors centered around shared goals and innovations (Adner, 2017; Jacobides et al., 2018).

This approach focuses on creating and nurturing a network of interdependent actors centered around shared goals and innovations. It leverages the combined resources and capabilities of multiple players to address specific challenges or opportunities within the ecosystem.

Creating and nurturing a network of interdependent actors centered around shared goals and innovations (Adner, 2017; Jacobides et al., 2018). Leverage the combined resources and capabilities of multiple players.

Platform-based approach (top-right quadrant): Utilizes digital platforms to facilitate interactions and transactions among ecosystem participants, enhancing value creation and exchange (Gawer & Cusumano, 2014; Parker et al., 2016).

Table 7.1 Comparing the Collaborate Strategies

Dimension	Ecosystem Approach	Platform Approach	Place-based Approach	Strategic Collaboration
Aim	Create and nurture a network of interdependent actors centered around shared goals and innovations	Create a digital environment that facilitates interactions between different user groups to drive innovation and competitive advantage	Leverage the unique attributes, resources, and needs of specific geographic areas to enhance innovation, knowledge sharing, and competitive advantage	Form alliances and partnerships to pursue shared objectives by combining resources and capabilities for mutual benefit
Core Logic	Firms are embedded in complex webs of relationships and interdependencies that shape their ability to create and capture value	Platforms create value by connecting different user groups and leveraging network effects	Benefits arise from spatial concentration of economic activities and collaboration among stakeholders	Firms can cooperate to jointly create value while also competing to capture part of that value
Assumptions	Ecosystems fundamentally alter the unit of analysis from the individual firm to the ecosystem as a whole	Multi-sided platforms create value by balancing the needs of various user groups	Agglomeration economics – firms and industries gain benefits by locating in close proximity	Coopetition – simultaneous pursuit of cooperation and competition is possible and beneficial
Strengths	Achieves competitive edge by leveraging combined resources and capabilities of multiple players	Drives innovation by facilitating interactions and fostering collaboration within platforms	Enhances regional development and competitiveness by leveraging local assets and promoting collaboration	Allows access to new markets, technologies, knowledge, and economies of scale/scope through collaboration

(*Continued*)

Table 7.1 (Continued)

Dimension	Ecosystem Approach	Platform Approach	Place-based Approach	Strategic Collaboration
Limitations	Requires careful consideration of ecosystem positioning and balance of collaboration vs. competition	Faces challenges in managing competition from other platforms and ensuring fair competition	Requires coordination across sectors and levels of government; may be difficult to replicate in other regions	Presents challenges in coordination, trust-building, and appropriation of jointly created value
Methods	• Ecosystem-based Model • Open Innovation Networks	• Multisided Platforms	• Clusters • Science Parks	• Strategic Alliances • Joint Ventures • Network Collaboration

Utilizes digital platforms to facilitate interactions and transactions among ecosystem participants. This approach enhances value creation and exchange by providing a structured environment that connects different user groups, fostering innovation and competitive advantage.

Place-based approach (bottom-left quadrant): Leverages the unique attributes, resources, and needs of specific geographic areas to enhance innovation, knowledge sharing, and competitive advantage and to foster sustainable economic growth and development (Barca et al., 2012).

Leverages the unique attributes, resources, and needs of specific geographic areas to enhance innovation, knowledge sharing, and competitive advantage. This approach focuses on tailoring interventions to local conditions and engaging community stakeholders to foster sustainable economic growth and development.

Strategic collaboration (bottom-left quadrant): Involves forming alliances and partnerships to pursue shared objectives, combining resources and capabilities for mutual benefit (Dyer & Singh, 1998; Lavie, 2006).

Involves forming alliances and partnerships to pursue shared objectives, combining resources and capabilities for mutual benefit. This approach emphasizes creating shared value through cooperative interactions while simultaneously competing.

Furthermore, their key characteristics are contrasted in Table 7.1.

7.2 Ecosystem Strategy Approach

7.2.1 Aim

The ecosystem strategy approach aims to create and nurture a network of interdependent actors centered around shared goals and innovations, leveraging combined resources and capabilities to achieve competitive advantage in complex, interconnected markets (Adner, 2017; Jacobides et al., 2018).

7.2.2 Core Logic

The ecosystem approach recognizes that firms are part of complex network of relationships and interdependencies that shape their ability to create and capture value (Iansiti & Levien, 2004). By furthering these interconnections, businesses can enhance their innovative capabilities and adapt more rapidly to market changes (Gawer & Cusumano, 2014). This approach shifts the unit of analysis from the individual firm to the entire ecosystem, emphasizing the importance of collaboration and network effects (Jacobides et al., 2018).

7.2.3 Key Elements

Shared goals and innovations: The ecosystem strategy is built around common objectives and collaborative innovations among participants (Adner, 2017).

Interdependence and relationships: Recognizes the interdependencies between different actors within the ecosystem, fostering a network of support and collaboration (Iansiti & Levien, 2004).

Resource and capability leveraging: Utilizes the combined resources and capabilities of multiple players to create value that individual firms could not achieve alone (Gawer & Cusumano, 2014).

Ecosystem positioning: Firms must strategically position themselves within the ecosystem to balance collaboration and competition effectively (Jacobides et al., 2018).

7.2.4 Applications and Examples

Ecosystem strategies have been successfully implemented in various industries. For example, Apple's iOS ecosystem, which includes developers, accessory makers, and other third-party providers, has created a robust platform that enhances the value of its products and services. This ecosystem approach has helped Apple maintain a competitive advantage and foster innovation (Gawer & Cusumano, 2014). Another example is Tesla's approach to electric vehicles and renewable energy, where the company collaborates with battery suppliers, charging infrastructure providers, and solar energy firms to create a comprehensive ecosystem. This interconnected network supports Tesla's strategic goals and enhances the overall value proposition to customers (Adner, 2017).

7.2.5 Challenges and Limitations

Implementing an ecosystem strategy involves several challenges. One major challenge is managing the balance between collaboration and competition within the ecosystem. Firms need to cooperate to create value collectively, but they also compete for market share and resources (Jacobides et al., 2018). Additionally, ensuring alignment of goals and maintaining trust among ecosystem partners can be difficult, requiring strong governance mechanisms and effective communication (Iansiti & Levien, 2004). Another limitation is the potential for dependency on key ecosystem players. If a central firm in the ecosystem faces difficulties, it can impact the entire network. This interdependence can create vulnerabilities and necessitate robust risk management practices.

7.2.6 Strategy Methods

Several strategy methods utilize the logic of the ecosystem approach. Ecosystem-based models focus on creating value through interconnected networks of firms, leveraging collective capabilities to innovate and compete effectively (Adner, 2017; Jacobides et al., 2018). Open innovation network is another method that involves collaboration with external partners, such as universities and research institutions, to drive innovation and explore new market opportunities (Chesbrough & Appleyard, 2007).

7.2.6.1 Ecosystem-Based Model

An ecosystem refers to a network of interconnected organizations and stakeholders that collaborate to create and capture value through shared goals, innovation, and interdependencies (Iansiti & Levien, 2004). Unlike a platform, which primarily facilitates interactions between different user groups, an ecosystem encompasses a broader and more dynamic set of relationships that extend beyond mere transactions to include co-innovation, resource sharing, and joint value creation (Adner, 2017). Ecosystems thrive on the synergistic potential of diverse participants, each contributing unique capabilities and resources to the collective whole (Jacobides et al., 2018).

The core logic of an ecosystem is rooted in mutual dependence and collective growth. For example, Apple's iOS ecosystem includes not just the app developers who create software for iPhones but also hardware manufacturers, service providers, and even accessory makers who contribute to and benefit from the iPhone's success (Gawer & Cusumano, 2014). Similarly, Google's Android ecosystem integrates a vast array of stakeholders, from smartphone manufacturers to app developers and end-users, fostering an environment where innovation and collaboration are key drivers of value (Tiwana, 2014).

Managing an ecosystem involves navigating complex interdependencies and ensuring that all participants are aligned toward common goals. This requires a deep understanding of each participant's role and value proposition within the ecosystem, as well as the ability to orchestrate activities and resources effectively (Moore, 1993). Successful ecosystems like Amazon's marketplace demonstrate how integrating diverse participants can lead to a robust platform that supports a wide range of products and services, driving continuous innovation and customer satisfaction (Hagiu & Wright, 2015).

7.2.6.2 Open Innovation Networks

Open innovation networks are a strategic approach that involves engaging with external sources of knowledge and expertise, such as universities, research institutions, startups, and other companies, to cocreate value and accelerate innovation (Chesbrough, 2003). This strategy approach recognizes that valuable knowledge and innovative ideas are widely distributed and that organizations can benefit from integrating these external insights with their internal capabilities (Chesbrough & Bogers, 2014). By leveraging external sources of innovation, firms share the risks and rewards of innovation, leverage complementary assets and skills, and reduce time-to-market for new products and services (Faems et al., 2005).

One of the examples of an open innovation network is IBM's Innovation Jam, a large-scale collaborative brainstorming session that brought together IBM employees, family members, business partners, and clients to generate and refine innovative ideas (Bjelland & Wood, 2008). Procter & Gamble's Connect & Develop program exemplifies the effectiveness of open innovation networks. This program seeks to build partnerships with external entities to discover, develop, and commercialize new products, significantly enhancing P&G's innovation pipeline and market presence (Huston & Sakkab, 2006). Lastly, the open innovation approach taken by Nokia in mobile telephone research and development (R&D) projects during the period 1985–2002 exemplifies how firms can leverage external collaborations to enhance innovation outcomes (Dittrich & Duysters, 2007).

This approach challenges the traditional, closed innovation model that relies solely on internal R&D, advocating instead for a more porous boundary between the firm and its external environment to capitalize on the collective expertise of a broader innovation ecosystem (Laursen & Salter, 2006). However, successful open innovation strategies require a strong emphasis on intellectual property management, trust-building, and the development of absorptive capacity (Cohen & Levinthal, 1990). An organizational culture that values collaboration, openness, and flexibility is crucial, along with robust mechanisms for managing external partnerships and integrating external innovations into the company's strategic framework (Gassmann et al., 2010).

7.3 Platform Strategy Approach

7.3.1 Aim

The platform strategy approach aims to create and capture value by developing digital environments that facilitate interactions between multiple user groups, leveraging network effects to drive innovation and competitive advantage (Gawer, 2014; Rochet & Tirole, 2003).

7.3.2 Core Logic

Platform-based strategies create a digital environment that acts as an intermediary, providing the infrastructure and tools necessary for interactions between multiple user groups (Gawer, 2014; Rochet & Tirole, 2003). The core logic involves understanding and leveraging network effects, where the value of the platform increases as more users join, creating a self-reinforcing cycle of growth and engagement (Gawer, 2021). This strategy focuses on balancing the needs of various user groups to achieve a critical mass, ensuring sustainability and growth (Rochet & Tirole, 2003).

7.3.3 Key Elements

Network effects: Leveraging the increased value that comes with a growing user base, which attracts even more users (Gawer, 2021).
Balancing user groups: Ensuring that the needs of different participants are met to maintain a critical mass and platform health (Rochet & Tirole, 2003).
Platform ownership: Deciding whether to directly provide services or focus on facilitating interactions between participants (Boudreau, 2017).
Ecosystem facilitation: Encouraging open innovation through collaboration and knowledge exchange within the platform's ecosystem (Chesbrough, 2003).
Regulatory compliance: Managing and adhering to regulations to ensure fair competition and protect user interests (Evans & Schmalensee, 2016).

7.3.4 Applications and Examples

Platform strategies are widely used in various industries to drive innovation and competitive advantage. For instance, Airbnb has revolutionized the hospitality industry by creating a platform that connects hosts with travellers, leveraging network effects to expand globally (Parker et al., 2016). Another example is Uber, which has challenged traditional taxi services by providing a platform that connects drivers with passengers. This platform strategy has allowed Uber to scale rapidly and become a dominant player in the ride-sharing market (Parker et al., 2016).

7.3.5 Challenges and Limitations

Implementing a platform strategy comes with several challenges. One of the primary challenges is managing competition from other platforms and traditional industry players, which requires continuous innovation and differentiation (Cennamo & Santalo, 2013). Moreover, the challenge is balancing interests of multiple user groups. Additionally, regulatory issues pose significant challenges, as platforms must navigate complex legal landscapes to ensure compliance and protect user interests (Evans & Schmalensee, 2016). Another limitation is the need for substantial initial investment in building and maintaining the platform infrastructure, as well as the ongoing effort required to balance the needs of diverse user groups (Gawer & Cusumano, 2014).

7.3.6 Strategy Methods

Multisided platforms utilize the platform approach by facilitating interactions between multiple user groups, leveraging network effects to create value (Hagiu & Wright, 2015; Rochet & Tirole, 2003).

7.3.6.1 Multisided Platforms

Multisided platforms are digital environments that connect and facilitate interactions between different user groups, such as buyers and sellers or content creators and consumers (Rochet & Tirole, 2003). These platforms create value by enabling direct interactions between two or more distinct sides, each of which is affiliated with the platform (Hagiu & Wright, 2015). The platform's success depends on its ability to attract and retain users on all sides, as the value for users on one side increases with the number of users on the other side(s), a phenomenon known as network effects (Eisenmann et al., 2006). To maintain a thriving ecosystem, multisided platforms must carefully design their architecture, governance rules, and pricing strategies to balance the interests of all participants (Tiwana, 2014). A prime example of a multisided platform is Airbnb, which connects travelers seeking accommodation with property owners willing to rent out their spaces, creating value for both sides by facilitating transactions and reducing search costs (Zervas et al., 2017).

7.4 Place-Based Approach

7.4.1 Aim

The aim of the place-based approach is to drive innovation, economic growth, and sustainable development by leveraging the unique characteristics, assets, and challenges of specific geographic areas.

The place-based approach aims to drive innovation, economic growth, and sustainable development by leveraging the unique characteristics, assets, and challenges of specific geographic areas (Barca et al., 2012). This approach tailors interventions to local contexts, fostering collaboration among stakeholders to unlock the full potential of each locality (Barca et al., 2012).

7.4.2 Core Logic

At its core, the place-based approach recognizes that innovation and economic development are intrinsically linked to the spatial concentration of resources, knowledge, and actors (Porter, 1998). By capitalizing on agglomeration economies, such as knowledge spillovers, specialized labor pools, and shared infrastructure, his strategy aims to create self-sustaining ecosystems that boost productivity and competitiveness (Delgado et al., 2014).

7.4.3 Key Elements

Local context understanding: A deep understanding of the local economic structure, social dynamics, institutional arrangements, and environmental conditions is crucial for identifying unique strengths and designing responsive interventions (Barca, 2009).

Stakeholder engagement: Engaging local businesses, universities, government agencies, and community organizations fosters collaboration and mobilizes local resources and expertise (Bentley & Pugalis, 2014).

Agglomeration economies: Facilitating knowledge spillovers, labor market pooling, and shared infrastructure to drive regional economic development (Duranton & Puga, 2004).

7.4.4 Applications and Examples

Place-based strategies have been successfully implemented in various regions worldwide – Silicon Valley's technology ecosystem in the United States (Engel, 2015). Other examples are Singapore's one-north research and business park (Wong & Bunnell, 2006) and Medicon Valley's life sciences cluster in Denmark-Sweden (Pålsson & Gregersen, 2011).

7.4.5 Challenges and Limitations

While the place-based approach offers significant benefits, it also faces challenges. Ensuring equitable development and avoiding the concentration of resources in already prosperous areas can be difficult. Additionally, coordinating among diverse local stakeholders and aligning their interests requires significant effort and governance (Barca et al., 2012). There is also the risk of dependence on specific industries, which can make regions vulnerable to sector-specific downturns (Bristow & Healy, 2014).

7.4.6 Strategy Methods

Several methods utilize the logic of the place-based approach. Clusters are geographic concentrations of interconnected companies, suppliers, and institutions in a particular field that enhance productivity and innovation through close proximity and collaboration (Porter, 1998). Science park is another method, which calls for dedicated areas that support the growth of technology-based firms by providing infrastructure, services, and networking opportunities to facilitate innovation and commercialization of research (Link & Scott, 2003a).

7.4.6.1 Clusters

Clusters are geographic concentrations of interconnected companies, specialized suppliers, service providers, and associated institutions in a specific field, driving innovation, productivity, and regional economic growth (Porter, 1998). These clusters form and grow through the co-location of related economic activities, generating agglomeration economies, attracting talent and investment, and stimulating entrepreneurship and innovation (Ketels & Memedovic, 2008).

Clusters provide firms with access to specialized skills, advanced technologies, and critical infrastructure through knowledge spillovers and shared resources, enhancing competitive advantage (Delgado et al., 2014).

Successful clusters exhibit high social capital, trust, and collaboration, facilitating knowledge sharing, joint problem-solving, and collective action (Sölvell et al., 2003).

Clusters foster innovation and efficiency by promoting collaboration and competition among firms, allowing them to adapt to changing market conditions and seize new opportunities (Ketels, 2013). They often involve universities, research institutions, and government agencies providing skilled labor, advanced technologies, and policy incentives (Porter, 2000). Examples include Silicon Valley, known for its dense network of tech companies, venture capitalists, and research institutions (Engel, 2014), and Medicon Valley, a leading life sciences cluster in the Øresund Region between Denmark and Sweden (Pålsson & Gregersen, 2011).

7.4.6.2 *Science Parks*

Science parks provide a supportive ecosystem, infrastructure, services, resource sharing and a collaborative environment by co-locating technology-based firms with universities, research institutions, and industry to facilitate the knowledge between them (Link & Scott, 2007). For example, Cambridge Science Park in the United Kingdom has successfully created a hub for high-tech firms and startups, leveraging its proximity to the University of Cambridge to facilitate knowledge exchange and innovation (Storey & Tether, 1998). Similarly, the Sophia Antipolis Science Park in France has become a leading site for research and technology, hosting numerous multinational companies and research centers that benefit from its collaborative environment (Longhi, 1999). Another example of a successful science park is the Research Triangle Park (RTP) in North Carolina, United States, which has been a driving force behind the region's economic transformation since its establishment in 1959 (Link & Scott, 2003b).

These parks accelerate the commercialization of research, encourage firms to engage in collaborative R&D activities and contribute significantly to regional economic development (Minguillo et al., 2015).

7.5 Strategic Collaboration Approach

7.5.1 Aim

The aim of the strategic collaboration approach is to form alliances and partnerships that allow firms to combine resources and capabilities, thereby achieving results beyond what could be accomplished independently. This strategy is particularly focused on leveraging complementary strengths to pursue shared objectives and enhance competitive positioning (Dyer & Singh, 1998; Lavie, 2006).

7.5.2 Core Logic

Strategic collaboration hinges on the concept of coopetition, which involves simultaneous cooperation and competition among firms. Coopetition allows economic actors to create value through cooperative interactions while competing to capture part of that value. This dynamic process leverages complementary resources, shares risks and costs, and accelerates innovation, making it a powerful strategy in complex and competitive markets (Bouncken et al., 2015; Brandenburger & Nalebuff, 1996).

7.5.3 Key Elements

Resource and capability sharing: Combining resources and capabilities across organizational boundaries to achieve enhanced results (Dyer et al., 2018; Gulati et al., 2000).

Coopetition: Engaging in both cooperative and competitive interactions to create and capture value (Bouncken et al., 2015; Brandenburger & Nalebuff, 1996).

Diverse collaborative forms: Utilizing various forms of collaboration, including joint ventures, strategic alliances, R&D partnerships, and co-branding initiatives (Gulati, 1998; Lavie, 2006).

Relational capabilities: Developing communication, conflict resolution, and governance mechanisms to foster alignment and minimize opportunistic behavior (Dyer & Singh, 1998; Schreiner et al., 2009).

7.5.4 Applications and Examples

One prominent example of strategic collaboration is the joint venture between Samsung and Sony in 2004, which led to the creation of S-LCD for advanced LCD panel development. This partnership combined Samsung's LCD expertise with Sony's TV technology, accelerating market presence and innovation for both companies while maintaining competitive dynamics in the market (Gnyawali & Park, 2011). Another example is Amazon's business model that involves partnering with competitors on its marketplace and through Amazon Web Services (AWS), increasing product variety and technological advancements while retaining a competitive edge (Ritala et al., 2014). Other expels include Renault-Nissan-Mitsubishi Alliance in the automotive industry (Segrestin, 2005) and the Star Alliance in the airline industry (Gomes-Casseres, 2003).

7.5.5 Challenges and Limitations

Strategic collaborations face challenges such as the need for effective coordination, trust-building, and the appropriation of jointly created value (Das & Teng, 2001). Firms must develop relational capabilities to mitigate these challenges, including effective communication, conflict resolution, and governance mechanisms. Moreover, there is a risk of opportunistic behavior, where one partner may seek to maximize its own gains at the expense of the other (Das & Teng, 2000; Gulati, 1998).

7.5.6 Strategy Methods

Several methods can be employed to implement the strategic collaboration approach. Strategic alliances use formal partnerships between firms allowing them to share resources and capabilities to achieve mutual goals while maintaining their independence (Gulati, 1998). Joint venture is another method that entails the creation of a new entity jointly owned by partnering firms to pursue specific objectives, allowing for deeper integration and resource sharing (Gulati, 1998; Lavie, 2006). Lastly, network collaboration leverages networks of multiple firms to drive innovation and competitiveness, benefiting from shared knowledge and resources across the network (Dyer et al., 2018).

7.5.6.1 Strategic Alliances

Strategic alliances are voluntary agreements between companies that involve the exchange, sharing, or co-development of products, technology, or services to achieve common strategic goals (Gulati, 1998). This strategic cooperation technique allows businesses to get access to new markets, technology, and expertise while taking advantage of economies of size and scope (Das & Teng, 2000; Dyer et al., 2018). Strategic partnerships enable businesses to harness complementary resources and talents, share risks and expenses, and accelerate innovation by pooling their strengths and experience. Successful strategic partnerships need careful partner selection, explicit objective alignment, and strong governance structures to manage collaboration and prevent possible risks like opportunistic behavior or information leaking (Dyer et al., 2018; Gulati, 1998).

One example of a strategic alliance is Microsoft and Intel's long-standing relationship, known as "Wintel", which has controlled the personal computer market for decades by coordinating their operating system and microprocessor technology (Casadesus-Masanell & Yoffie, 2007). Another example is the Star Alliance in the airline sector, which allows member airlines to provide passengers with worldwide connectivity, joint frequent flyer programs, and integrated services (Gomes-Casseres, 2003).

7.5.6.2 *Joint Ventures*

Joint ventures are a strategic collaboration method that involves two or more firms creating a separate legal entity by pooling a portion of their resources to pursue a common objective (Kogut, 1988). This method enables firms to share risks, costs, and rewards while maintaining some degree of control over the venture, allowing them to leverage complementary assets, knowledge, and capabilities to create value that would be difficult to achieve independently (Harrigan, 1988). Joint ventures are often formed to enter new markets, develop new products or technologies, or gain access to critical resources (Gulati, 1998). Successful joint ventures require careful partner selection, clear goal alignment, and effective governance mechanisms to manage the inherent challenges of shared decision-making and potential conflicts of interest (Beamish & Lupton, 2016).

An example of a joint venture is Sony Ericsson, formed in 2001 by Sony Corporation and Ericsson to combine their expertise in consumer electronics and telecommunications, respectively, to develop and market mobile phones (Luo, 2007). Another example is the Fuji Xerox joint venture between Xerox Corporation and Fuji Photo Film Co., Ltd., which has successfully collaborated for over 50 years in the development, production, and sale of document solutions (Inkpen, 2008).

7.5.6.3 *Network Collaboration*

Network collaboration is a strategic approach that involves multiple firms working together in a network structure to achieve common goals, share resources, and create value through collective action (Provan & Kenis, 2008). This method enables firms to leverage the diverse capabilities, knowledge, and assets of network members to address complex challenges, pursue innovation, and enhance their competitive positioning (Dhanaraj & Parkhe, 2006).

Network collaboration goes beyond traditional dyadic partnerships, focusing instead on the collective engagement of multiple actors in a shared value creation process (Provan et al., 2007). Successful network collaboration requires effective governance mechanisms, trust-building, and the alignment of interests among network members (Provan & Kenis, 2008).

An example of network collaboration is the Toyota supplier network, where Toyota fosters close relationships with its suppliers, encouraging knowledge sharing, joint problem-solving, and continuous improvement, resulting in enhanced innovation, quality, and efficiency across the entire network (Dyer & Nobeoka, 2000). Another example is the Bluetooth Special Interest Group (SIG) that was set up by Ericsson, IBM, Intel, Nokia, and Toshiba in 1998 to develop and promote the Bluetooth wireless technology standards, enabling interoperability across a wide range of devices and applications (Keil, 2002). The Bluetooth SIG is now a global community of over 40,000 companies.

References

Adner, R. (2017). Ecosystem as Structure: An Actionable Construct for Strategy. *Journal of Management*, *43*(1), 39–58.

Adner, R., & Kapoor, R. (2010). Value Creation in Innovation Ecosystems: How the Structure of Technological Interdependence Affects Firm Performance in New Technology Generations. *Strategic Management Journal*, *31*(3), 306–333.

Barca, F. (2009). *An Agenda for a Reformed Cohesion Policy: A Place-Based Approach to Meeting European Union Challenges and Expectations*. (Independent Report requested by Commissioner Danuta Hübner). European Parliament. www.europarl.europa.eu/meetdocs/2009_2014/documents/regi/dv/barca_report_/barca_report_en.pdf

Barca, F., McCann, P., & Rodríguez-Pose, A. (2012). The Case for Regional Development Intervention: Place-Based Versus Place-Neutral Approaches. *Journal of Regional Science*, *52*(1), 134–152.

Beamish, P. W., & Lupton, N. C. (2016). Cooperative Strategies in International Business and Management: Reflections on the Past 50 Years and Future Directions. *Journal of World Business*, *51*(1), 163–175.

Bentley, G., & Pugalis, L. (2014). Shifting Paradigms: People-Centred Models, Active Regional Development, Space-Blind Policies and Place-Based Approaches. *Local Economy*, 29(4-5), 283–294.

Bjelland, O. M., & Wood, R. C. (2008). An Inside View of IBM's 'Innovation Jam'. *MIT Sloan Management Review*, 50(1), 32–40.

Boudreau, K. J. (2017). Platform Boundary Choices & Governance: Opening-Up While Still Coordinating and Orchestrating☆. In J. Furman, A. Gawer, B. S. Silverman, & S. Stern (Eds.), *Entrepreneurship, Innovation, and Platforms* (Vol. 37, pp. 227–297). Emerald Publishing Limited.

Bouncken, R. B., Gast, J., Kraus, S., & Bogers, M. (2015). Coopetition: A Systematic Review, Synthesis, and Future Research Directions. *Review of Managerial Science*, 9(3), 577–601.

Brandenburger, A. M., & Nalebuff, B. J. (1996). *Co-Opetition: 1. A Revolutionary Mindset That Combines Competition and Co-Operation; 2. The Game Theory Strategy That's Changing the Game of Business* (1st ed.). Doubleday.

Bristow, G., & Healy, A. (2014). Regional Resilience: An Agency Perspective. *Regional Studies*, 48(5), 923–935.

Burt, R. S. (1992). *Structural Holes: The Social Structure of Competition*. Harvard University Press.

Casadesus-Masanell, R., & Yoffie, D. B. (2007). Wintel: Cooperation and Conflict. *Management Science*, 53(4), 584–598.

Cennamo, C., & Santalo, J. (2013). Platform Competition: Strategic Trade-Offs in Platform Markets. *Strategic Management Journal*, 34(11), 1331–1350.

Chesbrough, H. W. (2003). *Open Innovation: The New Imperative for Creating and Profiting from Technology*. Harvard Business School Press.

Chesbrough, H. W., & Appleyard, M. M. (2007). Open Innovation and Strategy. *California Management Review*, 50(1), 57–76.

Chesbrough, H. W., & Bogers, M. (2014). Explicating Open Innovation: Clarifying an Emerging Paradigm for Understanding Innovation. In H. W. Chesbrough, W. Vanhaverbeke, & J. West (Eds.), *New Frontiers in Open Innovation* (pp. 3–28). Oxford University Press.

Cohen, W. M., & Levinthal, D. A. (1990). Absorptive Capacity: A New Perspective on Learning and Innovation. *Administrative Science Quarterly*, 35(1), 128–152.

Das, T. K., & Teng, B.-S. (2000). A Resource-Based Theory of Strategic Alliances. *Journal of Management*, 26(1), 31–61.

Das, T. K., & Teng, B.-S. (2001). Trust, Control, and Risk in Strategic Alliances: An Integrated Framework. *Organization Studies*, 22(2), 251–283.

Delgado, M., Porter, M. E., & Stern, S. (2014). Clusters, Convergence, and Economic Performance. *Research Policy*, 43(10), 1785–1799.

Dhanaraj, C., & Parkhe, A. (2006). Orchestrating Innovation Networks. *Academy of Management Review*, 31(3), 659–669.

Dittrich, K., & Duysters, G. (2007). Networking As a Means to Strategy Change: The Case of Open Innovation in Mobile Telephony. *Journal of Product Innovation Management*, *24*(6), 510–521.

Duranton, G., & Puga, D. (2004). Micro-Foundations of Urban Agglomeration Economies. In J. V. Henderson & J.-F. Thisse (Eds.), *Handbook of Regional and Urban Economics* (Vol. 4, pp. 2063–2117). Elsevier.

Dyer, J. H., & Nobeoka, K. (2000). Creating and Managing a High-Performance Knowledge-Sharing Network: The Toyota Case. *Strategic Management Journal*, *21*(3), 345–367.

Dyer, J. H., & Singh, H. (1998). The Relational View: Cooperative Strategy and Sources of Interorganizational Competitive Advantage. *The Academy of Management Review*, *23*(4), 660–679.

Dyer, J. H., Singh, H., & Hesterly, W. S. (2018). The Relational View Revisited: A Dynamic Perspective on Value Creation and Value Capture. *Strategic Management Journal*, *39*(12), 3140–3162.

Eisenmann, T., Parker, G. G., & Van Alstyne, M. W. (2006). Strategies for Two-Sided Markets. *Harvard Business Review*, *84*(10), 92–101.

Engel, J. S. (2014). *Global Clusters of Innovation: Entrepreneurial Engines of Economic Growth around the World*. Edward Elgar Publishing.

Engel, J. S. (2015). Global Clusters of Innovation: Lessons from Silicon Valley. *California Management Review*, *57*(2), 36–65.

Evans, D. S., & Schmalensee, R. (2016). *Matchmakers: The New Economics of Multisided Platforms*. Harvard Business Review Press.

Faems, D., Van Looy, B., & Debackere, K. (2005). Interorganizational Collaboration and Innovation: Toward a Portfolio Approach. *Journal of Product Innovation Management*, *22*(3), 238–250.

Gassmann, O., Enkel, E., & Chesbrough, H. (2010). The Future of Open Innovation. *R&D Management*, *40*(3), 213–221.

Gawer, A. (2014). Bridging Differing Perspectives on Technological Platforms: Toward an Integrative Framework. *Research Policy*, *43*(7), 1239–1249.

Gawer, A. (2021). Digital Platforms' Boundaries: The interplay of Firm Scope, Platform Sides, and Digital Interfaces. *Long Range Planning*, *54*(5), 102045.

Gawer, A., & Cusumano, M. A. (2014). Industry Platforms and Ecosystem Innovation. *Journal of Product Innovation Management*, *31*(3), 417–433.

Gnyawali, D. R., & Park, B.-J. R. (2011). Co-Opetition Between Giants: Collaboration with Competitors for Technological Innovation. *Research Policy*, *40*(5), 650–663.

Gomes-Casseres, B. (2003). Constellation Strategy: Managing Alliance Groups. *Ivey Business Journal*, *67*(5), 1–6.

Granovetter, M. S. (1973). The Strength of Weak Ties. *American Journal of Sociology*, *78*(6), 1360–1380.

Gulati, R. (1998). Alliances and Networks. *Strategic Management Journal*, *19*(4), 293–317.

Gulati, R., Nohria, N., & Zaheer, A. (2000). Strategic Networks. *Strategic Management Journal*, *21*(3), 203–215.

Gulati, R., Puranam, P., & Tushman, M. (2012). Meta-Organization Design: Rethinking Design in Interorganizational and Community Contexts. *Strategic Management Journal*, *33*(6), 571–586.

Hagiu, A., & Wright, J. (2015). Multi-Sided Platforms. *International Journal of Industrial Organization*, *43*, 162–174.

Harrigan, K. R. (1988). Joint Ventures and Competitive Strategy. *Strategic Management Journal*, 9(2), 141–158.

Huston, L., & Sakkab, N. Y. (2006). Connect and Develop: Inside Procter & Gamble's New Model for Innovation. *Harvard Business Review*, *84*(3), 58–66.

Iansiti, M., & Levien, R. (2004). Strategy as Ecology. *Harvard Business Review*, *82*(3), 68–78.

Inkpen, A. C. (2008). Knowledge Transfer and International Joint Ventures: The Case of NUMMI and General Motors. *Strategic Management Journal*, *29*(4), 447–453.

Jacobides, M. G., Cennamo, C., & Gawer, A. (2018). Towards a Theory of Ecosystems. *Strategic Management Journal*, *39*(8), 2255–2276.

Katz, M. L., & Shapiro, C. (1985). Network Externalities, Competition, and Compatibility. *The American Economic Review*, *75*(3), 424–440.

Keil, T. (2002). De-Facto Standardization Through Alliances—Lessons from Bluetooth. *Telecommunications Policy*, *26*(3), 205–213.

Ketels, C. (2013). Recent Research on Competitiveness and Clusters: What Are the Implications for Regional Policy? *Cambridge Journal of Regions, Economy and Society*, 6(2), 269–284.

Ketels, C. H. M., & Memedovic, O. (2008). From Clusters to Cluster-Based Economic Development. *International Journal of Technological Learning, Innovation and Development*, *1*(3), 375–392.

Kogut, B. (1988). Joint Ventures: Theoretical and Empirical Perspectives. *Strategic Management Journal*, 9(4), 319–332.

Laursen, K., & Salter, A. (2006). Open for Innovation: The Role of Openness in Explaining Innovation Performance among U.K. Manufacturing Firms. *Strategic Management Journal, 27*(2), 131–150.

Lavie, D. (2006). The Competitive Advantage of Interconnected Firms: An Extension of the Resource-Based View. *The Academy of Management Review, 31*(3), 638–658.

Link, A. N., & Scott, J. T. (2003a). The Growth of Research Triangle Park. *Small Business Economics, 20*(2), 167–175.

Link, A. N., & Scott, J. T. (2003b). U.S. Science Parks: The Diffusion of an Innovation and Its Effects on the Academic Missions of Universities. *International Journal of Industrial Organization, 21*(9), 1323–1356.

Link, A. N., & Scott, J. T. (2007). The Economics of University Research Parks. *Oxford Review of Economic Policy, 23*(4), 661–674.

Longhi, C. (1999). Networks, Collective Learning and Technology Development in Innovative High Technology Regions: The Case of Sophia-Antipolis. *Regional Studies, 33*(4), 333–342.

Luo, Y. (2007). Are Joint Venture Partners More Opportunistic in a More Volatile Environment? *Strategic Management Journal, 28*(1), 39–60.

Minguillo, D., Tijssen, R., & Thelwall, M. (2015). Do Science Parks Promote Research and Technology? A Scientometric Analysis of the UK. *Scientometrics, 102*(1), 701–725.

Moore, J. F. (1993). Predators and Prey: A New Ecology of Competition. *Harvard Business Review, 71*(3), 75–86.

Pålsson, C. M., & Gregersen, B. (2011). Biotechnology in Denmark and Sweden. In B. Göransson & C. M. Pålsson (Eds.), *Biotechnology and Innovation Systems: The Role of Public Policy*. Edward Elgar Publishing.

Parker, G., Van Alstyne, M., & Choudary, S. P. (2016). *Platform Revolution: How Networked Markets Are Transforming the Economy – and How to Make Them Work for You* (1st ed.). W.W. Norton & Company.

Pfeffer, J., & Salancik, G. R. (1978). *The External Control of Organizations: A Resource Dependence Perspective*. Harper & Row.

Pisano, G. P., & Teece, D. J. (2007). How to Capture Value from Innovation: Shaping Intellectual Property and Industry Architecture. *California Management Review, 50*(1), 278–296.

Porter, M. E. (1998). Clusters and the New Economics of Competition. *Harvard Business Review, 76*(6), 77–90.

Porter, M. E. (2000). Location, Competition, and Economic Development: Local Clusters in a Global Economy. *Economic Development Quarterly*, *14*(1), 15–34.

Powell, W. W., Koput, K. W., & Smith-Doerr, L. (1996). Interorganizational Collaboration and the Locus of Innovation: Networks of Learning in Biotechnology. *Administrative Science Quarterly*, *41*(1), 116–145.

Provan, K. G., Fish, A., & Sydow, J. (2007). Interorganizational Networks at the Network Level: A Review of the Empirical Literature on Whole Networks. *Journal of Management*, *33*(3), 479–516.

Provan, K. G., & Kenis, P. (2008). Modes of Network Governance: Structure, Management, and Effectiveness. *Journal of Public Administration Research and Theory*, *18*(2), 229–252.

Raza-Ullah, T., Bengtsson, M., & Kock, S. (2014). The Coopetition Paradox and Tension in Coopetition at Multiple Levels. *Industrial Marketing Management*, *43*(2), 189–198.

Ritala, P., Golnam, A., & Wegmann, A. (2014). Coopetition-Based Business Models: The Case of Amazon.com. *Industrial Marketing Management*, *43*(2), 236–249.

Ritala, P., & Hurmelinna-Laukkanen, P. (2013). Incremental and Radical Innovation in Coopetition—The Role of Absorptive Capacity and Appropriability. *Journal of Product Innovation Management*, *30*(1), 154–169.

Rochet, J.-C., & Tirole, J. (2003). Platform Competition in Two-Sided Markets. *Journal of the European Economic Association*, *1*(4), 990–1029.

Schreiner, M., Kale, P., & Corsten, D. (2009). What Really Is Alliance Management Capability and How Does It Impact Alliance Outcomes and Success? *Strategic Management Journal*, *30*(13), 1395–1419.

Segrestin, B. (2005). Partnering to Explore: The Renault–Nissan Alliance As a Forerunner of New Cooperative Patterns. *Research Policy*, *34*(5), 657–672.

Shapiro, C., & Varian, H. R. (1999). *Information Rules: A Strategic Guide to the Network Economy*. Harvard Business School Press.

Sölvell, Ö., Lindqvist, G., & Ketels, C. (2003). *The Cluster Initiative Greenbook*. Ivory Tower.

Storey, D. J., & Tether, B. S. (1998). Public Policy Measures to Support New Technology-Based Firms in the European Union. *Research Policy*, *26*(9), 1037–1057.

Tiwana, A. (2014). *Platform Ecosystems: Aligning Architecture, Governance, and Strategy*. Morgan Kaufmann.

Wong, K. W., & Bunnell, T. (2006). 'New Economy' Discourse and Spaces in Singapore: A Case Study of One-North. *Environment and Planning A: Economy and Space*, *38*(1), 69–83.

Zervas, G., Proserpio, D., & Byers, J. W. (2017). The Rise of the Sharing Economy: Estimating the Impact of Airbnb on the Hotel Industry. *Journal of Marketing Research*, *54*(5), 687–705.

8 Conquering Strategic Posture

8.1 Overview

8.1.1 Introduction

The conquering or colonizing strategic posture focuses on building a common vision, mobilizing resources, stakeholders, and inventive activities to create revolutionary change and establish new paradigms (Kotter, 1996). It uses collective action and visionary thinking to promote systemic change and create new realities (Senge, 1990). This chapter delves into the conquering posture's major qualities and four primary strategy approaches: visioning, strategic renewal, strategic roadmapping, and transitions.

8.1.2 Key Characteristics

The aim of the conquering posture is to drive radical change and establish new standards, practices, or markets that align with a transformative vision of the future (Hamel & Prahalad, 1994).

Like the crafting posture, this posture is rooted in the belief that the future is not to be passively accepted but actively shaped, but it differs in the extent of change that is possible, its audacious and transformative vision-based approach, and often involves taking higher levels of risk. It seeks to mobilize resources, stakeholders, and innovative efforts to create entirely new paradigms and disrupt existing systems (Hamel, 2000). Furthermore, it views the future as a space for significant, transformative opportunities that can be seized and shaped through deliberate actions today (Godet, 2000).

The conquering strategic posture takes a transformative perspective, moving beyond the plausibility-based multiple futures used in the coping approach to possibility-based multiple futures (Van der Heijden, 2005). Since plausibility

DOI: 10.4324/9781003684060-8

logic is based on our understanding of the present, it limits the possibilities that can be imagined and pursued. The transformative stance opens up the possibilities space by creating images of the future and mobilizing actors within the organization or ecosystem to cocreate the desired futures (Loorbach et al., 2017).

An appropriate analogy for the conquering posture is the envisioning of a future mobility system where cars not only travel the roads but also the skies, and then mobilizing car manufacturers, government agencies, media, policy tanks, and other relevant stakeholders on the journey to shape the future mobility landscape.

Key actors in this posture are visionaries who can inspire collective action and marshal the resources and alliances necessary to realize ambitious futures (Westley & Mintzberg, 1989).

8.1.3 Key Theoretical Perspectives

The conquering strategic posture draws from several key theoretical perspectives that emphasize leadership and the dynamics of transformative change. **Visionary leadership** is central to this posture, focusing on leaders' ability to articulate a compelling and inspiring vision for the future (Nanus, 1992; Westley & Mintzberg, 1989). **Transformational leadership** further supports the visionary posture by emphasizing leaders' role in inspiring and motivating their followers to exceed their own self-interests for the sake of the organization (Bass, 1985, 1990). **Transitions theory** complements these leadership perspectives by offering a framework for understanding and managing large-scale transformations within organizations and society (Loorbach et al., 2017). This theory addresses the complexities of shifting from one stable state to another, highlighting the role of strategic vision and leadership in guiding the transition process.

8.1.4 Limitations

The conquering strategic posture, while powerful in its ability to drive transformative change and shape new market realities, has several limitations. First, its emphasis on bold, visionary leadership can lead to an underestimation of the risks and challenges associated with this posture (Conger, 1990). This is because visionary leaders tend to be overconfident (Russo & Schoemaker, 1992) and overoptimistic (Lovallo & Kahneman, 2003) in their ability to shape the future. Additionally, the conquering posture's focus on long-term, transformative goals may come at the expense of short-term performance and profitability, creating tensions with stakeholders who prioritize immediate results (March, 1991).

Finally, the success of this posture heavily relies on the presence of visionary leadership and the ability to mobilize significant resources and stakeholder support, which may not always be available or sustainable in the long run (Kotter, 2001).

8.1.5 Conquering Strategy Approaches

As illustrated in Figure 8.1, the conquering strategy approaches can be arranged in a matrix consisting of two dimensions. The vertical axis comprises the required coordination with actors outside the focal entity. Two dimensions are present in the horizontal axis: the strategy process dimension and the paths to achieving the desired future.

In the vertical axis, the required coordination with actors outside focal entity dimension has two categories: high and low. The high category signifies that a high level of coordination with key external stakeholders is required to formulate the strategy, while low denotes that a low level of coordination with external stakeholders is required.

The horizontal strategy process dimension has two categories: single path and multiple paths. The single path focuses on a singular, well-defined route to reach the desired future state, while the multiple paths category involves exploring

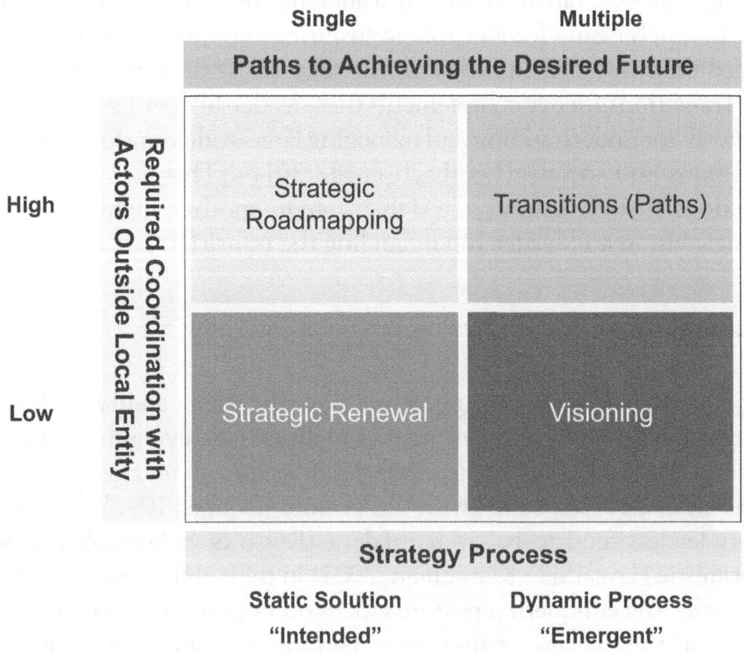

Figure 8.1 The Conquering Strategic Posture Matrix.

and pursuing various potential routes to achieve the desired future, acknowledging the complexity and unpredictability of the future. For the strategy process, the **static solution ("intended")** involves a predetermined and stable approach where the strategy is designed to achieve a specific, intended future state that maintains focus and robustness without regular adjustments. On the other hand, the **dynamic process ("emergent")** denotes that the strategy approach is adaptive and flexible, continuously evolving in response to changing circumstances and new information, leading to an emergent strategy.

As shown in the matrix, there are four key strategy approaches that can be used to achieve the conquer posture:

Strategic renewal (bottom-left quadrant): This strategy approach focuses on fundamentally reshaping the organization for a desired future through comprehensive and often radical changes in strategy and structure. Strategic renewal involves inherently altering an organization's strategy, structure, processes, and capabilities to achieve a desired future state (Agarwal & Helfat, 2009).

Strategic roadmapping (bottom-left quadrant): This strategy approach utilizes a structured visualization of strategic goals and timelines to anticipate and prepare for future challenges and opportunities (Phaal et al., 2004). It helps align resources, capabilities, and initiatives toward achieving the desired future by providing a clear and shared understanding of the organization's strategic direction (Phaal & Muller, 2009).

Transitions (paths) (bottom-left quadrant): This strategy approach entails achieving long-term sustainability goals through systemic changes, understanding the interconnectedness of technological, social, and cultural factors (Loorbach et al., 2017). It incorporates a participatory process of visioning, experimentation, and learning to guide transformative change across technological, organizational, economic, and cultural dimensions (Geels & Schot, 2010).

Visioning (bottom-left quadrant): This strategy approach emphasizes creating a desirable and transformative future state by leveraging collective imagination and bold leadership. Visioning is a process that involves developing a compelling, idealized image of the desired future state (Van der Helm, 2009). It leverages the power of collective imagination and bold leadership to inspire action toward realizing the vision (Nanus, 1992). Visioning often serves as the starting point for other conquering approaches, setting the direction for transformative change (McDowall & Eames, 2006).

Their key characteristics are contrasted in Table 8.1.

Table 8.1 Comparing the Conquering Strategies

Dimension	Visioning	Strategic Renewal	Strategic Roadmapping	Transitions
Aim	Create a desirable and transformative future state	Fundamentally transform the organization for a desired future	Aims to develop a structured visualization of an organization's strategic goals, objectives, and timelines.	Use the transitions to drive long-term, sustainable change in complex socio-technical systems.
Core Logic	Leveraging collective imagination and bold leadership	Aligning strategy with evolving context and opportunities	The roadmaps are "time-based pathways" from the current state to the future vision	Understanding interconnectedness of technological, social, and cultural factors
Assumptions	Future is shaped by collective action and visionary thinking	Alignment with the environment is necessary for competitiveness	Structured systems thinking and visual methods aid strategy formulation	Long-term processes across multiple levels are needed for socio-technical transitions
Strengths	Inspires action and drives transformative change	Creates new capabilities and competitive advantage through transformation	Provides clear understanding and alignment of strategic goals	Enhances mobilization and guides long-term sustainable development
Limitations	Requires high coordination with stakeholders	Requires significant investment and change management	Can be complex and require continuous updates	Long-term nature may face resistance and require sustained effort
Methods	• Backcasting • Scenario planning	• Strategic Transformation • Digital transformation • Corporate turnaround	• Technology roadmapping • Strategy roadmaps • Scenario-based roadmapping	• Multilevel perspective • Transition management • Three Horizons

8.2 Visioning

8.2.1 Aim

The visioning approach aims to create a preferred and transformative future state by developing a compelling, idealized vision that mobilizes stakeholders and resources to pursue a new reality (Johnson & Suskewicz, 2020; Van der Helm, 2009).

8.2.2 Core Logic

Visioning involves the development of an idealized and aspirational view of the future, leveraging collective imagination and strategic foresight. It emphasizes the power of possibility-based futures, enabling organizations to envision and work toward significant transformations (Van Der Steen, 2022). The process often includes normative or prospective scenarios that guide and shape strategic initiatives.

8.2.3 Key Elements

Normative scenarios: They are also referred to as prospective scenarios, strategic scenarios, policy-driven scenarios, or intervention-based scenarios. They explicitly incorporate norms, values, and desired outcomes into the exploration of possible futures. These scenarios are designed to describe probable or preferable futures based on specific policy interventions, strategies, or normative assumptions, laden and reflect the interests, goals, and preferences of the scenario developers (Van Notten et al., 2003).

Descriptive scenarios: They are also known as baseline cases, reference projections, or scenarios assuming no intervention – scenarios that explore possible futures without expressing explicit preferences or value judgments. They focus on what could happen, rather than what should happen (Van Notten et al., 2003).

Vision criteria: Criteria such as visionary, sustainable, systemic, coherent, plausible, tangible, relevant, nuanced, motivational, and shared help translate bold ideas into actionable strategies (Wiek & Iwaniec, 2014).

8.2.4 Applications and Examples

Visioning is effectively applied in various contexts where transformative change is needed. For example, sustainability initiatives often use visioning to create long-term goals that inspire collective action. Another use is corporate strategy development, where visionary leaders articulate future states that inspire organizational change. The CEO of Tesla, Elon Musk, believes that instead of only using analogy based on what is currently known, one should reason from fundamental principles to imagine what may be. Because of this, he was able to envision electric car possibilities that went beyond simply improving upon gas-powered cars (Stringham et al., 2015). Singapore's vision of becoming a "Smart Nation" was announced in December, 2014 by the prime minister and it aims to improve people lives and create innovative solution through the use of information and communication technologies (Hoe, 2016).

8.2.5 Challenges and Limitations

While visioning is powerful, it faces several challenges. It requires bold and inspirational leadership capable of articulating and sustaining a compelling vision (Bass, 1985, 1990). Additionally, transforming visionary ideas into practical applications involves navigating complex social, political, and economic landscapes. It demands high levels of coordination among diverse stakeholders, which can be challenging to manage (Grin & Grunwald, 2000). Visioning also needs to be adaptable, evolving in response to new information and changing circumstances (Mintzberg, 2007).

8.2.6 Strategy Methods

Several methods utilize visioning as their core approach. Backcasting starts with the desired future state and works backward to identify necessary steps and milestones needed to achieve the vision (Quist & Vergragt, 2006). The use of vision workshops is another approach used to engage stakeholders in cocreating a shared vision through collaborative workshops and strategic dialogues (Weisbord & Janoff, 2010).

8.2.6.1 Backcasting

Backcasting is a strategy method that begins by defining a desirable future state (prospective scenario) and then works backward to identify the necessary steps, policies, initiatives, and strategies to connect that future to the present (Robinson, 1990). This contrasts with traditional forecasting, which projects current trends forward to create a projective scenario (Dreborg, 1996). While projective scenarios look forward in time, prospective scenarios work backward from a future scenario (Van Der Steen, 2022).

The process of backcasting involves several stages. Initially, it requires the creation of a normative vision of the future, which is typically idealistic and transformative (Quist & Vergragt, 2006). This vision serves as a guiding star for the entire planning process. Subsequently, planners work backward to identify the strategic actions and pathways required to achieve this vision, considering both short-term and long-term objectives (Robinson et al., 2011). By focusing on the end goal, backcasting encourages innovative thinking and the exploration of alternative solutions that might be overlooked in conventional strategic planning approaches (Bibri, 2018).

An example of backcasting is Tesla's strategy since its founding in 2004, where the company has envisioned a future with widespread electric vehicle adoption and works backward to develop solutions addressing barriers and leveraging current opportunities (Kim & Srivastava, 2024).

8.2.6.2 *Vision Workshops*

Vision workshops are dynamic, collaborative methods designed to bring together diverse stakeholders to cocreate a shared vision of the future. These workshops leverage collective imagination, insights, and expertise to develop a compelling vision that guides organizational strategy and transformation (Stewart, 1993; Wilson, 1992).

At the heart of vision workshops is participatory planning (Bryson, 2018). By engaging stakeholders in the process, organizations can tap into a wealth of knowledge and creativity, ensuring that the resulting vision is both innovative and grounded in practical reality. This approach enhances the quality of the vision and strengthens buy-in and commitment from participants, which is crucial for successful implementation (Shipley & Michela, 2006).

Vision workshops are particularly valuable in fostering innovation within organizations. By creating a space where participants feel empowered to think creatively and challenge existing assumptions, these workshops can generate breakthrough ideas and novel solutions to complex problems.

An example of their application is NASA's "Vision for Space Exploration" initiative, which brought together various stakeholders to develop a long-term vision for space exploration, shaping the agency's strategic direction.

8.3 Strategic Renewal

8.3.1 Aim

The aim of the strategic renewal approach is to fundamentally reshape an organization to adapt to a changing environment or pursue new opportunities, ensuring long-term competitiveness and relevance. It does this by radically changing the strategy, structure, processes, and capabilities to reach a desired future state (Agarwal & Helfat, 2009).

8.3.2 Core Logic

Strategic renewal is based on the premise that to remain competitive and relevant in a dynamic business landscape, organizations must be willing to question and transform their core assumptions, purpose, business models, and competencies. It seeks to align an organization's strategy with its evolving context (Floyd & Lane, 2000).

8.3.3 Key Elements

Purposeful direction: Renewal is not merely a reactive adjustment but a deliberate process aimed at altering a firm's strategic trajectory and overcoming path dependency (Schmitt et al., 2018). This element reflects a proactive orientation wherein organizations formulate renewal strategies in anticipation of or in response to fundamental shifts in their environment (Nguyen et al., 2022).

Reconfiguration of capabilities and realignment of resources: Organizations usually need to modify their core competencies and business models to remain competitive. This includes developing dynamic capabilities and orchestrating internal and external resource flows to support innovation and adaptation (Schmitt et al., 2018; Volberda et al., 2001).

Multilevel and multi-actor process: Strategic renewal requires coordinated engagement across corporate, business unit, and frontline management levels. Rather than being confined to top-down directives, effective renewal strategies integrate bottom-up initiatives and cross-level knowledge flows, fostering coevolutionary learning within the firm (Schmitt et al., 2018; Volberda et al., 2001).

Contextual and temporal fit: Effective renewal strategies are those aligned with both the external environment and the firm's internal development stage. Organizations must time and pace their renewal initiatives to match environmental turbulence and organizational readiness, often shifting between different renewal modes as conditions evolve (Nguyen et al., 2022; Volberda et al., 2001).

8.3.4 Applications and Examples

Strategic renewal is evident in Nokia's transformation from a rubber and paper company to a telecommunications leader in the 1990s (Häikiö, 2002). Another example is LEGO's approach to undertaking many strategic transformations using the LEGO way (Jakobsen, 2023).

8.3.5 Challenges and Limitations

Implementing strategic renewal poses several challenges associate with most large-scale change strategies and initiatives. These challenges include managing resistance to change from employees and stakeholders who may feel threatened by the transformation (Kotter & Schlesinger, 2008). Moreover, effective change management processes, robust communication, training, and support are essential to managing these challenges (Jakobsen, 2023). Additionally, shifting organizational mindsets from a focus on the exploitation of current circumstances to the exploration of new futures requires letting go of past success formulas and embracing novel ways of thinking and working (Floyd & Lane, 2000).

8.3.6 Strategy Methods

Several methods utilize strategic renewal as their core approach. Strategic transformation involves a fundamental redesign of an organization's strategy, business model, structure, workforce, and operational practices (Faeste & Hemerling, 2016). Digital transformation is another method where organizations fundamentally reconfigure their business models, operations, and value creation processes by embedding digital technologies throughout all areas of the organization (Vial, 2019). Third, corporate turnaround is the process of reversing a firm's decline and restoring profitability and strategic stability, typically in response to severe performance or financial challenges (Hofer, 1980).

8.3.6.1 Strategic Transformation

Strategic transformation represents a comprehensive overhaul of an organization's strategy, business model, structure, human resources, and operational processes that can affect the entire enterprise or specific operational segments. This approach extends beyond gradual improvements to constitute a complete reimagining of business fundamentals, designed to deliver significant and sustainable performance enhancements and increased shareholder returns. In contrast to continuous improvement methodologies, which typically involve minor adjustments originated by frontline employees that gradually influence the broader organization, transformation initiatives encompass extensive, interconnected changes that are deliberately orchestrated by executive leadership (Faeste & Hemerling, 2016).

While various transformation methodologies exist, most can be illustrated by McKinsey's 5A framework. McKinsey outlines five stages for performance and health during a transformation. The initial stage, Aspire, involves defining the desired future and setting ambitious goals. Next, Assess evaluates the organization's current capabilities and readiness. In the Architect phase, specific initiatives and strategies are developed. Act focuses on the execution and effective management of the change process. Finally, Advance emphasizes continuous monitoring, adjustments, and embedding a culture of ongoing improvement to sustain the transformation's gains (Keller & Price, 2011).

Strategic transformation has been successfully applied in various industries and contexts. One example is the LEGO Group, which used its transformation method called the LEGO Way of Change to move from financial crisis to market leadership under CEO Jørgen Vig Knudstorp (Jakobsen, 2023). Another example is Adobe, the multinational software company that executed a successful strategic transformation from a traditional software licensing model to a subscription-based cloud computing model. Adobe launched Adobe Creative Cloud, a subscription-based service providing access to its suite of innovative tools and services via the cloud. This strategic shift transformed Adobe's revenue model from one-time sales to recurring subscription revenues and enhanced customer value by providing continuous updates, new features, and seamless collaboration capabilities (Anthony et al., 2017).

8.3.6.2 Digital Transformation

Digital transformation is a strategic process through which organizations fundamentally reshape their business models, operations, and value creation mechanisms by integrating digital technologies across all functions (Vial, 2019). It extends beyond simple digitization or the adoption of new IT systems, it entails rethinking organizational structures, capabilities, and cultures to leverage digital innovation for sustained competitiveness and growth (Bharadwaj et al., 2013). Digital transformation is as much about leadership and strategic vision as it is about technology; it requires aligning digital initiatives with long-term business goals and fostering an organizational mindset receptive to continuous change and innovation (Kane et al., 2015).

The journey of digital transformation typically unfolds across several distinct phases. Initially, organizations digitize existing processes and customer interfaces to improve efficiency and accessibility. This is followed by a phase of integration, where digital technologies connect previously siloed systems, functions, and data sources, enabling more agile and informed decision-making (Sebastian et al., 2017). The final stage involves strategic transformation, in which the organization reimagines its value proposition, customer relationships, and operating model, often leading to the creation of entirely new revenue streams, business ecosystems, or market spaces (Westerman et al., 2014). Successful digital transformation hinges on several critical enablers: visionary leadership, a coherent digital strategy, enterprise-wide collaboration, technological flexibility, and the capability to navigate organizational change and overcome cultural resistance (Fitzgerald et al., 2013).

DBS Bank's digital transformation focused on building a robust digital platform and operational backbone to enable agility and innovation. By synchronizing people, processes, data, and technology, DBS successfully delivered innovative customer solutions and became a leading example of digital reinvention among established banks (Ross et al., 2019). Another example is Nike's digital transformation, which involved creating the Nike Digital Sport unit to drive innovation in digital products and customer engagement. Through initiatives like Nike+, personalized online ordering, and digital tools for design and manufacturing, Nike improved operational efficiency, deepened customer relationships, and positioned itself as an integral part of athletes' lives (Westerman et al., 2014).

8.3.6.3 Corporate Turnaround

Corporate turnaround refers to the process of reversing a firm's performance decline and restoring it to a path of sustained profitability and strategic health. It typically applies to firms facing serious threats to their survival due to prolonged poor performance, financial distress, or competitive disadvantage (Hofer, 1980). Turnaround strategies are distinct from routine performance improvement initiatives; they are comprehensive efforts to stop decline and reposition the firm for viability. As Hopkins (2008) notes, the success of such strategies depends on correctly diagnosing the root cause of the firm's problems, be it operational inefficiency, strategic misalignment, or external shocks, and selecting a strategy consistent with that diagnosis. Barker III and Duhaime (1997) further emphasize that strategic reorientation, rather than mere retrenchment, is often essential for recovery when decline stems from a weak strategic position.

The turnaround process typically unfolds in stages. Hofer (1980) distinguishes between strategic turnarounds, which involve fundamental changes to a firm's competitive positioning (e.g., market repositioning, new product strategies), and operating turnarounds, which focus on short-term performance improvements (e.g., cost reduction, asset downsizing, or revenue recovery). Barker III and Duhaime (1997) offer a contingency framework suggesting that the extent of strategic change required varies with the nature and severity of the decline. Firms facing industry downturns may succeed through efficiency improvements and retrenchment, while those with firm-specific strategic weaknesses often require more radical strategic reorientation.

Several examples illustrate the application of corporate turnaround strategies. One of the classic cases discussed by Hofer (1980) is American Motors Corporation, which pursued cost-cutting, product simplification, and aggressive marketing to recover from near collapse in the 1950s. Another example is IBM's turnaround in the 1990s under CEO Lou Gerstner, which involved shifting from a hardware-centric business to a services and solutions firm, illustrating a successful strategic reorientation in response to competitive decline (Gerstner, 2002).

8.4 Strategic Roadmapping

8.4.1 Aim

Strategic roadmapping aims to develop a structured visualization of an organization's strategic goals, objectives, and timelines, enabling anticipation and preparation for future challenges and opportunities while aligning resources, capabilities, and initiatives toward achieving those goals (Phaal et al., 2004; Phaal & Muller, 2009).

8.4.2 Core Logic

At its core, strategic roadmapping is "[a] process that mobilizes structured systems thinking, visual methods (e.g. roadmap 'canvas') and participative approaches to address organizational challenges and opportunities, supporting communication and alignment for strategic planning and innovation management within and between organizations at firm and sector levels." (Park et al., 2020, p. 2). The roadmaps are "time-based pathways" from the current state to the future vision (Schimpf et al., 2023, p. 3).

8.4.3 Key Elements

Framework structure: The roadmap typically features a horizontal, time-based axis that encompasses past, short-, medium-, and long-term horizons, including the vision, and a vertical axis representing perspectives or dimensions relevant to the roadmap's focal point (Phaal et al., 2009).

Alignment and integration: Roadmaps align different perspectives across a broad time range, facilitating the exploration of short-term initiatives and long-term market trends (Kerr & Phaal, 2015).

Normative and action-oriented: Unlike descriptive scenarios and forecasts, roadmaps are both normative and action-oriented, providing a vision of a desirable future and a pathway of actions toward it (McDowall & Eames, 2006).

Workshop-led process: Although techniques like Delphi, Scenario Planning, or computer-based methods can facilitate the roadmapping process, the workshop-led approach that engages cross-functional teams with members from various organizational levels remains the most prevalent (Vatananan & Gerdsri, 2012).

8.4.4 Applications and Examples

Strategic roadmapping is used across various industries to align corporate, sector, or national strategies with anticipated future developments. For instance, in the technology sector, Honeywell has made roadmapping a key part of its annual strategic and technology planning, integrating both functional and strategic initiatives (Whalen, 2007). Similarly, in the electronics industry, Philips Electronics uses roadmapping to integrate business and technology strategies, enhance cross-functional communication, and improve the early stages of the product creation process by aligning product and technology development over a five-year period (Groenveld, 1997).

8.4.5 Challenges and Limitations

A recently published work on the challenges of roadmapping highlighted several challenges (Siebelink et al., 2021). First, developing a high-quality roadmap requires considerable effort, time, and resources and analytic, strategic, creative, and visualization skills. These requirements are usually lacking in many organizations. Second, there is a tension between short- and long-term orientations. They may suffer from myopia (focusing too much on short-term gains) or hyperopia (focusing too much on long-term goals) to the detriment of overall performance. Third, effective roadmapping requires integrating insights from various functional disciplines, such as technology, marketing, finance, human resources, and information technology. This integration is often lacking, leading to fragmented strategies.

8.4.6 Strategy Methods

There are many roadmapping methods. In a recent review, researchers identified seven roadmapping schools that are complementary and combinable (Park et al., 2020). We describe here three methods. First, strategy roadmaps are described. They focus on corporate strategy through visual representations that align strategic goals with actions and timelines (Phaal & Muller, 2009). Technology roadmapping (TRM) focuses on aligning technological developments with business goals (Phaal et al., 2004). Lastly, scenario-based roadmapping combines scenario planning with roadmapping to address multiple potential futures (Saritas & Aylen, 2010).

8.4.6.1 Technology Roadmapping

TRM is a method designed to support strategy formulation across market, product, technology development, and investments over the planning horizon (Phaal et al., 2004). It helps organizations identify, evaluate, and choose between alternative technology development paths to meet long-term strategic goals and visions (Vatananan & Gerdsri, 2012). TRM can be applied at two levels: organizational, where it graphically explores and communicates the relationships between markets, products, and technologies over time, and industry, where it involves multiple organizations focusing on shared needs (Chakraborty et al., 2022).

One of the key benefits of TRM is its ability to foster communication and collaboration among diverse stakeholders, such as R&D, marketing, sales, and strategic planning (Kerr et al., 2012). By providing a common language and framework for discussing technology-related issues, TRM helps break down silos and promote cross-functional integration. Additionally, it supports strategic decision-making by providing a structured approach for evaluating and prioritizing technology investments based on their alignment with business goals and market needs (Cosner et al., 2007).

TRM has been successfully applied at the corporate and industry levels (Chakraborty et al., 2022). At the corporate level, Motorola, a major player in the semiconductor industry, uses TRM roadmapping as a common process across the company to create, build, and share technology visions, product plans, and business strategies in a collaborative digital environment (Richey & Grinnell, 2004). In the automotive industry, General Motors uses TRM as a key visual tool in its technology management process to prioritize projects, eliminate duplication, improve communications, and link technology readiness with vehicle product plans (Grossman, 2004). Similarly, Samsung has employed TRM to guide its product development efforts in the highly competitive smartphone market, enabling the company to maintain its technological leadership and market share (Lee et al., 2009).

At the industry level, many national and international initiatives have created TRMs to mobilize industry players to achieve their strategic visions. This is illustrated by the Korea Institute of Energy Research utilizing TRM to establish a long-term strategic energy technology roadmap for Korea from 2006 to 2015 (Lee et al., 2009). This provided direction for the country's national energy technology development and policy by focusing on core technologies in three major sectors. The EU serves as another example, using TRM through the BATTERY 2030+ initiative to invent sustainable, high-performance batteries. It brought together stakeholders across academia, industry, and research institutions to address long-term research directions and support the European Green Deal and the Strategic Energy Technology Plan (SET Plan) (Edström, 2020).

8.4.6.2 *Strategy Roadmaps*

Strategy roadmaps build upon the traditional TRM approach by incorporating additional strategic elements and perspectives (Phaal et al., 2010). The multiple perspectives they consider include market trends, customer needs, competitive landscape, and internal capabilities, integrating these to form a coherent and actionable plan. By providing a structured visual framework for aligning these perspectives across different time horizons, they help organizations better communicate their strategic vision, goals, and plans and enable them to take better resource allocation decisions (Phaal & Muller, 2009). Furthermore, strategy roadmaps help organizations anticipate and prepare for future challenges and opportunities, while ensuring that short-term actions support long-term goals (Phaal & Muller, 2009).

According to the Cambridge practical school (Phaal et al., 2007), the strategy roadmapping process involves six steps: planning the roadmapping process, developing a "strategic landscape", identifying and prioritizing strategic opportunities, exploring priority opportunities then presenting and discussing "first-cut" roadmaps, reviewing opportunities, agreeing on the way forward and actions, and, lastly, organizing and reviewing the progress. This flexible process is typically facilitated through collaborative workshops that bring together cross-functional teams to share knowledge, generate ideas, and build consensus around the organization's strategic direction (Kerr et al., 2012).

Strategy roadmaps have been successfully applied in various industries and contexts. One example is the Lego Group's use of roadmapping to build a foundation for a more integrative and cross-functional approach to driving strategic innovation (Kerr et al., 2019).

8.4.6.3 Scenario-Driven Roadmapping

Scenario-driven roadmapping is a method that combines the benefits of scenario planning and strategic roadmapping to help organizations navigate uncertain futures (Hussain et al., 2017). By developing multiple scenarios and corresponding roadmaps, organizations adopt a systematic approach that goes beyond merely listing trends and drivers. Through this method, they obtain a deeper understanding of and better alignment with future uncertainties. This helps overcome the limitations of the individual methods of scenario planning and roadmapping, equipping organizations to explore alternative paths to achieve their strategic goals and make more informed decisions (Strauss & Radnor, 2004). It has been successfully applied in the UK National Health Service to develop the RFID technology adoption roadmap (Hussain et al., 2017).

The scenario-driven roadmapping process involves two phases. In the first phase, plausible scenarios are developed. Subsequently, the second phase deploys these scenarios as a foundation in the construction of roadmaps. A key step here is to identify the "flex points" that would signal transitions along specific pathways in the roadmap (Hussain et al., 2017). The purpose of flex points is to allow for adaptability to fit with various scenarios. Throughout the process, it is important to engage stakeholders to foster shared understanding and consensus, ensuring the roadmap remains relevant and useful over time (Hussain et al., 2017).

8.5 Transitions Strategy Approach

8.5.1 Aim

Organizations and governments use the transitions strategy approach to drive long-term, sustainable change in complex socio-technical systems. Socio-technical systems consist of networks of actors, institutions, material artifacts, and knowledge (Geels, 2004; Markard, 2011), and understanding these interconnected elements is essential for driving sustainable transformations.

8.5.2 Core Logic

This approach, rooted in the field of sustainability transitions, recognizes the interconnectedness of technological, social, and cultural factors in shaping the future (Loorbach et al., 2017). By understanding and leveraging these dynamics, the transitions approach enables strategic interventions that can guide systems toward a strategic vision or destination.

8.5.3 Key Elements

There are four common concepts in the transition approach (Grin et al., 2010):

Coevolution: Refers to the mutual influence and reinforcement between different societal subsystems (economic, cultural, technological, ecological, and institutional) during a transition. It helps make sense of transition dynamics and informs management approaches (Kemp et al., 2007).

Multilevel perspective (MLP): Regards transitions as interactions between three functional levels: niche experiments (innovative practices), regime (existing structures), and landscape (long-term exogenous trends). This perspective aids in depicting and potentially influencing transitions (Geels, 2005).

Multi-phase: Describes transitions as a sequence of four phases: predevelopment, take-off, acceleration, and stabilization. While not strictly predictive, this concept helps recognize transition stages and guide intervention efforts (Rotmans et al., 2001).

Codesign and Learning: Emphasizes the importance of interactive knowledge development involving multiple stakeholders through social learning. This process aims to reframe perspectives and find shared problem perceptions and sustainable solutions (Grin & Loeber, 2007).

Other elements include:

Visioning: Visioning is integral to transitions, as it helps create a compelling image of the future that can guide the process of change (Van der Helm, 2009).

Pathways: Pathways involve exploring and pursuing various routes to achieve the desired future, recognizing the complexity and unpredictability of the process (Sharpe et al., 2016).

Long-term, systemic, and fundamental change: Transitions involve achieving long-term visions or sustainability goals through systemic, fundamental changes that call for understanding the interconnectedness of technological, social, and cultural factors (Geels & Schot, 2010).

Guidance and governance: These play a pivotal role in directing change and fostering collaboration. For instance, the goal to achieve climate neutrality by 2050 is set within the EU's Green Deal, a policy framework designed for this purpose (Muiderman et al., 2020).

Participatory and adaptive processes: Transitions require participatory processes involving diverse stakeholders to cocreate the desired future (Loorbach et al., 2017).

8.5.4 Applications and Examples

The transitions approach has been applied in various domains, including energy (Verbong & Geels, 2007), transportation (Geels, 2005), health (Sharpe, 2020), education (Leicester et al., 2013), and urban sustainability (Loorbach & Wijsman, 2013). An example of a successful sustainability transition is the German Energiewende. This long-term energy and climate strategy involves a fundamental shift from a fossil fuel-based energy system to one centered on renewable energy sources, aiming to reduce greenhouse gas emissions and phase out nuclear power. The Energiewende has been driven by a combination of government policies, technological innovations, and changes in social norms and behaviours, illustrating the multi-dimensional nature of sustainability transitions (Geels et al., 2016).

8.5.5 Challenges and Limitations

The transitions approach offers a valuable framework, but it is not without its challenges. The interconnectedness of socio-technical systems means that changes in one area can have unexpected ripple effects on others (Markard et al., 2012). Moreover, aligning short-term actions with long-term goals is difficult, as the benefits of sustainability transitions may not be immediately apparent or evenly distributed (Loorbach et al., 2017). This issue is exacerbated when managing complex multi-stakeholder processes, as it requires coordinating among a wide range of actors with diverse and often conflicting interests and priorities (Köhler et al., 2019).

8.5.6 Strategy Methods

There are several strategy methods that utilize the logic of transitions. The MLP highlights the interplay between niche innovations, socio-technical regimes, and broader landscape developments (Geels, 2011). Transition management (TM) is a key governance framework that offers a prescriptive, complexity-based approach to steering long-term change (Loorbach, 2010). The three horizons (3H) framework is another valuable tool within the transitions approach that helps organizations and governments navigate the complex dynamics of change, taking into account the current dominant system, emerging innovations, and desired future states (Sharpe et al., 2016).

8.5.6.1 Multilevel Perspective

The MLP is a widely used framework in transitions research that provides a structured approach to analyzing the complex dynamics of socio-technical systems change (Geels, 2002, 2004, 2011). The MLP distinguishes between three interrelated levels: niches, socio-technical regimes, and landscape developments.

Niches are protected spaces for radical innovations that challenge the status quo, often emerging from entrepreneurs, startups, and grassroots initiatives focused on sustainability. Examples include renewable energy technologies and sharing economy platforms. Socio-technical regimes are the dominant ways of fulfilling societal functions, stabilized by rules, institutions, infrastructures, and actor networks, leading to resistance to change. Examples include the fossil fuel-based energy system and industrialized food production. Finally, landscape developments are external factors that pressure regimes and create opportunities for niche innovations, such as climate change, digitalization, and the COVID-19 pandemic.

The MLP posits that transitions occur through the alignment of developments at all three levels (Geels, 2005). Niche innovations build up internal momentum, taking advantage of landscape pressures and destabilization of the regime. As niche innovations mature and gain traction, they can break through and reconfigure the regime, leading to a new sustainable equilibrium (Geels & Schot, 2007).

Recent examples of the use of MLP can be found in the UK's ongoing low-carbon transitions across the electricity, mobility, and heat sectors (Geels & Turnheim, 2022). In the electricity sector, a preference exists for large-scale wind and photovoltaic (PV) systems over smaller solutions; in the mobility sector, there has been a rise of electric vehicles driven by declining battery costs, and in the heat sector, there is a transition from traditional to sustainable heating technologies (Geels & Turnheim, 2022).

The MLP provides a valuable framework for analyzing the complex dynamics of transitions and identifying opportunities for strategic interventions (Geels, 2011). However, the MLP also has its limitations and critiques (Geels, 2011). There are three main leveled against MLP: (1) ambiguity in empirically applying the conceptual levels of niche, regime, and landscape; (2) an overly functionalistic view of regime transformation that neglects agency and context; and (3) overemphasis on technological niches as the primary driver of regime change at the expense of top-down landscape influences or direct regime-level changes (Smith et al., 2010). Moreover, MLP was critiqued for overemphasizing stability and incremental change, insufficiently addressing power dynamics and political processes, and simplifying the role of agency by neglecting the complexity and diversity of actor motivations and interactions in sustainability transitions (Loorbach et al., 2017).

8.5.6.2 Transition Management

TM is a policy-directed governance method prescribing a participatory process of visioning, experimentation, and learning to guide sustainability transitions (Loorbach, 2010; Rotmans et al., 2001). This method emphasizes the development of transition arenas, where diverse stakeholders collaborate to develop shared visions, transition pathways, and experiments to test innovative solutions (Rotmans & Loorbach, 2009).

TM facilitates and accelerates sustainability transitions through a process that consists of four main nested phases: strategic, tactical, operational, and reflexive. The strategic phase focuses on developing long-term visions, setting collective goals, and engaging in strategic discussions to shape the overall direction of societal transitions. The tactical phase focuses on creating the necessary structures, regulations, and networks to support these long-term goals, involving mid-term planning and coordination among various actors and institutions. The operational phase is where concrete experiments and innovations are implemented, often on a short-term basis, to test new ideas and practices that align with the strategic vision. Finally, the reflexive phase involves continuous monitoring, evaluation, and learning from these experiments and actions, ensuring that insights are integrated back into the strategic and tactical planning processes to adapt and refine the TM approach (Loorbach, 2010).

At the national level, an example of TM is the managed transition of the waste management subsystem in the Netherlands from uncontrolled landfilling to a structured system of recycling, incineration, and controlled landfilling (Kemp, 2007). At the industry level, the Dutch Ministry of Economic Affairs implemented TM to guide the energy transition in the Netherlands toward a more sustainable energy system (Kern & Smith, 2008). At the corporate level, ESHA Group, a producer of bituminous roofing products, used TM to initiate a "roof transition" by setting up a transition arena (the Earth Recovery Open Platform) to develop a new paradigm focused on transforming roofs to contribute to sustainability. A variety of stakeholders were involved in co-developing experiments and changing business practices in the roofing sector (Loorbach & Rotmans, 2010).

8.5.6.3 Three Horizons

The 3H method helps organizations navigate transitions by considering three distinct horizons: the current dominant system (Horizon 1), emerging innovations (Horizon 2), and desired future states (Horizon 3) (Sharpe, 2020; Sharpe et al., 2016). This method provides a framework for understanding and managing the complex interplay between short-term operational demands, medium-term innovation opportunities, and long-term transformative change (Curry & Hodgson, 2008). By considering these 3H simultaneously, organizations can develop strategies that balance the need for continuity and stability with the imperative for adaptation and transformation (Sharpe & Hodgson, 2019).

Horizon 1 represents the current dominant system, which is often characterized by established technologies, business models, and institutional structures (Sharpe et al., 2016). While Horizon 1 provides the foundation for current success, it may also face increasing challenges and risks as external conditions change (Curry & Hodgson, 2008). Horizon 2 represents emerging innovations that have the potential to disrupt the dominant system and create new opportunities for growth and value creation (Sharpe, 2020). These innovations may be technological, social, or organizational in nature and often require experimentation, learning, and adaptation to realize their full potential (Sharpe & Hodgson, 2019). Horizon 3 represents desired future states that align with long-term goals and aspirations, such as sustainability, resilience, or social justice (Sharpe et al., 2016). While Horizon 3 may seem distant and uncertain, it provides a guiding vision and direction for strategic decision-making and innovation efforts (Curry & Hodgson, 2008).

The 3H framework has been applied in various contexts. The former UK Government's Office for Science & Technology Foresight Unit used 3H to explore how science and technology could enhance infrastructure over the next 50 years to meet the changing demands for UK transport (Sharpe & Hodgson, 2006). In another example, the Nordic Center for Sustainable Healthcare, in collaboration with a diverse group of stakeholders, including health industries, health providers, managing authorities, universities and research centers, clusters, NGOs, and healthcare networks, used 3H to structure and integrate multi-stakeholder perspectives on sustainable healthcare. The output was three scenarios: sustaining innovation, disruptive innovation, and transformative innovation, which identified key drivers and strategies for the transition toward desirable futures (Pereno & Eriksson, 2020).

References

Agarwal, R., & Helfat, C. E. (2009). Strategic Renewal of Organizations. *Organization Science*, *20*(2), 281–293.

Anthony, S. D., Clark, G. W., & Johnson, M. W. (2017). *Dual Transformation: How to Reposition Today's Business While Creating the Future*. Harvard Business Review Press.

Barker III, V. L., & Duhaime, I. M. (1997). Strategic Change in the Turnaround Process: Theory and Empirical Evidence. *Strategic Management Journal*, *18*(1), 13–38.

Bass, B. M. (1985). *Leadership and Performance Beyond Expectations*. Free Press.

Bass, B. M. (1990). From transactional to transformational Leadership: Learning to Share the Vision. *Organizational Dynamics*, *18*(3), 19–31.

Bharadwaj, A., El Sawy, O. A., Pavlou, P. A., & Venkatraman, N. V. (2013). Digital Business Strategy: Toward a Next Generation of Insights. *MIS Quarterly*, *37*(2), 471–482.

Bibri, S. E. (2018). Backcasting in Futures Studies: A Synthesized Scholarly and Planning Approach to Strategic Smart Sustainable City Development. *European Journal of Futures Research*, 6(1), 13.

Bryson, J. M. (2018). *Strategic Planning for Public and Nonprofit Organizations: A Guide to Strengthening and Sustaining Organizational Achievement* (5th ed.). John Wiley & Sons.

Chakraborty, S., Nijssen, E. J., & Valkenburg, R. (2022). A Systematic Review of Industry-Level Applications of Technology Roadmapping: Evaluation and Design Propositions for Roadmapping Practitioners. *Technological Forecasting and Social Change*, *179*, 121141.

Conger, J. A. (1990). The Dark Side of Leadership. *Organizational Dynamics*, *19*(2), 44–55.

Cosner, R. R., Hynds, E. J., Fusfeld, A. R., Loweth, C. V., Scouten, C., & Albright, R. (2007). Integrating Roadmapping into Technical Planning. *Research Technology Management*, *50*(6), 31–48.

Curry, A., & Hodgson, A. (2008). Seeing in Multiple Horizons: Connecting Futures to Strategy. *Journal of Futures Studies*, *13*(1), 1–20.

Dreborg, K. H. (1996). Essence of Backcasting. *Futures*, *28*(9), 813–828.

Edström, K. (2020). *Battery 2030+ Roadmap*.

Faeste, L., & Hemerling, J. (2016). *Transformation: Delivering and Sustaining Breakthrough Performance*. Boston Consulting Group.

Fitzgerald, M., Kruschwitz, N., Bonnet, D., & Welch, M. (2013). Embracing Digital Technology: A New Strategic Imperative. *MIT Sloan Management Review*, *55*(2), 1–12.

Floyd, S. W., & Lane, P. J. (2000). Strategizing Throughout the Organization: Managing Role Conflict in Strategic Renewal. *Academy of Management Review*, *25*(1), 154–177.

Geels, F. W. (2002). Technological Transitions As Evolutionary Reconfiguration Processes: A Multi-Level Perspective and a Case-Study. *Research Policy*, *31*(8), 1257–1274.

Geels, F. W. (2004). From Sectoral Systems of Innovation to Socio-Technical Systems: Insights About Dynamics and Change from Sociology and Institutional Theory. *Research Policy*, 33(6-7), 897–920.

Geels, F. W. (2005). *Technological Transitions And System Innovations: A Co-Evolutionary and Socio-Technical Analysis*. Edward Elgar Publishing.

Geels, F. W. (2011). The Multi-Level Perspective on Sustainability Transitions: Responses to Seven Criticisms. *Environmental Innovation and Societal Transitions*, *1*(1), 24–40.

Geels, F. W., Kern, F., Fuchs, G., Hinderer, N., Kungl, G., Mylan, J., Neukirch, M., & Wassermann, S. (2016). The Enactment of Socio-Technical Transition Pathways: A Reformulated Typology and a Comparative Multi-Level Analysis of the German and UK Low-Carbon Electricity Transitions (1990–2014). *Research Policy*, 45(4), 896–913.

Geels, F. W., & Schot, J. (2007). Typology of Sociotechnical Transition Pathways. *Research Policy*, 36(3), 399–417.

Geels, F. W., & Schot, J. (2010). The Dynamics of Transitions: A Socio-Technical Perspective. In J. Grin, J. Rotmans, & J. Schot (Eds.), *Transitions to Sustainable Development: New Directions in the Study of Long Term Transformative Change* (1st ed., pp. 11–101). Routledge.

Geels, F. W., & Turnheim, B. (2022). *The Great Reconfiguration: A Socio-Technical Analysis of Low-Carbon Transitions in UK Electricity, Heat, and Mobility Systems*. Cambridge University Press.

Gerstner, L. V. (2002). *Who Says Elephants Can't Dance? Inside IBM's Historic Turnaround*. HarperCollins Publishers.

Godet, M. (2000). The Art of Scenarios and Strategic Planning: Tools and Pitfalls. *Technological Forecasting and Social Change*, *65*(1), 3–22.

Grin, J., & Grunwald, A. (Eds.). (2000). *Vision Assessment: Shaping Technology in 21st Century Society*. Springer.

Grin, J., & Loeber, A. (2007). Theories of Policy Learning: Agency, Structure, and Change. In F. Fischer, G. J. Miller, & M. S. Sidney (Eds.), *Handbook of Public Policy Analysis: Theory, Politics, and Methods* (1st ed., pp. 201–222). CRC Press.

Grin, J., Rotmans, J., & Schot, J. (2010). From Persistent Problems to System Innovations and Transitions. In J. Grin, J. Rotmans, & J. Schot (Eds.), *Transitions to Sustainable Development: New Directions in the Study of Long Term Transformative Change* (1st ed., pp. 1–10). Routledge.

Groenveld, P. (1997). Roadmapping Integrates Business and Technology. *Research Technology Management*, *40*(5), 48–55.

Grossman, D. S. (2004). Putting Technology on the Road. *Research-Technology Management*, *47*(2), 41–46.

Häikiö, M. (2002). *Nokia: The Inside Story*. Financial Times.

Hamel, G. (2000). *Leading the Revolution*. Harvard Business School Press.

Hamel, G., & Prahalad, C. K. (1994). *Competing for the Future*. Harvard Business School Press.

Hoe, S. L. (2016). Defining a Smart Nation: The Case of Singapore. *Journal of Information, Communication and Ethics in Society*, *14*(4), 323–333.

Hofer, C. W. (1980). Turnaround Strategies. *Journal of Business Strategy*, *1*(1), 19–31.

Hopkins, D. H. (2008). Successful Turnaround Strategies. *Strategic Direction*, *24*(8), 3–5.

Hussain, M., Tapinos, E., & Knight, L. (2017). Scenario-Driven Roadmapping for Technology Foresight. *Technological Forecasting and Social Change*, *124*, 160–177.

Jakobsen, G. (2023). *Leading Transformations: Using the LEGO® Way of Change to Drive Transformations Effectively and Successfully* (1st ed.). Routledge.

Johnson, M. W., & Suskewicz, J. (2020). *Lead from the Future: How to Turn Visionary Thinking Into Breakthrough Growth*. Harvard Business Review Press.

Kane, G. C., Palmer, D., Phillips, A. N., Kiron, D., & Buckley, N. (2015). *Strategy, not Technology, Drives Digital Transformation*. MIT Sloan Management Review.

Keller, S., & Price, C. (2011). *Beyond Performance: How Great Organizations Build Ultimate Competitive Advantage*. John Wiley & Sons.

Kemp, R. (2007). An Example of a "Managed Transition": The Transformation of the Waste Management Subsystem in the Netherlands (1960–2000). In M. Lehmann-Waffenschmidt (Ed.), *Innovations Towards Sustainability: Conditions and Consequences* (pp. 87–94). Physica-Verlag HD.

Kemp, R., Loorbach, D., & Rotmans, J. (2007). Transition Management As a Model for Managing Processes of Co-evolution Towards Sustainable Development. *International Journal of Sustainable Development & World Ecology*, *14*(1), 78–91.

Kern, F., & Smith, A. (2008). Restructuring Energy Systems for Sustainability? Energy Transition Policy in the Netherlands. *Energy Policy*, *36*(11), 4093–4103.

Kerr, C., & Phaal, R. (2015). Visualizing Roadmaps: A Design-Driven Approach. *Research-Technology Management*, *58*(4), 45–54.

Kerr, C., Phaal, R., & Probert, D. (2012). Cogitate, Articulate, Communicate: The Psychosocial Reality of Technology Roadmapping and Roadmaps. *R&D Management*, *42*(1), 1–13.

Kerr, C., Phaal, R., & Thams, K. (2019). Customising and Deploying Roadmapping in an Organisational Setting: The LEGO Group Experience. *Journal of Engineering and Technology Management*, *52*, 48–60

Kim, F. D., & Srivastava, R. (2024). Backcasting from the Future: Strategies for Accelerating and De-Risking Discontinuous Innovations. *California Management Review*. [online]. Available at: https://cmr.berkeley.edu/2024/03/backcasting-from-the-future-strategies-for-accelerating-and-de-risking-discontinuous-innovations/ [Accessed 10 May 2024].

Köhler, J., Geels, F. W., Kern, F., Markard, J., Onsongo, E., Wieczorek, A., Alkemade, F., Avelino, F., Bergek, A., Boons, F., Fünfschilling, L., Hess, D., Holtz, G., Hyysalo, S., Jenkins, K., Kivimaa, P., Martiskainen, M., McMeekin, A., Mühlemeier, M. S., … Wells, P. (2019). An Agenda for Sustainability Transitions Research: State of the Art and Future Directions. *Environmental Innovation and Societal Transitions*, *31*, 1–32.

Kotter, J. P. (1996). *Leading Change*. Harvard Business School Press.

Kotter, J. P. (2001). What Leaders Really Do. *Harvard Business Review*, *79*(11), 85–96.

Kotter, J. P., & Schlesinger, L. A. (2008). Choosing Strategies for Change. *Harvard Business Review*, *86*(7–8), 130–139.

Lee, S. K., Mogi, G., & Kim, J. W. (2009). Energy Technology Roadmap for the Next 10 years: The Case of Korea. *Energy Policy*, *37*(2), 588–596.

Leicester, G., Stewart, D., Bloomer, K., & Ewing, J. (2013). *Transformative Innovation in Education: A Playbook for Pragmatic Visionaries* (2nd ed.). Triarchy Press.

Loorbach, D. (2010). Transition Management for Sustainable Development: A Prescriptive, Complexity-Based Governance Framework. *Governance*, *23*(1), 161–183.

Loorbach, D., Frantzeskaki, N., & Avelino, F. (2017). Sustainability Transitions Research: Transforming Science and Practice for Societal Change. *Annual Review of Environment and Resources*, *42*, 599–626.

Loorbach, D., & Rotmans, J. (2010). The Practice of Transition Management: Examples and Lessons from Four Distinct Cases. *Futures*, *42*(3), 237–246.

Loorbach, D., & Wijsman, K. (2013). Business Transition Management: Exploring a New Role for Business in Sustainability Transitions. *Journal of Cleaner Production*, *45*, 20–28.

Lovallo, D., & Kahneman, D. (2003). Delusions of Success: How Optimism Undermines Executives' Decisions. *81*(7), 56–63.

March, J. G. (1991). Exploration and Exploitation in Organizational Learning. *Organization Science*, *2*(1), 71–87.

Markard, J. (2011). Transformation of Infrastructures: Sector Characteristics and Implications for Fundamental Change. *Journal of Infrastructure Systems*, *17*(3), 107–117.

Markard, J., Raven, R., & Truffer, B. (2012). Sustainability Transitions: An Emerging Field of Research and Its Prospects. *Research Policy*, *41*(6), 955–967.

McDowall, W., & Eames, M. (2006). Forecasts, Scenarios, Visions, Backcasts and Roadmaps to the Hydrogen Economy: A Review of the Hydrogen Futures Literature. *Energy Policy*, *34*(11), 1236–1250.

Mintzberg, H. (2007). *Tracking Strategies: Toward a General Theory*. Oxford University Press.

Muiderman, K., Gupta, A., Vervoort, J., & Biermann, F. (2020). Four Approaches to Anticipatory Climate Governance: Different Conceptions of the Future and Implications for the Present. *WIREs Climate Change*, *11*(6), e673.

Nanus, B. (1992). *Visionary Leadership: Creating a Compelling Sense of Direction for Your Organization* (1st ed.). Jossey-Bass.

Nguyen, K., Peltoniemi, M., & Lamberg, J.-A. (2022). Strategic Renewal: Can It Be Done Profitably? *Long Range Planning*, *55*(6), 102179.

Park, H., Phaal, R., Ho, J.-Y., & O'Sullivan, E. (2020). Twenty Years of Technology and Strategic Roadmapping Research: A School of Thought Perspective. *Technological Forecasting and Social Change*, *154*, 119965.

Pereno, A., & Eriksson, D. (2020). A Multi-Stakeholder Perspective on Sustainable Healthcare: From 2030 Onwards. *Futures*, *122*, 102605.

Phaal, R., Farrukh, C., & Probert, D. (2004). Customizing Roadmapping. *Research-Technology Management*, *47*(2), 26–37.

Phaal, R., Farrukh, C., & Probert, D. (2010). *Roadmapping for Strategy and Innovation: Aligning Technology and Markets in a Dynamic World.* Centre for Technology Management, Institute for Manufacturing, University of Cambridge.

Phaal, R., Farrukh, C. J. P., & Probert, D. R. (2007). Strategic Roadmapping: A Workshop-Based Approach for Identifying and Exploring Strategic Issues and Opportunities. *Engineering Management Journal*, *19*(1), 3–12.

Phaal, R., Farrukh, C. J. P., & Probert, D. R. (2009). Visualising strategy: A Classification of Graphical Roadmap Forms. *International Journal of Technology Management*, *47*(4), 286.

Phaal, R., & Muller, G. (2009). An Architectural Framework for Roadmapping: Towards Visual Strategy. *Technological Forecasting and Social Change*, *76*(1), 39–49.

Quist, J., & Vergragt, P. (2006). Past and Future of Backcasting: The Shift to Stakeholder Participation and a Proposal for a Methodological Framework. *Futures*, 38(9), 1027–1045.

Richey, J. M., & Grinnell, M. (2004). Evolution of Roadmapping at Motorola. *Research-Technology Management*, *47*(2), 37–41

Robinson, J., Burch, S., Talwar, S., O'Shea, M., & Walsh, M. (2011). Envisioning Sustainability: Recent Progress in the Use of Participatory Backcasting Approaches for Sustainability Research. *Technological Forecasting and Social Change*, *78*(5), 756–768

Robinson, J. B. (1990). Futures Under Glass: A recipe for People Who Hate to Predict. *Futures*, *22*(8), 820–842.

Ross, J. W., Beath, C. M., & Mocker, M. (2019). *Designed for Digital: How to Architect Your Business for Sustained Success*. MIT Press.

Rotmans, J., Kemp, R., & Van Asselt, M. (2001). More Evolution Than Revolution: Transition Management in Public Policy. *Foresight*, 3(1), 15–31.

Rotmans, J., & Loorbach, D. (2009). Complexity and Transition Management. *Journal of Industrial Ecology*, *13*(2), 184–196.

Russo, J. E., & Schoemaker, P. J. H. (1992). Managing Overconfidence. *MIT Sloan Management Review*, *33*(2), 7–17.

Saritas, O., & Aylen, J. (2010). Using scenarios for roadmapping: The case of clean production. *Technological Forecasting and Social Change*, *77*(7), 1061–1075.

Schimpf, S., Phaal, R., de Weck, O. L., & Abele, T. (2023). *Roadmapping Field Study Update 2023*.

Schmitt, A., Raisch, S., & Volberda, H. W. (2018). Strategic Renewal: Past Research, Theoretical Tensions and Future Challenges. *International Journal of Management Reviews*, *20*(1), 81–98.

Sebastian, I. M., Ross, J. W., Beath, C. M., Mocker, M., & Moloney, K. G. (2017). How Big Old Companies Navigate Digital Transformation *MIS Quarterly Executive*, 16(3), 197–213.

Senge, P. M. (1990). *The Fifth Discipline: The Art & Practice of the Learning Organisation* (1st ed.). Doubleday.

Sharpe, B. (2020). *Three Horizons: The Patterning of Hope* (2nd ed.). Triarchy Press.

Sharpe, B., & Hodgson, A. (2006). *Intelligent Infrastructure Futures: Technology Forward Look*. Foresight Directorate, UK Department of Trade & Industry.

Sharpe, B., & Hodgson, A. (2019). Anticipation in Three Horizons. In R. Poli (Ed.), *Handbook of Anticipation: Theoretical and Applied Aspects of the Use of Future in Decision Making* (pp. 1071–1088). Springer International Publishing.

Sharpe, B., Hodgson, A., Leicester, G., Lyon, A., & Fazey, I. (2016). Three Horizons: A Pathways Practice for Transformation. *Ecology and Society*, *21*(2).

Shipley, R., & Michela, J. L. (2006). Can Vision Motivate Planning Action? *Planning Practice & Research*, *21*(2), 223–244.

Siebelink, R., Hofman, E., Halman, J. I. M., & Nee, I. (2021). Roadmapping: (Missed) Opportunities to Overcome Strategic Challenges. *Business Horizons*, 64(4), 501–512.

Smith, A., Voß, J.-P., & Grin, J. (2010). Innovation Studies and Sustainability Transitions: The Allure of the Multi-Level Perspective and Its Challenges. *Research Policy*, 39(4), 435–448.

Stewart, J. M. (1993). Future State Visioning—A Powerful Leadership Process. *Long Range Planning*, 26(6), 89–98.

Strauss, J. D., & Radnor, M. (2004). Roadmapping for Dynamic and Uncertain Environments. *Research-Technology Management*, 47(2), 51–58.

Stringham, E. P., Miller, J. K., & Clark, J. R. (2015). Overcoming Barriers to Entry in an Established Industry: Tesla Motors. *California Management Review*, 57(4), 85–103.

Van der Heijden, K. (2005). *Scenarios: The Art of Strategic Conversation* (2nd ed.). John Wiley & Sons.

Van der Helm, R. (2009). The Vision Phenomenon: Towards a Theoretical Underpinning of Visions of the Future and the Process of Envisioning. *Futures, 41*(2), 96–104.

Van der Steen, M. (2022). Scenario Analysis, Forecasting and Backcasting as Policy Tools. In M. Howlett (Ed.), *The Routledge Handbook of Policy Tools* (1st ed., pp. 245–256). Routledge.

Van Notten, P. W. F., Rotmans, J., Van Asselt, M. B. A., & Rothman, D. S. (2003). An Updated Scenario Typology. *Futures, 35*(5), 423–443.

Vatananan, R. S., & Gerdsri, N. (2012). The Current State of Technology Roadmapping Research and Practice. *International Journal of Innovation and Technology Management*, 09(04), 1–20.

Verbong, G., & Geels, F. (2007). The Ongoing Energy Transition: Lessons from a Socio-Technical, Multi-Level Analysis of the Dutch Electricity System (1960–2004). *Energy Policy, 35*(2), 1025–1037.

Vial, G. (2019). Understanding Digital Transformation: A Review and a Research Agenda. *The Journal of Strategic Information Systems, 28*(2), 118–144.

Volberda, H. W., Baden-Fuller, C., & Van den Bosch, F. A. J. (2001). Mastering Strategic Renewal: Mobilising Renewal Journeys in Multi-Unit Firms. *Long Range Planning, 34*(2), 159–178.

Weisbord, M. R., & Janoff, S. (2010). *Future Search: Getting the Whole System in the Room for Vision, Commitment, and Action*. Berrett-Koehler.

Westerman, G., Bonnet, D., & McAfee, A. (2014). *Leading Digital: Turning Technology into Business Transformation*. Harvard Business Review Press.

Westley, F., & Mintzberg, H. (1989). Visionary Leadership and Strategic Management. *Strategic Management Journal, 10*(S1), 17–32.

Whalen, P. J. (2007). Strategic and Technology Planning on a Roadmapping Foundation. *Research-Technology Management, 50*(3), 40–51.

Wick, A., & Iwaniec, D. (2014). Quality Criteria for Visions and Visioning in Sustainability Science. *Sustainability Science*, 9(4), 497–512.

Wilson, I. (1992). Realizing the Power of Strategic Vision. *Long Range Planning, 25*(5), 18–28.

9
Challenging Strategic Posture

9.1 Overview

9.1.1 Introduction

In an increasingly divided and uncertain world riddled with polarized discourse, a growing need emerges for strategic approaches that challenge dominant strategic narratives, question underlying assumptions, and explore alternative futures (Levy et al., 2003; Slaughter, 2004). The challenging strategic posture represents a radical paradigm shift in strategy formulation, emphasizing critical interrogation, examining political interest and dynamics, challenging assumptions, and exploring pluralistic futures (Ezzamel & Willmott, 2010). This chapter explores the key characteristics of the challenging posture and its associated strategy approaches, the critical analytic approach, the discourse analytic approach, the critical scenario approach, and the narrative-based approach.

9.1.2 Key Characteristics

The challenging posture recognizes the shortcomings of the current strategy approaches and perspectives that rely heavily on rational instrumentality, objectivity, and economic logic but largely ignore the social, political, and ideological aspects of strategy (Knights & Morgan, 1991). It does not stop at explaining what is wrong with current strategies but also offers alternative strategy approaches (Phillips & Dar, 2009). Unlike the other mainstream strategic postures, the challenging posture takes a critical perspective that views strategy formulation "as a set of practices and discourses embedded within broader asymmetrical power relations, which systematically privilege the interests and viewpoints of some groups while silencing and marginalizing others" (Levy et al., 2003, p. 93).

DOI: 10.4324/9781003684060-9

The strategy approaches employing the challenging strategic posture emphasize several themes. First, they emphasize *power and domination*, critiquing how strategy often serves to perpetuate existing power imbalances within organizations and society (Knights & Morgan, 1991). They explore how strategic practices and strategies are deeply embedded within and serve to reinforce dominant power structures, whether through economic, political, or ideological means (Ezzamel & Willmott, 2010). Second, this posture delves into the political implications of strategies and future visions. It highlights the role of strategy formulation in shaping present-day choices through the *performative effects* of strategic discourse (Ezzamel & Willmott, 2010) and future imaginaries (2015), advocating for a critical examination of how strategic discourses and imaginaries frame and influence strategy trajectories and choices. Third, the challenging approaches engage in an *ideological critique*, highlighting that strategies are not neutral or objective but are instead shaped by specific values, beliefs, and interests that reflect and sustain the dominance of specific groups (Shrivastava, 1986). Fourth, these critical approaches also consider the potential for *resistance and change* within strategic practices, viewing strategy as a site of contestation where dominant practices can be challenged, and alternative strategies proposed (Ezzamel & Willmott, 2010; Knights & Morgan, 1991). Fifth, they emphasize the *contextual and relational nature of strategy*, critiquing the notion of strategy as a purely rational or objective practice and instead highlighting its contingent and socially constructed nature, deeply embedded within specific historical, economic, and discursive contexts (Jarzabkowski, 2004; Whittington, 1996). Finally, the challenging posture advocates for a more **inclusive, equitable, and critically engaged process of strategy-making**, where diverse perspectives are valued, and hegemonic narratives are questioned (Inayatullah, 2008).

9.1.3 Key Theoretical Perspectives

The challenging strategic posture is underpinned by a rich tapestry of theoretical perspectives that interrogate and disrupt established paradigms. **Critical theory** examines power, ideology, and domination within organizations, aiming for human emancipation by challenging oppressive structures. Rooted in the Frankfurt School (Theodor Adorno, Max Horkheimer, Herbert Marcuse, Jürgen Habermas) (Alvesson & Deetz, 2006), it critiques the managerial focus on control and instrumental reason, emphasizing rational communication and democratic processes (Habermas, 1984). It highlights how strategic decisions often reinforce existing power dynamics and calls for strategies that promote social justice and inclusivity (Scherer, 2009). **Poststructuralism** further informs this posture by deconstructing traditional narratives and exploring the fluid and contested nature of knowledge and power (Derrida, 1976; Foucault, 1972). It questions the stability of meaning, emphasizing the role of language, discourse, and power in constructing organizational realities. It destabilizes the concept of a coherent subject and critiques essentialist views, arguing that strategy should be flexible, context-dependent, and aware of the fluidity of identities (Foucault, 1980). In strategy, poststructuralism encourages a focus on discourse and power relations, urging leaders to recognize the contingent nature of organizational decisions (Jones, 2009). The **sociology of the future** offers another vital lens, focusing on the temporal dimensions of social life and the ways in which future possibilities are envisioned and enacted, as well as concentrating on the performative aspects of the futures thinking (Adam, 2004; Adam & Groves, 2007; Anderson, 2010; Jasanoff & Kim, 2015; Selin, 2008).

9.1.4 Limitations

The challenging strategic posture, while offering a critical and transformative approach to strategy making, also has some limitations. One of the main challenges is the potential resistance to change and the difficulty in overcoming deeply entrenched assumptions, power structures, and dominant narratives (Ezzamel & Willmott, 2008). Engaging diverse stakeholders and challenging existing paradigms can be a complex and time-consuming process, requiring significant resources and commitment (Ahlqvist & Rhisiart, 2015). Therefore, the challenging posture's effectiveness may be limited by the willingness and capacity of organizations and institutions to embrace radical change and disruptive thinking (Ahlqvist & Rhisiart, 2015). Additionally, the critical and deconstructive nature of this posture may lead to a focus on critique rather than constructive action, potentially hindering the development of concrete strategies and solutions (Levy et al., 2003). The emphasis on exploring multiple, transformative futures may also create ambiguity, making it challenging to reach consensus and implement coherent strategies.

9.1.5 Challenging Strategy Approaches

The challenging strategy approaches can be arranged in a matrix consisting of two dimensions: analytical and scenario-based (normative), as illustrated in Figure 9.1.

The vertical analytical dimension has two categories: critical and discourse. Analytical approaches to strategy aim primarily to explore, analyze, and understand possibilities without necessarily promoting a particular preferred future even though they do open up new possibilities. The critical analytical

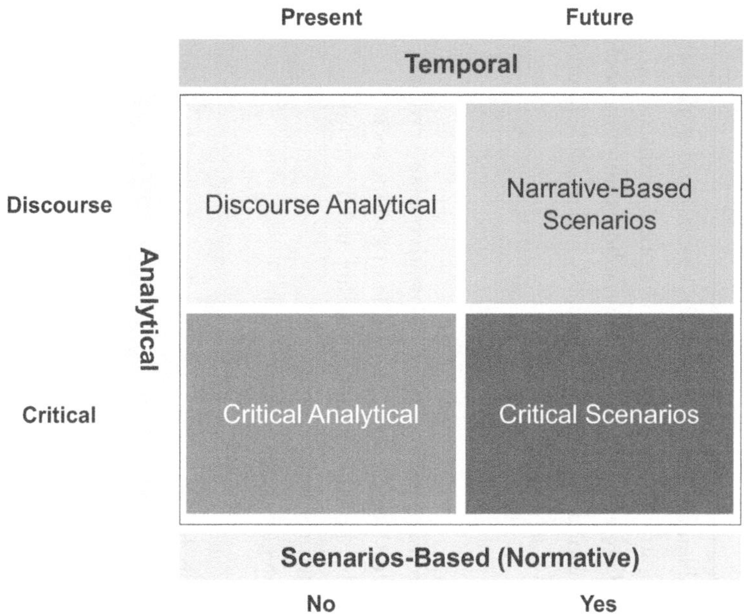

Figure 9.1 The Challenging Strategic Posture Matrix.

approaches broaden the analysis from merely examining the economic structure and rationale to examining political, ideological, and cultural structures. They involve scrutinizing and questioning the political interests of key stakeholders in the strategy formulation process. They also seek to uncover the underlying ideological assumptions that shape strategy and support political agendas. The discourse analytic approaches aim to explore the linguistic and communicative aspects of strategy making, highlighting how the use of language shapes and limits the range of strategic options available. They tend to deepen the analysis by examining strategy at multiple levels of reality (Inayatullah, 1998, 2008).

The horizontal scenario-based (normative) dimension has two categories: not scenario-based (No) and scenario-based (Yes). The scenario-based (normative) dimension differentiates between strategy approaches that use scenarios in strategy formulation to explicitly aim to steer the organization in a particular direction based on certain values or ethical considerations. Their primary goal is to actively intervene and create change toward what is considered desirable or preferable future.

It is worth noting that the distinction between analytical and normative is not absolute. Analytical approaches are still underpinned by certain normative

Table 9.1 Comparing the Challenging Strategy Approaches

Dimension	Critical Analytical	Discourse Analytical	Critical Scenarios	Narrative-Based Approach
Aim	Analyze economic, political, and ideological structures to uncover hidden assumptions, challenge the interests of dominant coalitions, and open up new possibilities	Unpack the linguistic and communicative dimensions of strategy-making, revealing how discourses enable and constrain strategic possibilities	Problematize the status quo, strategies, visions, and preferred futures to transform the present and the future	Understand and work with the stories, myths and metaphors that shape social reality and possible futures
Core Logic	Strategy as a political project	Discourses play a constitutive role in the formation of strategies and policies	Dominant ideologies, discursive practices, and political-economic structures actively shape strategies and potential future outcomes	Narratives play a crucial role in shaping social reality and the future
Assumptions	Dominant ideologies can be challenged and changed	By negotiating and renegotiating meaning, a consensus can be reached	By including many diverse stakeholders, deeper understanding and inclusive scenarios could be achieved	Myths and metaphors are powerful devices that shape our worldviews

Output	Critical analysis	Discourse analysis	Critical inclusive scenarios	Narratives; stories, metaphors; myths
Timing of Action	Present	Present	Present and future	Present and future
Time Horizon	Short to medium term	Short to medium term	Medium to long-term	Medium to long-term
Strengths	Broaden the analysis to include political, social, ideological, and institutional factors	Deepen the analysis of strategic issue by examining them at multiple levels of reality	Creating critical scenarios	Creating new narratives to inform strategy
Limitations	Potential for paralysis by analysis; ideological bias	Potential for excessive focus on language while ignoring material elements	Extensive resources to engage diverse stakeholders; need to manage conflict; increasing ambiguity	Relies heavily on the interpretive capacities of those crafting new narratives
Methods	• Cultural political economy • Sociotechnical imaginaries	• Causal layered analysis • Critical discourse Analysis	• Critical scenario method • Transformative scenario planning	• Narrative Foresight • Six Pillars Method

assumptions and values, but these normative underpinnings remain mostly in the background, while the forefront focus is on understanding rather than directing.

As shown in the matrix, there are four key strategy approaches that can be used to achieve the challenging posture:

Critical analytical approach (bottom-left quadrant): This approach analyzes economic, political, and ideological structures to uncover hidden assumptions and challenge the interests of dominant coalitions. By questioning power, norms, and domination, it seeks to open up new possibilities.

Discourse analytical approach (top-left quadrant): This approach seeks to explore the linguistic and communicative aspects of strategy-making, revealing how discourses shape and limit strategic options (Balogun et al., 2014). It examines how certain strategic ideas gain support, face resistance, and influence organizational realities (Mantere & Vaara, 2008).

Critical scenarios approach (bottom-right quadrant): This approach critically examines the assumptions and power dynamics underlying conventional strategic narratives, challenging accepted ideas of what is realistic in strategic thinking. By doing so, it encourages strategists to consider transformative possibilities, including those that may initially seem improbable or unconventional.

Narrative-based approach (top-right quadrant): This approach seeks to understand and engage with the stories, myths, and metaphors that shape social reality and future possibilities (Milojević & Inayatullah, 2015). It aims to challenge dominant narratives and create alternative ones that broaden future options (Inayatullah, 2008).

Their key characteristics are contrasted in Table 9.1.

9.2 Critical Analytical Approach

9.2.1 Aim

The critical analytical approach aims to critically examine how political, economic, and ideological structures shape and are shaped by the processes and practices of strategizing or policy development. It examines the current paradigm and economic and political forces to reveal hidden ideological assumptions, thereby challenging the political interests of the dominant coalition. By confronting power and domination and questioning and destabilizing norms, it aims to open new possibilities.

9.2.2 Core Logic

The critical analytical approach recognizes that strategy operates within broader social, economic, and political dynamics, challenging the conventional views of strategy as a neutral or purely technical process. At its core, it views "strategy as a political project" (Levy et al., 2003, p. 105) that serves to reinforce and legitimize the status quo (Shrivastava, 1986). Strategy has been defined as "the art of creating power" (Freedman, 2013, p. xi). Hence, this approach goes beyond analyzing the economic structure and economic logic and incorporates analyzing and challenging the political interests of the dominant players in strategy formulation by unearthing the ideological assumptions that underpin strategy and serve political interests (Levy et al., 2003).

9.2.3 Key Elements

Power and ideology: The critical analytical approaches view organizations as political entities where power dynamics play a central role. They examine how power is distributed, exercised, and maintained within organizations and analyze their power relations that underlie strategy making. Their analysis encompasses how dominant ideologies shape organizational practices, values, and beliefs, as well as how power structures are reproduced and legitimized through ideological means (Shrivastava, 1986).

Ideology: In the strategy context, it refers to the set of beliefs and assumptions that shape strategic discourses and practices and perspectives, often aligning with dominant economic and political interests. Strategy formulation is inherently ideological as it promotes a worldview that prioritizes efficiency, competition, and profit maximization, thereby legitimizing existing power structures (e.g., top executives). This ideology tends to marginalize alternative perspectives that emphasize social welfare, equity, and environmental sustainability, reinforcing managerial control and capitalist values (Shrivastava, 1986).

Power analysis: It is a central tenet of the critical analytical approaches to strategy, focusing on how power relations shape strategic decisions, practices, and outcomes (Levy et al., 2003). This perspective examines how strategic discourses and practices can reinforce existing power structures within organizations and society (Alvesson & Willmott, 2003). Power analysis in strategy reveals how certain voices are privileged while others are marginalized in strategic processes (Ezzamel & Willmott, 2010). It also explores how strategy can be used as a tool for domination or resistance, highlighting the political nature of strategy (Hardy & Thomas, 2014).

Emancipatory intent: It aims to liberate individuals and organizations from oppressive structures and practices (Alvesson & Willmott, 2003). It seeks to unmask and challenge power relations that constrain human potential and perpetuate social inequalities within strategic contexts (Levy et al., 2003). Furthermore, it attempts to create spaces for alternative voices and perspectives, fostering more inclusive and equitable organizational environments (Spicer et al., 2009). It encourages the reimagination of strategy as a vehicle for positive social change and individual empowerment (Fournier & Grey, 2000).

Dominant strategic discourses: It refers to the prevailing narratives and practices in the strategy formulation that prioritizes efficiency, competition, and market success, often aligning with capitalist ideologies (Knights & Morgan, 1991). These discourses shape what is considered legitimate strategy, marginalizing alternative perspectives that might emphasize ethics, sustainability, or stakeholder inclusivity (Ezzamel & Willmott, 2010). Critical analytical approaches critique these dominant discourses for reinforcing power structures and limiting the scope of strategic thinking to narrow economic objectives (Phillips & Dar, 2009).

Reflexivity: It involves a continuous, critical self-examination of one's own assumptions, values, and actions in the practice of strategy (Alvesson & Willmott, 2003). Reflexivity encourages strategists to critically examine their own assumptions, biases, and their role in knowledge production (Cunliffe, 2003). Reflexivity challenges leaders and strategists to question the power dynamics and ideological underpinnings of their strategies, promoting a more ethical and transparent approach to knowledge production (Hardy et al., 2001).

Hegemony: According to the Gramscian perspective (Gramsci, 1971; Sassoon, 2000), hegemony refers to the historically specific alignment of economic, political, and ideological forces that coordinates major social groups into a dominant alliance. Hegemony is never total or complete, and dissent persists due to the complex, fragmented nature of hegemonic formations. This fragility provides opportunities for subordinate groups to challenge the dominant bloc through counter-hegemonic strategies that exploit tensions and contradictions within the existing hegemonic order (Levy et al., 2003).

Critique of instrumental rationality: Critical analysis challenges the dominant focus on efficiency, profit maximization, and means-end calculations in strategic management (Alvesson & Willmott, 2003). This perspective argues that an overemphasis on instrumental rationality can lead to the neglect of ethical considerations, social responsibility, and human values in strategic decision-making (Adler et al., 2007). Critical theorists contend that instrumental rationality in strategy often serves to legitimize managerial control and reinforce existing power structures (Levy et al., 2003). They advocate for a more holistic approach to strategy that considers broader social, environmental, and ethical implications (Ezzamel & Willmott, 2010).

Denaturalization: It refers to the process of critically examining and challenging the taken-for-granted assumptions that underpin organizational practices and beliefs, revealing them as socially constructed rather than inherent or inevitable (Alvesson & Willmott, 2003). This concept is central to Critical Management Studies, as it seeks to unearth how certain management norms, such as hierarchical authority or market rationality, are maintained as "natural" to legitimize existing power structures and marginalize alternative perspectives (Adler et al., 2007).

Performativity: It examines how strategic theories and models don't merely describe reality but actively shape and produce it (Cabantous & Gond, 2011). This concept, derived from Austin's speech act theory, suggests that strategic discourse and practices perform the realities they claim to represent (MacKenzie & Millo, 2003). Critical scholars argue that strategy research and tools can become self-fulfilling prophecies, influencing organizational behaviors and market dynamics (Kornberger & Clegg, 2011). Performativity analysis in strategy reveals how strategic knowledge interacts with and transforms the social world it purports to objectively study (Vaara & Whittington, 2012).

9.2.4 Applications and Examples

The critical analytical approach can be used to critically analyze complex socioeconomic or sociotechnical systems to open possibilities. For example, using one of its methods, Cultural Political Economy (CPE), was used to analyze the housing policies in Türkiye and the main organization responsible for implementing these policies, the Housing Development Administration of the Republic of Türkiye (TOKİ). Furthermore, the Sociotechnical Imaginaries (STIs), another method utilizing the critical analytical approach, was used to examine how technologies shape policies and strategies across a wide range of economic sectors such as energy policies (Jasanoff & Kim, 2013; Rudek, 2022) and national Artificial Intelligence strategies (Bareis & Katzenbach, 2022).

9.2.5 Challenges and Limitations

Using a critical analytical approach involves several challenges. Critics of the critical analytical approaches argue that these approaches often focus more on critique than on providing actionable insights for practitioners, limiting their practical utility and adoption in business settings (Alvesson & Willmott, 2012; Levy et al., 2003). While critical analytical approaches emphasize the role of power and ideology in shaping strategic decision-making, they can sometimes overlook the practical aspects of strategy formulation. Also, these approaches often carry their own ideological biases, which can influence their critiques and interpretations of strategic issues, strategies, and futures. This risk of ideological bias can lead to accusations that critical strategy approaches are just as partial and subjective as the mainstream approaches they critique (Levy et al., 2003).

9.2.6 Strategy Methods

Several strategy methods utilize the critical analytical approach. CPE analyzes power structures, social relations, and economic systems to critique the dominant economic and political narratives (Jessop, 2010). STI is another method to analyze future visions and examine their performative effects in the present (2015).

9.2.6.1 *Cultural Political Economy*

The principles and analytical framework of CPE extend far beyond its namesake field, offering a versatile and robust toolkit for understanding and shaping complex social systems across various sectors (Jessop, 2010). CPE is rooted in the idea of complexity reduction, recognizing that the social world is too complex to be fully understood in all its details. Instead, social actors must simplify and selectively interpret the world to act within it. This selective interpretation takes place in two primary modes: semiosis (sensemaking and meaning-making – how meanings are created and contested) and structuration (institutionalization and social forms – how these meanings become embedded in institutions and practices) (Sum & Jessop, 2013). Furthermore, CPE uses the strategic-relational approach to bridge the structure-agency divide, considering how structures selectively privilege certain actions and how actors strategically navigate these structures. Moreover, CPE uses the evolutionary mechanisms of variation, selection, and retention to understand how certain imaginaries, strategies, and practices emerge, gain prominence, and become institutionalized while others do not (Sum & Jessop, 2013).

The developers of CPE, Bob Jessob, and Ngai-Ling Sum propose a four-step process that can be used to challenge strategy proposals and suggest alternatives (Jessop & Sum, 2023). First, critique the internal logic of strategy and policy proposals by identifying deficiencies in their assumptions, categories, problematization, and argumentation, revealing empirical inadequacies, anomalies, or practical failings. Second, trace these issues to inconsistencies in the underlying paradigms or knowledge brands (dominant ways of framing policy or strategy issues). Third, analyze the role of policies in perpetuating social domination by investigating how specific strategies or policies may contribute to reproducing entrenched forms of social domination and hierarchy. Fourth, envision emancipatory alternatives by proposing alternative interpretations, policies, and strategies that aim to liberate subordinated social groups (and potentially dominant ones too) from the oppressive effects of domination, challenging the naturalization and legitimation of domination by the current strategy approaches.

9.2.6.2 Sociotechnical Imaginaries

STIs as an analytical framework were initially developed to help in the understanding of the development of Science and Technology (S&T) policies and strategies at the national level (Jasanoff & Kim, 2009). Later, its developers, Jasanoff and Kim, refined the analytical concept so it could be used by corporations, social movements, and professional societies to critically analyze S&T-based innovations, industrial and economic development policies, and strategies. They define STIs as "collectively held, institutionally stabilized, and publicly performed visions of desirable futures, animated by shared understandings of forms of social life and social order attainable through, and supportive of, advances in science and technology" (Jasanoff, 2015, p. 4). STIs can start as visions of individuals or corporations and then become collectively shared through coalition building or explicit power exercises. The STI framework "situate(s) technologies within the integrated material, moral, and social landscapes (Jasanoff, 2015, p. 3). This framework allows us to critically analyze how visions of scientific and technological progress intersect with social, political, and cultural dynamics.

There are several key considerations when using this powerful analytical framework – identifying the dominant imaginaries shaping the trajectory of scientific and technological development within the specific context under examination, as these imaginaries often reflect the priorities and visions of powerful social groups or institutions (1995); recognizing that STIs are rooted in a specific historical and cultural context; and examining how these imaginaries have emerged from and are shaped by the specific social, political, and economic conditions (Jasanoff, 2015). Analyzing how these STIs are co-produced through the interaction of science, technology, and society (2004). Critically assessing how these imaginaries can reinforce or challenge existing power structures and inequalities by considering whose interests and values are represented in these imaginaries and whose are marginalized or excluded (Jasanoff, 2015). Looking for examples of resistance to dominant STIs and the articulation of alternative visions, then analyzing how these counter-imaginaries challenge prevailing assumptions and propose different pathways for scientific and technological development (Fujimura, 2003). Comparing STIs across different national, regional, or institutional contexts to understand how these imaginaries are shaped by local conditions and how they interact with or diverge from global trends (Jasanoff, 2015). Lastly, reflecting on the how insights from the analysis could inform how the dominant visions can be reimagined (Jasanoff, 2015).

9.3 Discourse Analytical Approach

9.3.1 Aim

The aim of a discourse-based approach is to unpack the linguistic and communicative dimensions of strategy making, revealing how discourses enable and constrain strategic possibilities (Balogun et al., 2014). It seeks to understand how particular strategic ideas gain traction, how they are resisted, and how they shape organizational realities (Mantere & Vaara, 2008).

9.3.2 Core Logic

The core logic is that discourses, the structured collections of texts, speech acts, and symbolic representations play a constitutive role in the formation of strategies and policies (Knights & Morgan, 1991; Phillips et al., 2004). Strategy discourses do not simply reflect an objective reality, but they actively construct social reality by framing issues in certain ways, legitimizing particular perspectives, and reproducing or challenging power relations (Hardy & Phillips, 2004; Vaara & Whittington, 2012).

9.3.3 Key Elements

Power/knowledge: Foucault understands power and knowledge to be intimately connected. Power operates through the development of knowledge and "discourses of truth" that shape social reality. Power is not just repressive but productive, constituting the domains of knowledge and rituals of truth that form individual subjectivities. Discursive practices, informed by power relations, systematically form the very objects of which they speak. Power and knowledge are fundamentally intertwined in the production of social meanings, identities, and truths (Ezzamel & Willmott, 2008).

Strategic discourse: It is a set of ideas and practices that shape how organizations and individuals understand and approach strategy. This discourse is not merely descriptive but actively constitutes the problems it claims to solve, and the identities of those who engage with it. Strategic discourse is seen as a power/knowledge nexus that produces its own truth effects, transforming managers into subjects who derive meaning and security from participating in its practices.

Discursive practices: The processes of text production, distribution, and consumption through which strategies are formed (Vaara et al., 2004). Examples of discursive practices include metaphors, narratives, jargons, framing, rhetorical devices, silence or omission, and nominalization.

Deconstruction: Discourse analysis involves deconstructing texts and discourses to uncover underlying assumptions, hidden meanings, contradictions, and power structures. It argues that meanings are not fixed but are always in flux, dependent on context and interpretation. Deconstruction reveals how seemingly stable structures are actually unstable and open to different interpretations (Inayatullah, 1998).

Genealogy: Inspired by Foucault, genealogy is a method of analyzing the historical development of discourses by examining the diverse conditions that contribute to their formation and transformation. It involves identifying discrete discourses and practices that have been adapted and changed to create new ways of thinking and acting. Genealogical analysis focuses on the relationships between power, knowledge, and discourse and is concerned with recording specific, unique events rather than broad, overarching narratives (Knights & Morgan, 1991).

Myths and metaphors: Myths and metaphors play a role in shaping our understanding of strategic issues and strategy (Inayatullah, 1998). Myths and metaphors "are the deep stories, the collective archetypes, the unconscious dimensions of the problem or the paradox" (Inayatullah, 1998, p. 820). They use evocative language and imagery that resonates on an emotional level, rather than focusing solely on analytical or intellectual engagement (Inayatullah, 1998).

Grand narratives: Discourse analysis challenges the idea of grand narratives or overarching explanations that claim to capture the entirety of organizational life. They argue that such narratives often obscure the complexity and diversity of experiences within organizations. (Alvesson & Deetz, 2006).

Plurality and fragmentation: Discourse analysis highlights the plurality and fragmentation of realities within organizations. It challenges the notion of a single, unified truth, instead advocating for multiple perspectives and interpretations (Alvesson & Deetz, 2006).

9.3.4 Applications and Examples

One example illustrating the use of the discursive analytic approach is StitchCo, a global retailer, who constructed its strategy through discursive practices involving accounting and performance metrics, demonstrating how these practices shaped strategic decisions and organizational power dynamics (Ezzamel & Willmott, 2008). Another example is the analysis of corporate strategy discourse in business schools and organizations was found to perpetuate certain power structures and managerial ideologies, framing strategic decisions in ways that align with the interests of dominant groups (Knights & Morgan, 1991).

9.3.5 Challenges and Limitations

The discourse-based approach may overemphasize the role of language at the expense of other material factors, such as economic conditions, technological capabilities, or structural constraints. The academic nature and complexity of discourse analysis can make it difficult for practitioners to understand and apply, limiting its accessibility and practical relevance in everyday strategic management contexts (Hardy & Maguire, 2016). Also, by focusing on the power of discourse, this approach might underplay the agency of individual actors to enact change and resist dominant narratives within strategic contexts (Phillips et al., 2004).

9.3.6 Strategy Methods

Several strategy methods use the discourse analytic approach. Two of these methods are causal layered analysis (CLA) and critical discourse analysis (CDA). CLA critically analyzes strategic issues, strategies, and futures at four levels: litany, systemic causes, discourse/worldviews, and myths/metaphors, to gain deeper insights and develop more effective long-term strategies and policies (Inayatullah, 1998). CDA examines how language and communication influence the formation, legitimization, and contestation of strategies, uncovering the power dynamics and ideological underpinnings that shape strategic decision-making and organizational practices (Vaara & Tienar, 2008).

9.3.6.1 *Causal Layered Analysis*

CLA, developed by Sohail Inayatullah, is a method that adopts a rich, multi-layered approach to deconstructing and analyzing phenomena, strategic issues, strategies, and futures at four levels. In doing so, it moves beyond surface-level analysis to the deeper, often hidden, layers of meaning and power dynamics using poststructuralism thinking (Inayatullah, 1998, 2004). The four layers of CLA are litany, systemic causes, discourse/worldview, and myth/metaphor (Inayatullah, 1998, 2004). Litany is the surface level where issues are often presented in simplistic and decontextualized ways, typically through media. It represents the immediate, visible aspects of problems. The second level, systemic causes, addresses the systemic and structural causes of strategic issues, including economic, political, and cultural factors. The third level is discourse/worldview, which focuses on the underlying worldviews and discourses that shape how issues are framed and understood. The fourth level is the myth/metaphor level. This represents the deepest level, exploring the cultural myths and metaphors that underpin our understanding of issues, revealing the unconscious narratives that influence perceptions and actions. By deconstructing narratives at these different levels and then reconstructing alternative narratives, CLA helps to create transformative spaces for alternative futures (Inayatullah, 1998, 2004).

While CLA considers historical context, it is often utilized to examine proposed future scenarios, explore alternative future scenarios, and challenge present assumptions. Moreover, as it uses poststructuralism that takes a constructivist stance, emphasizing how reality is socially constructed through language, myths, and worldviews, it primarily employs qualitative methods, focusing on discourse, narrative, and metaphor analysis. It also uses participatory workshops to involve stakeholders in the analysis process, potentially leading to collective transformation of perspectives. CLA also examines how different worldviews and deep cultural myths shape power structures.

9.3.6.2 *Critical Discourse Analysis*

CDA is a powerful method for critically examining the linguistic, meaning-making, and power dimensions of strategy formulation (Fairclough, 2003). By situating strategy discourse within its multilevel contexts, exposing the contestation and political dynamics inherent in strategizing, and unveiling its material and constitutive effects, CDA offers a more reflexive and socially attuned understanding of how strategies emerge and take shape through discursive practices (Balogun et al., 2014; Hardy & Thomas, 2014). Rather than merely reflecting or describing strategic issues, strategic discourses actively construct and frame them in particular ways, legitimizing certain perspectives while marginalizing others (Vaara & Whittington, 2012).

At the institutional level, CDA examines how widely shared strategic discourses, such as those around globalization or sustainability, enable and constrain strategic choices (Vaara et al., 2004). At the organizational level, it investigates how local discourses, narratives, and rhetorical strategies are deployed by different actors to influence strategic agendas (Hardy & Thomas, 2014; Paroutis & Heracleous, 2013). Finally, at the interactional level, CDA unpacks the micro-level linguistic practices and conversational dynamics through which strategic issues are discursively negotiated and constructed (Samra-Fredericks, 2003).

A key focus of CDA is to illuminate the power dynamics and political struggles that underlie strategy discourse (Levy et al., 2003; Mantere & Vaara, 2008). It recognizes that strategic sensemaking is a contested process, where different actors mobilize discursive resources to frame issues, advocate their positions, and establish legitimacy (Kaplan, 2008; Maitlis & Lawrence, 2007). By examining the discursive strategies employed by various stakeholders, CDA can uncover how certain voices and interests come to dominate the strategy process while others are silenced or marginalized (Ezzamel & Willmott, 2008; Laine & Vaara, 2007).

Moreover, CDA highlights the material consequences of strategy discourse in terms of enabling or constraining particular courses of action, allocating resources, and shaping organizational practices (Balogun et al., 2014; Hardy et al., 2000). It also attends to the ways in which discourses construct the subjectivities and identities of strategists and other stakeholders, influencing how they perceive their roles and engage in the strategy process (Knights & Morgan, 1991; Mantere & Vaara, 2008).

9.4 Critical Scenarios Approach

9.4.1 Aim

By problematizing the status quo, strategies, visions, and preferred futures, the critical scenarios approach seeks to transform the present and the future.

9.4.2 Core Logic

The critical scenarios approach emphasizes how dominant ideologies, discursive practices, and political-economic structures actively shape strategies and potential future outcomes from within the complex reality of the present moment. They focus on the open-ended, contested nature of the future and the wide range of possibilities that arise from the dynamic interplay of social, political, and economic forces. These approaches are less concerned with making probabilistic predictions and more interested in critically examining the assumptions and power dynamics that underpin conventional strategic narratives. They challenge taken-for-granted notions about what is considered realistic or plausible in strategic thinking. In doing so, critical scenario approaches push strategists to explore transformative strategic possibilities – even those that might initially seem far-fetched or "preposterous". The goal is to expand the boundaries of strategic imagination and open up space for alternative futures that break from the status quo.

9.4.3 Key Elements

In addition to the key elements that were discussed in the critical analytic approach (power and ideology, domination, emancipatory intent, discourse and communication, contradictions and ambiguity, historical and contextual analysis, hegemony, and ethical and normative considerations), these are further elements that should be considered.

Transformation: The approach aims to challenge existing power structures and promote change toward more sustainable and equitable practices.

Participation of marginalized voices: The approach emphasizes involving a wide range of stakeholders in the strategy-making process, particularly those who are often excluded from traditional business discourse. This involves analyzing the costs and benefits to all stakeholders and can even extend to incorporating stakeholders' voices and inputs within strategy formulation.

9.4.4 Applications and Examples

The critical scenario approach has been used to encourage students to explore multiple possible futures, consider broader societal and environmental impacts, and analyze issues from various stakeholder perspectives beyond just profit (Cairns et al., 2010).

9.4.5 Challenges and Limitations

The critical scenario approach faces several challenges, including its time-intensive nature and the complexity of integrating diverse social, environmental, and business factors. Ensuring engagement from all stakeholders, especially when unfamiliar with reflective techniques, can also be difficult (Cairns et al., 2010). Additionally, there is a risk of overemphasizing ethical considerations at the expense of practical business concerns, and power dynamics may bias the process (Flyvbjerg, 2001).

9.4.6 Strategy Methods

Several strategy methods use the critical scenarios approach. Two of these methods are the critical scenario method (CSM) and transformative scenario planning (TSP). The CSM integrates scenario planning with phronetic inquiry to explore multiple futures, emphasizing the broader societal and environmental impacts beyond profit maximization (Cairns & Wright, 2018). TSP is a critical and a collaborative approach that engages diverse stakeholders to explore alternative futures and co-create strategies for systemic change by addressing complex, shared challenges (Kahane, 2012).

9.4.6.1 *Critical Scenario Method*

CSM builds on the basic intuitive logic scenario method (Van der Heijden et al., 2002). It aims to challenge assumptions, bring power dynamics to the surface, foster a deeper understanding of complex problems, and consider ethical implications and impacts on a wide range of stakeholders (Cairns et al., 2010; Cairns & Wright, 2018).

At the heart of CSM is the integration of a "broad" stakeholder analysis (Freeman & Reed, 1983), which considers the effects of scenarios on all parties, including those who may be remote, excluded, or lacking in power (Cairns & Wright, 2017). This is particularly crucial in a contemporary context of heightened awareness of corporate social responsibility, environmental sustainability, and ethical consumption and investment (Cairns & Wright, 2017).

CSM is grounded in the Aristotelian concept of phronēsis, or practical wisdom, and operationalized through (Flyvbjerg, 2001; 2003) value-rational question framework for phronetic social science. This involves interrogating each scenario using four key questions (Cairns et al., 2010; Cairns & Wright, 2018): (1) Where are we going? (2) Is this development desirable? (3) What, if anything, should we do about it? (4) Who gains and who loses, and by which mechanisms of power? The method is implemented using a matrix, with scenarios along the top row and stakeholders down the left-hand column. For each scenario-stakeholder intersection, participants consider the impact on the stakeholder's interests and values, and their likely action or reaction. The final question of gains, losses, and power is then debated for each scenario across all stakeholders (Cairns & Wright, 2017).

By surfacing power relationships and the distribution of benefits and costs, CSM supports decision-making grounded in broad social and environmental considerations, beyond mere financial or shareholder concerns. It makes transparent when other criteria, such as short-term gains, are being prioritized (Cairns & Wright, 2017). As such, CSM enables a form of "responsible management" that looks beyond narrow profit maximization to consider the wider public good (Cairns & Wright, 2018).

9.4.6.2 *Transformative Scenario Planning*

TSP was developed by Adam Kahane's work in South Africa in the early 1990s. It is an approach to address complex societal challenges, particularly in conflictual contexts where stakeholders need to work together to transform an unacceptable status quo. The TSP process steps involve convening a diverse team, observing the current situation, constructing scenario stories, discovering implications, and acting.

There are several critical characteristics of TSP (Kahane, 2012, 2013). First, it emphasizes diverse perspectives as it brings together stakeholders from across the system, including marginalized voices, which resonates with critical theory's focus on power dynamics and inclusivity. Second, the TSP process encourages participants to question current assumptions and mental models, a key aspect of critical thinking. Third, it is action-oriented with its ultimate goal to inspire action to transform systems, aligning with critical theory's emphasis on praxis. Fourth, it emphasizes the participation of diverse stakeholders. It stresses the importance of assembling a team that represents the "whole system" being addressed, including those with conflicting views.

9.5 Narrative-Based Approach

9.5.1 Aim

The aim of the narrative-based approach is to understand and work with the stories, myths, and metaphors that shape social reality and possible futures (Milojević & Inayatullah, 2015). It seeks to challenge dominant narratives and articulate alternative narratives that open up new possibilities for the future (Inayatullah, 2008).

9.5.2 Core Logic

The narrative-based approach builds on the premise that narratives play a crucial role in shaping social reality and the future (Milojević & Inayatullah, 2015). They provide the mental structures through which we make sense of the world and shape what we see as possible, desirable, and actionable (Milojević & Inayatullah, 2015). By working with narratives, we can thus bridge the gap between abstract scenarios and images of future and strategies (Jarva, 2014).

9.5.3 Key Elements

In addition to the key elements that were discussed in the discourse analytic approach (power and knowledge, discourses, discursive practices, deconstruction, genealogy, myths and metaphors, grand narratives, plurality and fragmentation), there are additional elements that should be considered.

Storytelling: Storytelling lies at the heart of strategy development and organizational practices (Küpers et al., 2013; Raven & Elahi, 2015). It is a fundamental, embodied method for creating, analyzing, critiquing, and enacting narratives about possible futures and organizational realities (Barry & Elmes, 1997; Küpers et al., 2013). Storytelling is not just about the content of the story but also about how that story is lived, experienced, and told through the bodies and emotions of organizational members (Küpers et al., 2013).

Metaphor analysis: Examining the metaphors used to describe an issue, strategy, or the future can reveal underlying assumptions and worldviews. Metaphor analysis involves identifying and critiquing dominant metaphors and articulating new metaphors that support the new narrative (Milojević & Inayatullah, 2015).

Contextual embeddedness: Narratives consider the broader social, cultural, and political contexts that shape and are shaped by discourse. This contextual embeddedness is crucial for understanding how discourse influences strategy and policymaking beyond the immediate organizational setting. Fairclough explains that "a piece of discourse is embedded within sociocultural practice at a number of levels; in the immediate situation, in the wider institution or organization, and at a societal level" (Fairclough, 1995, p. 97) (Phillips & Oswick, 2012).

9.5.4 Applications and Examples

The narrative-based approach was used in the articulation of alternative narratives about the futures of education, cities, and technology (Inayatullah, 2008). The approach was also used to create new stories to support new strategies (Milojević & Inayatullah, 2015; 2021).

9.5.5 Challenges and Limitations

The narrative-based approaches focus primarily on the story level and may neglect how narratives interact with material realities and system structures (Milojević & Inayatullah, 2015). They rely heavily on the interpretive capacities of those crafting new narratives and may be less suited for predictive or probabilistic futures work (Raven & Elahi, 2015). They can also be time and resource intensive if carried out in a fully participatory manner (Inayatullah, 2008).

9.5.6 Strategy Methods

Several strategy methods use the narrative-based approach. Two of these methods are the Narrative Foresight method and the Six Pillars method. The

Narrative Foresight method aims to uncover, deconstruct, and transform the deep narratives and cognitive frameworks that underlie assumptions about strategies and the future. It moves beyond traditional forecasting to explore how worldviews, metaphors, and myths shape perceptions of what is possible or desirable in the future (Milojević & Inayatullah, 2015). The Six Pillars method is a structured futures thinking framework that helps explore, anticipate, and shape multiple possible futures through the following pillars: mapping, anticipating, timing, deepening, creating alternatives, and transforming strategic visions into actions (Inayatullah, 2008).

9.5.6.1 *Narrative Foresight*

The Narrative Foresight method focuses on the stories, metaphors, and myths that shape how individuals, organizations, and societies envision and construct their futures (Milojević & Inayatullah, 2015). Drawing on poststructuralist and postmodernist perspectives, narrative foresight recognizes that reality is constantly negotiated and constructed through language and discourse, rather than existing as an objective truth to be discovered (Milojević & Inayatullah, 2015).

By integrating the Narrative Foresight method into strategy making, organizations can critically examine the assumptions and values underlying their existing narratives, making room for new stories that are more adaptable to changing circumstances. This approach is particularly relevant in complex and uncertain environments where traditional strategic models may fall short. By combining it with methods such as CLA that examines issues across four levels: litany, systemic causes, worldview, and myth/metaphor (Inayatullah, 2004), Narrative Foresight unearths the deep myths and metaphors that shape current strategies, allowing strategists to reframe issues and identify novel pathways forward (Milojević & Inayatullah, 2015).

For instance, in the context of public sector responses to crises such as COVID-19, Narrative Foresight has highlighted the importance of collective narratives that foster global solidarity, planning, and social inclusion, contrasting with narratives of blame and exceptionalism that hinder effective preparedness and response (Milojević & Inayatullah, 2021). Thus, Narrative Foresight not only aids in envisioning alternative futures but also serves as a strategic tool to navigate complex challenges through a lens that values diversity, adaptability, and collective action. Another example of using the Narrative Foresight method includes storytelling projects in Serbia that promoted cultural pluralism and peace by revising traditional narratives and constructing alternative futures that emphasize partnership, gender equity, and social inclusion (Milojević & Izgarjan, 2014).

9.5.6.2 *Six Pillars Method*

The Six Pillars method, developed by Sohail Inayatullah, provides a comprehensive framework for futures thinking and strategy development (Inayatullah, 2008). The six pillars are mapping, anticipation, timing, deepening, creating alternatives, and transforming. Mapping involves creating a shared understanding of the present by exploring the historical context and identifying current trends and drivers. This step uses tools such as the Futures Triangle (Inayatullah, 2023), which examines the forces that push the present, pull the future, and weigh down with past constraints (Inayatullah, 2008). It establishes a baseline from which strategic possibilities can be developed. Anticipation focuses on scanning for emerging issues and weak signals that may disrupt or influence future trajectories. Techniques such as emerging issues analysis (Molitor, 2003) and the Futures Wheel (Glenn, 2009) are employed to identify and evaluate these early indicators of change (Inayatullah, 2013). This pillar encourages a proactive stance toward future developments, enhancing the strategic capacity to respond to potential challenges and opportunities. Timing addresses when to act by understanding the timing and cycles of change. By examining historical patterns and using macrohistorical and microhistorical analyses (Galtung & Inayatullah, 1997), strategists can better align their actions with optimal moments for intervention (Inayatullah, 2008). This pillar aids in prioritizing strategic initiatives based on the rhythms of change. Deepening employs CLA (Inayatullah, 1998, 2004) to delve into the deeper narratives, worldviews, and myths that shape current challenges. This approach uncovers the underlying causes of issues, allowing for a more nuanced and transformative strategic response (Inayatullah, 2013). Creating alternatives emphasizes generating diverse scenarios to explore a range of potential futures rather than settling on a single predicted outcome. Scenario planning and other creative methods help in developing robust strategies that can adapt to various possible futures (Inayatullah, 2008). Lastly, transforming focuses on implementing preferred futures through visioning, backcasting, and strategic planning. This final pillar encourages a shift from reactive to transformative strategies by setting clear goals and identifying the steps needed to achieve desired outcomes (Inayatullah, 2013).

Examples of the Six Pillars method in practice include its application in e-health futures in Bangladesh (Sheraz et al., 2013), democratic governance in Asia (Inayatullah & Song, 2014), and city futures (Cruz & Villanueva, 2014).

References

Adam, B. (2004). Memory of Futures. *KronoScope*, *4*(2), 297–315.

Adam, B., & Groves, C. (2007). *Future Matters: Action, Knowledge, Ethics*. Brill.

Adler, P. S., Forbes, L. C., & Willmott, H. (2007). Critical Management Studies. *Academy of Management Annals*, *1*(1), 119–179.

Ahlqvist, T., & Rhisiart, M. (2015). Emerging Pathways for Critical Futures Research: Changing Contexts and Impacts of Social Theory. *Futures*, *71*, 91–104.

Alvesson, M., & Deetz, S. A. (2006). Critical Theory and Postmodernism Approaches to Organizational Studies. In S. R. H. Clegg, Cynthia, T. B. Lawrence, & W. R. Nord (Eds.), *The SAGE Handbook of Organization Studies* (2nd ed., pp. 255–283). Sage Publications.

Alvesson, M., & Willmott, H. (2003). Introduction. In M. Alvesson & H. Willmott (Eds.), *Studying Management Critically* (pp. 1–22). Sage Publications.

Alvesson, M., & Willmott, H. (2012). *Making Sense of Management: A Critical Introduction* (2nd ed.). Sage Publications.

Anderson, B. (2010). Security and the Future: Anticipating the Event of Terror. *Geoforum*, *41*(2), 227–235.

Balogun, J., Jacobs, C., Jarzabkowski, P., Mantere, S., & Vaara, E. (2014). Placing Strategy Discourse in Context: Sociomateriality, Sensemaking, and Power. *Journal of Management Studies*, *51*(2), 175–201.

Bareis, J., & Katzenbach, C. (2022). Talking AI into Being: The Narratives and Imaginaries of National AI Strategies and Their Performative Politics. *Science, Technology, & Human Values*, *47*(5), 855–881.

Barry, D., & Elmes, M. (1997). Strategy Retold: Toward a Narrative View of Strategic Discourse. *The Academy of Management Review*, *22*(2), 429–452.

Cabantous, L., & Gond, J.-P. (2011). Rational Decision Making as Performative Praxis: Explaining Rationality's Éternel Retour. *Organization Science*, *22*(3), 573–586.

Cairns, G., Śliwa, M., & Wright, G. (2010). Problematizing International Business Futures Through a 'Critical Scenario Method'. *Futures*, *42*(9), 971–979.

Cairns, G., & Wright, G. (2017). *Scenario Thinking: Preparing Your Organization for the Future in an Unpredictable World* (2nd ed.). Springer.

Cairns, G., & Wright, G. (2018). *Scenario Thinking: Preparing Your Organization for the Future in an Unpredictable World* (2nd ed.). Palgrave Macmillan.

Cruz, S., & Villanueva, C., H. (2014). City Futures for City Leaders Penang Malaysia. *Journal of Futures Studies, 19*(1), 115–125.

Cunliffe, A. L. (2003). Reflexive Inquiry in Organizational Research: Questions and Possibilities. *Human Relations*, 56(8), 983–1003.

Derrida, J. (1976). *Of Grammatology*. Johns Hopkins University Press.

Ezzamel, M., & Willmott, H. (2008). Strategy as Discourse in a Global Retailer: A Supplement to Rationalist and Interpretive Accounts. *Organization Studies, 29*(2), 191–217.

Ezzamel, M., & Willmott, H. (2010). Strategy and Strategizing: A Poststructuralist Perspective. In B. Joel A.C. & J. Lampel (Eds.), *The Globalization of Strategy Research* (Vol. 27, pp. 75–109). Emerald Group Publishing Limited.

Fairclough, N. (1995). *Critical Discourse Analysis: The Critical Study of Language*. London: Longman.

Flyvbjerg, B. (2001). *Making Social Science Matter: Why Social Inquiry Fails and How It Can Succeed Again*. Cambridge University Press.

Flyvbjerg, B. (2003). Making Organization Research Matter: Power, Values and Phronesis. In B. Czarniawska & G. Sevón (Eds.), *The Northern Lights: Organization Theory in Scandinavia* (pp. 357–382). Copenhagen Business School Press.

Foucault, M. (1972). *The Archaeology of Knowledge: And the Discourse on Language*. Pantheon Books.

Foucault, M. (1980). *Power/Knowledge: Selected Interviews and Other Writings 1972-1977* (C. Gordon, Ed.). Pantheon Books.

Fournier, V., & Grey, C. (2000). At the Critical Moment: Conditions and Prospects for Critical Management Studies. *Human Relations*, 53(1), 7–32.

Freedman, L. (2013). *Strategy: A History*. Oxford University Press.

Freeman, R. E., & Reed, D. L. (1983). Stockholders and Stakeholders: A New Perspective on Corporate Governance. *California Management Review, 25*(3), 88–106.

Fujimura, J. H. (2003). Chapter 9. Future Imaginaries: Genome Scientists as Sociocultural Entrepreneurs. In H. G. Alan, H. Deborah, & M. S. Lindee (Eds.), *Genetic Nature/Culture* (pp. 176–199). University of California Press.

Galtung, J., & Inayatullah, S. (1997). *Macrohistory and Macrohistorians: Perspectives on Individual, Social, and Civilizational Change*. Praeger.

Glenn, J. C. (2009). The Futures Wheel. In J. C. Glenn & T. J. Gordon (Eds.), *Futures Research Methodology, Version 3.0* (pp. 1–17). The Millennium Project.

Gramsci, A. (1971). *Selections from the Prison Notebooks of Antonio Gramsci*. Lawrence & Wishart.

Habermas, J. (1984). *The Theory of Communicative Action: Reason and the Rationalization of Society* (1st ed.). Beacon Press.

Hardy, C., & Maguire, S. (2016). Organizing Risk: Discourse, Power, and "Riskification". *Academy of Management Review, 41*(1), 80–108.

Hardy, C., Palmer, I., & Phillips, N. (2000). Discourse as a Strategic Resource. *Human Relations, 53*(9), 1227–1248.

Hardy, C., & Phillips, N. (2004). Discourse and Power. In D. Grant, C. Hardy, C. Oswick, & L. Putnam (Eds.), *The SAGE Handbook of Organizational Discourse* (pp. 299–316). Sage Publications.

Hardy, C., Phillips, N., & Clegg, S. (2001). Reflexivity in Organization and Management Theory: A Study of the Production of the Research 'Subject'. *Human Relations, 54*(5), 531–560.

Hardy, C., & Thomas, R. (2014). Strategy, Discourse and Practice: The Intensification of Power. *Journal of Management Studies, 51*(2), 320–348.

Inayatullah, S. (1998). Causal Layered Analysis: Poststructuralism As Method. *Futures, 30*(8), 815–829.

Inayatullah, S. (2004). Causal Layered Analysis: Theory, Historical Context, and Case Studies. In S. Inayatullah (Ed.), *The Causal Layered Analysis Reader: Theory and Case Studies of an Integrative and Transformative Methodology* (pp. 1–51). Tamkang University Press.

Inayatullah, S. (2008). Six Pillars: Futures Thinking for Transforming. *Foresight, 10*(1), 4–21.

Inayatullah, S. (2013). Futures Studies: Theories and Methods. In F. G. Jonquiere (Ed.), *There's a Future: Visions for a Better World* (pp. 36–66). BBVA.

Inayatullah, S. (2023). The Futures Triangle: Origins and Iterations. *World Futures Review, 15*(2-4), 112–121.

Inayatullah, S., & Song, M.-M. (2014). Visions and Scenarios of Democratic Governance in Asia 2030. *Futures*, 60, 1–13.

Jarva, V. (2014). Introduction to Narrative for Futures Studies. *Journal of Futures Studies, 18*(3).

Jarzabkowski, P. (2004). Strategy as Practice: Recursiveness, Adaptation, and Practices-in-Use. *Organization Studies, 25*(4), 529–560.

Jasanoff, S. (2015). Future Imperfect: Science, Technology, and the Imaginations of Modernity. In S. Jasanoff & S.-H. Kim (Eds.), *Dreamscapes of Modernity: Sociotechnical Imaginaries and the Fabrication of Power* (pp. 1–33). University of Chicago Press.

Jasanoff, S., & Kim, S.-H. (2009). Containing the Atom: Sociotechnical Imaginaries and Nuclear Power in the United States and South Korea. *Minerva*, *47*(2), 119–146.

Jasanoff, S., & Kim, S.-H. (2013). Sociotechnical Imaginaries and National Energy Policies. *Science as Culture*, *22*(2), 189–196.

Jasanoff, S., & Kim, S.-H. (2015). *Dreamscapes of Modernity: Sociotechnical Imaginaries and the Fabrication of Power*. The University of Chicago Press.

Jessop, B. (2010). Cultural Political Economy and Critical Policy Studies. *Critical Policy Studies*, *3*(3-4), 336–356.

Jessop, B., & Sum, N.-L. (2023). The Cultural Political Economy Approach to Public Policy. In C. Scherrer, A. Garcia, & J. Wullweber (Eds.), *Handbook on Critical Political Economy and Public Policy* (pp. 36–48). Edward Elgar Publishing.

Jones, C. (2009). Poststructuralism in Critical Management Studies. In M. Alvesson, T. Bridgman, & H. Willmott (Eds.), *The Oxford Handbook of Critical Management Studies* (pp. 76–98). Oxford University Press.

Kahane, A. (2012). Transformative Scenario Planning: Changing the Future by Exploring Alternatives. *Strategy & Leadership*, *40*(5), 19–23.

Kahane, A. (2013). Transformative Scenario Planning: A Tool for Systemic Change. *Social Space*, 16–22.

Kaplan, S. (2008). Framing Contests: Strategy Making Under Uncertainty. *Organization Science*, *19*(5), 729–752.

Knights, D., & Morgan, G. (1991). Corporate Strategy, Organizations, and Subjectivity: A Critique. *Organization Studies*, *12*(2), 251–273

Kornberger, M., & Clegg, S. (2011). Strategy as Performative Practice: The Case of Sydney 2030. *Strategic Organization*, *9*(2), 136–162.

Küpers, W., Mantere, S., & Statler, M. (2013). Strategy as Storytelling: A Phenomenological Collaboration. *Journal of Management Inquiry*, *22*(1), 83–100.

Laine, P.-M., & Vaara, E. (2007). Struggling Over Subjectivity: A Discursive Analysis of Strategic Development in an Engineering Group. *Human Relations*, *60*(1), 29–58.

Levy, D. L., Alvesson, M., & Willmott, H. (2003). Critical Approaches to Strategic Management. In M. Alvesson & H. Willmott (Eds.), *Studying Management Critically* (pp. 92–110). Sage Publications.

MacKenzie, D., & Millo, Y. (2003). Constructing a Market, Performing Theory: The Historical Sociology of a Financial Derivatives Exchange. *American Journal of Sociology*, *109*(1), 107–145.

Maitlis, S., & Lawrence, T. B. (2007). Triggers and Enablers of Sensegiving in Organizations. *Academy of Management Journal*, *50*(1), 57–84.

Mantere, S., & Vaara, E. (2008). On the Problem of Participation in Strategy: A Critical Discursive Perspective. *Organization Science*, *19*(2), 341–358.

Milojević, I., & Inayatullah, S. (2015). Narrative Foresight. *Futures*, *73*, 151–162.

Milojević, I., & Izgarjan, A. (2014). Creating Alternative Futures Through Storytelling: A Case Study from Serbia. *Futures*, *57*, 51–61.

Milojević, I. S., & Inayatullah, S. (2021). Narrative Foresight and Covid-19: Successes and Failures in Managing the Pandemic. *Journal of Futures Studies*, *25*(3), 79–84.

Molitor, G. T. T. (2003). *Power to Change the World: The Art of Forecasting*. World Future Society.

Paroutis, S., & Heracleous, L. (2013). Discourse Revisited: Dimensions and Employment of First-Order Strategy Discourse During Onstitutional Adoption. *Strategic Management Journal*, *34*(8), 935–956.

Phillips, N., & Dar, S. (2009). Strategy. In M. Alvesson, T. Bridgman, & H. Willmott (Eds.), *The Oxford Handbook of Critical Management Studies* (pp. 414–432). Oxford University Press.

Phillips, N., Lawrence, T. B., & Hardy, C. (2004). Discourse and Institutions. *The Academy of Management Review*, *29*(4), 635–652.

Phillips, N., & Oswick, C. (2012). Organizational Discourse: Domains, Debates, and Directions. *Academy of Management Annals*, 6(1), 435–481.

Raven, P. G., & Elahi, S. (2015). The New Narrative: Applying Narratology to the Shaping of Futures Outputs. *Futures*, *74*, 49–61.

Rudek, T. J. (2022). Capturing the Invisible. Sociotechnical Imaginaries of Energy. The Critical Overview. *Science and Public Policy*, 49(2), 219–245.

Samra-Fredericks, D. (2003). Strategizing as Lived Experience and Strategists' Everyday Efforts to Shape Strategic Direction. *Journal of Management Studies*, 40(1), 141–174.

Sassoon, A. S. (2000). *Gramsci and Contemporary Politics: Beyond Pessimism of the Intellect*. Routledge.

Scherer, A. G. (2009). Critical Theory and its Contribution to Critical Management Studies. In M. Alvesson, T. Bridgman, & H. Willmott (Eds.), *The Oxford Handbook of Critical Management Studies* (pp. 29–51). Oxford University Press.

Selin, C. (2008). The Sociology of the Future: Tracing Stories of Technology and Time. *Sociology Compass*, 2(6), 1878–1895.

Sheraz, U., Inayatullah, S., & Shah, A. (2013). E-health Futures in Bangladesh. *Foresight*, *15*(3), 177–189.

Shrivastava, P. (1986). Is Strategic Management Ideological? *Journal of Management*, *12*(3), 363–377.

Slaughter, R. (2004). *Futures Beyond Dystopia: Creating Social Foresight*. Routledge.

Spicer, A., Alvesson, M., & Kärreman, D. (2009). Critical Performativity: The Unfinished Business of Critical Management Studies. *Human Relations*, 62(4), 537–560.

Sum, N.-L., & Jessop, B. (2013). *Towards a Cultural Political Economy: Putting Culture in its Place in Political Economy*. Edward Elgar Publishing.

Vaara, E., Kleymann, B., & Seristö, H. (2004). Strategies as Discursive Constructions: The Case of Airline Alliances. *Journal of Management Studies*, *41*(1), 1–35.

Vaara, E., & Tienar, J. (2008). A Discursive Perspective on Legitimation Strategies in Multinational Corporations. *Academy of Management Review*, 33(4), 985–993.

Vaara, E., & Whittington, R. (2012). Strategy-As-Practice: Taking Social Practices Seriously. *The Academy of Management Annals*, 6(1), 285–336.

Van der Heijden, K., Bradfield, R., Burt, G., Cairns, G., & Wright, G. (2002). *The Sixth Sense: Accelerating Organizational Learning with Scenarios*. John Wiley & Sons.

Whittington, R. (1996). Strategy as Practice. *Long Range Planning*, 29(5), 731–735.

Index

Note: Figures are indicated by *italics*. Tables are indicated by **bold**.

For Product Safety Concerns and Information please contact our EU representative GPSR@taylorandfrancis.com Taylor & Francis Verlag GmbH, Kaufingerstraße 24, 80331 München, Germany